Dharma and the Preservation of Liberty

The Globalist Threat to Our Freedom
And What to Do About It

By Kedarji

I0093063

The Bhakta School of Transformation, Inc.
Youngstown, Ohio

Dharma and
the Preservation of Liberty

The Globalist Threat to Our Freedom
And What to Do About It

Copies of this book may be ordered through booksellers or by contacting:

The Bhakta School of Transformation, Inc.
330-623-7388 Ext. 10

https://yoursacredstore.org/books-by-sadguru-kedarji/

ISBN: 979-8-218-37169-2

Printed in the United States of America

Contents

Introduction

We live on a rock that hangs in a void of space, spinning on an axis in an orbit around a fireball! This phenomenon has been going on for longer than anyone knows. And there is an order to it all that no nation, no standing army, no President, no dictator, no corporate conglomerate and no sovereign wealth trust can influence or change. It is a higher order, a greater law. Wherever there is law, there is a lawgiver. Now, let that fact sink in for a moment.

As human beings, as spiritual entities and as a species we are evolving in every way. We are evolving back into That Supreme Being that is embodied in the energy substratum of everything and everyone.

It is a fact that, in any evolutionary process, only the species that adapts will survive. Therefore, the key to our survival, growth and freedom is in our ability to adapt.

We cannot move toward the fulfillment of any potentiality that is not already inherent in our existence, no more than a caterpillar can decide to, one day, become a frog, rather than a butterfly.

So, our ability to adapt must be founded on this inherent potentiality. *This inherent potentiality is based on fearlessness.*

"Fearlessness is the first requisite of spirituality. Cowards can never be moral."
~ *Mahatma Gandhi*

Shri Jnaneshwar Maharaj, in his commentary on the Bhagavad Gita of Shri Krishna, states the following:

"Now, of all the divine qualities, fearlessness holds the highest place. Listen to what it is.

One who does not leap into a flood can have no fear of being drowned, nor can one who lives a temperate life be in dread of illness.

So the person who does not allow egotism to arise in connection with good and evil deeds and abandons the anxieties of worldly life, and through the realization of non-duality knows all others to be one with himself, casts out all fear.

When salt is thrown into water, it becomes one with it; so also he who realizes his unity with all, destroys fear.

This is what is called fearlessness; thou shouldst know this to be the servant of true perception."

Attachment to people, places and things, along with attachment to outcomes - these cause many diverse fears to manifest, from the most insignificant to the most traumatic. Over many, many lifetimes these fears are embedded in your memory and manifest as your Karmas. They culminate in your clinging to life out of fear of loss and death. To eliminate all fears one has to take total refuge in God with the intention of merging with the Absolute, just as a river merges with the ocean.

Love and the intelligence that comes with knowledge and direct experience of one's true nature, the Self: these are the antidote to fear.

Kali Yuga

Kali Yuga, the fourth age of each world cycle, is described in the scriptures and sacred texts of the Siddha lineage (the Siddha Nation) as the age in which brainwashing (as in mind control) and lewd sex dominate the activity of the masses. It is also a time when women are defiled and the sacredness of motherhood is denigrated. It is described as a time in which what it is to be human is distorted in order to further manipulate and control the masses. We are in the advanced stages of Kali Yuga and this is that time.

How did we get here? If you don't know who you are, you will become whoever others want you to be. That same lawgiver who has established the sacred law here that I spoke of at the start of this introduction dwells within you. That is the One God who dwells equally in all. God is your nature. God, the Self is who you really are. Lack of direct knowledge and experience of this fact is how we got here. Turning away from God, discarding the means to know God and to remember God is how we got here. This contrived separation between humankind and God is the foundation for the madness of this age.

Socio-Economic Control of the World

The word *Liberty* is defined as free choice, freedom to do as one chooses, freedom from the bondage of ignorance, free will, civil or political freedom and the state of being free from arbitrary, despotic, or autocratic rule or control.

The human species is at risk. Our Liberty is being forced into extinction. And this is intentional. The declared pandemic, the proposed global pandemic treaty, the attacks on our health freedom, the recurring fraud of usury in our monetary system and the push for digital IDs and central bank digital currency – these are measures to support a global agenda for the socio-economic control of the masses by the wealthy elite and big government. If we allow their implementation, these measures will be irreversible. *This is the globalist threat to our freedom.*

Today, there is a great push by the wealthy elite to secure complete socio-economic control of the masses. The execution of this massive plan is occurring out in the open, with organizations and corporations like the United Nations, the World Economic Forum (WEF), the World Health Organization (WHO), the Council On Foreign Relations (CFR), Blackrock, Vanguard and State Street leading the way in establishing globalism.

Globalism is *collectivism*, also established as socialism, fascism and communism, as these are all forms of collectivism. Globalism is a central-planning scheme that relies on big, central government, in lock step with large corporate conglomerates, to take control of us all by way of controlling our thinking and behavior, to hand over socio-economic control to a small group of wealthy elite.

These wealthy elite are those same people, without whose funding, the organizations named above, along with agencies within the governments of nations would not exist. For example, the WHO gets the majority of its funding from Bill Gates. The U.S. Food and Drug Administration (FDA), relies on licensing fees from Big Pharma for almost 60% of its budget. Without those fees, the FDA would not exist. These are just two of many examples the world over. The wealthy elite have enough money to buy governments. And that's exactly what most of them do.

In addition, the economies of the world are directed and managed by central banks. Central banks are private corporations run by wealthy elite. So, the financial foundation for the world's money on which we rely for our mundane existence is controlled, not by our elected officials, but by corporations and wealthy individuals who have executed regulatory capture of most government agencies. In their minds, full socio-economic control of the masses is the next, logical step. *They actually believe that we want to be ruled, not governed.* They believe we are just rabble, too stupid to think for ourselves and govern ourselves. They think that, due to their monetary wealth, they are superior to the masses in every way, and more intelligent.

These corporations and wealthy elite, fueled by globalist think tanks like the WEF, the UN, the CFR and the Bilderberg Group, have determined that it is far easier to exact tyranny over the masses by way of socio-economic control mandated by governments that have been bought, rather than resort to war by military force.

The new war is the war to control our minds and bodies through propaganda, censorship, medical biologics that are mandated, and runaway technology that aims at controlling our lives through surveillance tools like digital IDs, vaccine passports, digital money and Environmental Social Governance (ESG) which is the lead up to establishing a world-wide social credit system based on the one currently used by the Chinese Communist Party (CCP) in China. Their final solution is Transhumanism by way of Artificial Intelligence (AI) designed to merge human beings with machines, under the control of robots that they manage.

All of this is dependent on keeping us in a state of constant fear and includes the age-old formula of creating a problem that they have already designed a solution for – a solution that they, government and the wealthy elite, control. I will provide examples of this in the chapters that follow.

The Growing Push to Control Our Minds and Bodies

Wealthy technocrats who have developed and own platforms like Facebook (the parent company of which is Meta), Twitter and Google are engaged in censoring free speech and enforcing partnerships with Big Government to fully control the information we get online, and to manipulate narratives on which the available information is based. As an example, Meta has hired a CIA agent to head up their election censorship division [1]. In an ongoing lawsuit, a federal judge has ruled that President Biden likely violated the First Amendment of the U.S. Constitution during the COVID-19 pandemic. Google, Meta and Twitter were all named in the lawsuits. [2] Biden is not only challenging the lawsuit, but wants to be able to order censorship on these platforms in the future and has hired a legal team to get the lawsuit reversed.

Mainstream media is entrenched in this scheme. By accepting billions of dollars in advertising revenue from Big Pharma, Big Agra and Big Tech, mainstream media outlets enter into a contractual agreement as to content that they cannot present and stories they cannot report on, based on what their major advertisers find objectionable.

The mass censorship of critical information pertaining to Covid-19, its origins and inexpensive, effective treatments for Covid-19 that do not require Covid shots is one major example of the growing push to control our minds and bodies. Now under legal indictment for global censorship, the Trusted News Initiative (TNI) is a media partnership initiated by the governments of the U.S. and Great Britain [3,4]. This initiative was designed to control the narrative and reporting on Covid-19, and to label doctors, scientists and researchers who differed with their narrative as quacks and enemies of the state.

I have friends who are world-renowned medical professionals who were targeted by TNI and the U.S. Department of Homeland Security (DHS) for publicly speaking out about alternative, available treatments for Covid-19, and for publicly sharing their knowledge of the origins of SARS-CoV-2 and its development as a bioweapon. Some of them are excellent doctors whose licenses were permanently revoked for saving lives using Ivermectin and Hydroxychloroquine to treat Covid-19. Others are medical professionals, scientists and researchers who have first-hand knowledge of the lab origin of SARS-CoV-2.

These people were targeted as part of the so called 'disinformation dozen' – a publicized list generated by the now defunct Disinformation Governance Board of the U.S. federal government that sought to not only censor their speech, but to defame them and ruin their careers. Some of them have been stripped of all their professional awards and associations after the list was published by media around the world. Are we the United States of China now?

Why would they censor medical professionals with very long track records of treating and healing patients? Could it be that they don't want Covid shots upstaged by other effective, inexpensive treatments? Why would they censor people with first-hand knowledge of the origins of SARS-CoV-2? They did it because SARS-CoV-2 is a manmade virus developed in a lab as part of gain of function research for the testing of bioweapons. What more are they hiding and why are they going to such great lengths to hide it?

Meta, now the parent of Facebook and owned by Mark Zuckerberg, is now experimenting with technology that alters brain waves and thought processes via a headset that covers your face. Meta Quest [5], as the device is known, gives users access to the Metaverse, a virtual reality universe providing access to everything from video games to fitness programs to advertising. However, this device hooks up people's brains directly to computers and the Internet, and the device is also designed to surveil the user's thoughts. This data is then collected, mined and sold to any and all interested parties. This is Orwell's *1984* on steroids!

Klaus Schwab of the WEF is posting videos [6] online of WEF conferences where he is encouraging people to have chips put in their brains that will automatically connect them to the Internet. Elon Musk/Tesla has already perfected this brain chip technology, originally designed for certain medical applications. [7,8] The U.S. government has a similar chip technology that has been used on livestock and other animals for decades. These chips have since gone commercial. Companies like Verichip [9] have developed and are now distributing microchip implants for humans. Are we livestock now?

Perhaps it is summed up best by Yuval Noah Harari, historian and adviser to Klaus Schwab and the WEF:

"Covid is critical because this is what convinces people to accept, to legitimize, total biometric surveillance. If we want to stop this epidemic, we need not just to monitor people, we need to monitor what's happening under their skin. .....What we have seen so far is corporations and governments collecting data about where we go, who we meet, what movies we watch. The next phase is the surveillance going under our skin."

"We now see mass surveillance systems established even in democratic countries, which previously rejected them. And we also see a change in the nature of surveillance. Previously, surveillance was mainly above the skin; now it's going under the skin. Governments want to know not just where we go or who we meet; above all, they want to know what is happening under our skin: what's our body temperature? What's our blood pressure? What is our medical condition? Humans are now hackable animals. You know, the whole idea that humans have this soul or spirit, and they have free will, and nobody knows what's happening inside me, so, whatever I choose, whether in the election or whether in the supermarket, this is my free will. That's over." [10]

The Push To Destroy Honor, Love for God and Spirituality

"There is no such thing as free will. Science is familiar with just two kinds of processes in nature. You have deterministic processes and you have random processes, and of course you have combinations of randomness and determinism which result in a probabilistic outcome, but none of that is freedom. Freedom has absolutely no meaning from a physical or biological perspective. It's just another myth, another empty term that humans have invented. Humans have invented God, and humans have invented heaven and hell, and humans have invented free will. But there is no more truth to free will than there is to heaven and hell. And as for feelings, they are definitely real; they are not a fiction of our imagination. But feelings are really just biochemical algorithms, and there is nothing metaphysical or supernatural about them. There is no

obvious reason to consider them as the highest authority in the world. And most importantly, what scientists and engineers are telling us more and more, is that if we only have enough data, and enough computing power, we can create external algorithms that understand humans and their feelings much better than humans can understand themselves. And once you have an algorithm that understands you, and understands your feeling better than you understand yourself, this is the point when authority really shifts away from humans to algorithms." [11]
~ *Yuval Noah Harari, Historian,*
  Adviser to Klaus Schwab and the WEF

Do you remember that, during Covid pandemic lockdowns, churches, spiritual centers and other houses of worship were deemed non-essential services and forced to lock down? Houses of worship and spiritual centers that did not comply were raided by law enforcement and forced to close. At the same time, topless bars and strip clubs were deemed essential businesses and allowed to remain open during the lockdowns.

Humanity is at a crossroads like never before. With respect to the environment, public health policy, food, water and energy, we are putting the human species at ever-increasing risk. The Covid crisis that has ushered in the Coronavirus Era brings with it the corruption of our most trusted institutions and government itself. Never before in recent history have we seen such a rapid decline in human and civil rights around the globe, with entire governments and nations acting in lockstep to dictate what we put on and in our bodies. My spiritual mentor once said that the source of the destruction of humanity will not require bombs, but *will proceed from greed.*

If not arrested, greed corrupts, both individually and collectively. It strikes at the heart of humankind by destroying human dignity and overriding conscience – our natural connection to ethics and morality, to God. This can only degrade the quality of life on our planet by dehumanizing entire populations. To be clear, greed is a spiritual disease. Therefore, it is important to understand how greed corrupts so that we can embrace and nurture principles for wholistic living, in recognition of the Creator, the true possessor of this place we call Earth.

Honoring the Creator is a necessity for upholding Human Dignity, protecting Humanity and cherishing all of Life. When we don't embrace Honor in this way, maniacal egoism becomes the order of the day, reigning down havoc, hysteria and tyranny everywhere.

What's God got to do with it? Everything. Under Covid, we have clearly experienced that many of our government officials have lost their moral and ethical compass. In addition, we have seen a growing loss of respect for human life and a corresponding denigration of Humanity. As a result, this is taking us in the direction of tyranny, fostered by a growing nihilism.

Without belief in and experience of the highest power (recognized by whatever label works for you - God, the Self, Yaweh, Great Spirit, the Creator, etc.), there can be no respect for human life and no willingness to preserve human and civil rights. This respect and desire to preserve life, liberty and the pursuit of happiness comes from the faith in and direct experience of God. This respect is nurtured by Conscience, an innate presence of the Divine that can and is overridden when we turn our backs on God.

History has taught us the devastating effects of this colossal blunder. From Nazism to Fascism to Communism, we already know what happens when maniacal egoism is allowed to replace reverence for God. Under Covid, the reemergence of this idiocy has taken many lives, while also resulting in the destruction of our Humanity and our God-given rights, as elucidated in the United States Constitution, the constitutions of other nations and the Nuremberg Code.

Without reverence for God, human life has no value and, therefore, can easily be reduced to enslavement at the whim of oppressors with plans to control the world.

Acknowledgements

I offer my gratitude and praise to my Guru, Muktananda Paramahamsa, for inspiring me to write this book and leading me in the presentation of its contents.

I also offer my heartfelt thanks to Kambra McConnel and Shanti Harkness for proofreading the chapters of this book.

I also offer my gratitude to all those who I worked with in fighting to preserve our God-given rights and Liberty by co-authoring and advocating for citizens bills introduced to the Ohio State Legislature. These people include Nadera Lopez-Garrity, Deana Tareshawty, and the staff at Health Freedom Ohio and Children's Health Defense Ohio.

Chapter 1
What Is Dharma?

Many spiritual traditions speak of Dharma. **Dharma is the act of loving the Truth, loving Righteousness more than mundane life itself.** Many of those who have gone before us lived by this principle. And many of those who did so gave their lives so that we can have Liberty under God. Down through the ages, there are countless examples of the Siddhas of my lineage facing challenges to Dharma and being victorious in protecting it.

We have great examples of Dharma in the *Mahabharata*, a great sacred text that my own Guru quoted and read from often. The centerpiece of the Mahabharata is the *Bhagavad Gita* of Shri Krishna. We have a similar epic and sacred text in the *Ramayana* where Shri Rama goes into battle against the demon king Ravana to restore righteousness to Ayodhya.

We live in trying times that are testing our desire and ability to preserve Dharma in the face of the evil of greed and the desire to control and manipulate the masses. People everywhere are in the habit of trading the truth for convenience and this has eroded Dharma before our very eyes.

"He who passively accepts evil is as much involved in it as he who helps to perpetrate it. He who accepts evil without protesting against it is really cooperating with it....The time is always right to do what is right."
~ *Dr. Martin Luther King, Jr.*

1

Individual Dharma

"Independence of will and judgment alone cause one to stand upright like God."
~ *Muktananda Paramahamsa*

Dharma is first based on Integrity. Without Integrity there is no courage and without courage there can be no fearlessness. Moral and ethical principles are innate in the direct experience of God. These are innate in the direct experience of fearlessness that is founded on spiritual principles and love for humankind. Honesty is the result. Individual Dharma comes with the understanding that action creates a reverberation in Consciousness that has present and future ramifications for one's thinking and behavior. This reverberation is known as Karma. Indeed, you reap what you sow.

Therefore, Dharma begins with every person adhering to ethics, morality and personal integrity in every situation and circumstance, and as a matter of personal strength and transformation. It is better not to speak than to lie. It is better to be moral and ethical, even if persecuted for it. It is better to employ stealth in difficult situations and circumstances rather than resort to dishonesty. By stealth I do not mean acting in a covert or clandestine manner. When I speak of stealth, I mean first to understand the present and future ramifications of a thing, and then to act in alignment with that understanding *as to the timing of your actions*, in alignment with Dharma.

For example, in the *Mahabharata*, the Pandava brothers, the rightful heirs to the throne are forced into exile by the Kauravas, their own family members who refuse to recognize their right to the throne and decide to take it by force. The Pandava brothers, feeling that the timing was not right to go to war with the Kauravas, agreed to remain in exile in the Kamyaka forest for 13 years. Further, the Pandavas agreed that, if at any time they were spotted while in exile before the 13 years was up, they would have to go back into exile for another 13 years. This agreement prompted the unethical, immoral Kauravas to take extensive measures to determine their whereabouts in the forest in order to spot them, to extend the period of exile. The Pandava brothers kept changing their location and the Kauravas continued attempts to track them. For the Pandavas war was a last resort, and they did not want their exile extended.

So, at one point in the 12th year, the Pandavas decided to dress in costumes and change their identities to reduce the possibility of them being spotted before the end of the 13th year of their exile. While under assumed identities in a King's court, the King began to suspect who they really were and then questioned them. The Pandavas admitted their true identities, explained their situation to the King and gained the King and his forces as an ally.

Another example is Nelson Mandela. Mandela, before becoming the first African President of the free South Africa, was a leader of the African National Congress (ANC). The ANC formed the resistance to the Afrikaner government that instituted and enforced Apartheid. Afrikaners were Dutch, German and French immigrants who colonized South Africa under Apartheid by forming the Afrikaner government of South Africa.

Mandela was arrested and imprisoned on Robben Island for 27 years. While the ANC weighed all measures to overthrow the Afrikaner government that ordered the execution of millions of South Africans, Mandela insisted on non-violent resistance. Further, in order to win his freedom and set the example for non-violent resistance and reform, Mandela began counseling the prison guards, hearing and helping them to address their personal problems and spiritual challenges. For this, he was released from prison early and the Afrikaner government agreed to enter into negotiations with Mandela and the ANC for a peaceful transition to abolish Apartheid and to hand the government over to South African rule by native South Africans, rather than Afrikaners.

Mandela not only wanted a free Republic in South Africa where native South Africans would have full and fair participation in their governance, but he recognized Afrikaners (the oppressors) as South Africans also. Not wanting there to be violent retaliation against white South Africans for the vicious crimes committed under Apartheid, and not wanting to see a mass exodus of white South Africans from South Africa, under the new South African government run by native South Africans, Mandela created *The Truth and Reconciliation Commission* (TRC). [1]

The TRC was established to allow Afrikaners who were engaged in atrocities against native South Africans to face their accusers in a public forum to confess their crimes. Those who confessed their crimes were not charged and were allowed to go free and remain living in South Africa, if that was their choice. The TRC was an incredible healing gesture of Love and Compassion and it worked. *Stealth.*

Another very important aspect of Individual Dharma is *Liberty*. It's important for you to understand your freedom to use your free will to make choices in your life, based on being fully informed - choices that do not harm others unless you are engaged in self-preservation or self-defense. This freedom must be protected from the pressure of the "group," the majority. This is why the framers of the United States Constitution insisted on drafting this highest law in America based on the premise that the individual who may be in the minority must be protected from the will of the majority. Otherwise, collectivism becomes the rule of law where the sacredness of the individual is replaced by the worship of and submission to the state. Therefore, it is essential that you understand what your constitutional and human rights are so that you can be constantly on your guard to protect those rights.

Understand this: Freedom is not free. And, particularly on the mundane level, there is no time in history where freedom has not required an extended and sometimes massive effort to protect.

Collective Dharma

It is past time for us to come together in solidarity to protect our God-given rights by ensuring Liberty for all, not just for a consenting majority. Collective Dharma is upheld when people everywhere understand the ramifications of collective Karmas created by a group, society or nation of people. In this regard, we have a duty to each other to be courageous, to be fearless, to be honest and to preserve ethics and morality in government and society. This is collective Dharma. Without it all nations will descend into tyranny.

In the United States, the framers of the U.S. constitution knew this all too well from the experiences that drove them out of England to establish a new government in America. The framers of the U.S. Constitution understood the duty they had to come together in solidarity by working out their differences, of which there were many (read the Federalist and Anti-Federalist papers), in order to engage ethics and morality in the building of a Republic under Liberty. These beings yielded to courage, honed by fearlessness. Although they were not perfect, they consistently aspired to a collective Dharma.

As of this year of 2023, we the people face many challenges to our Liberty. These challenges are mounting because big government and the wealthy elite have learned from the past that people are easily frightened and can easily be led into a prison without walls, by way of fear. The Covid-19 pandemic proved this. However, the pandemic of 2019-2023 was based on a very old playbook that yielded like results in other historic challenges in America and around the world.

- The assassination of President John F. Kennedy
- The assassination of Robert F. Kennedy
- The assassination of Dr. Martin Luther King, Jr.
- The fabricated story of WMDs in Iraq that led to the Iraq War [2]
- The NSA/CIA files leaked by Edward Snowden [3]
- Operation Dark Winter [4]
- The SARS-COV1 plandemic [5,6]

This is just to name a few. There are others – enough to raise the question *Is a government that consistently lies to the people it is tasked with serving worth preserving?* Today, as a society, we are suffering the collective Karmas created by our actions and inaction in the challenges I list above. There are other, additional examples that will be addressed in this and later chapters.

It is an absolute necessity for Collective Dharma to be nurtured and protected if we are to get to the truth behind what our present challenges represent. Some of these present challenges are addressed in this book. If we do not act in solidarity, if we do not recognize and engage our Collective Dharma, we will pay the price in a total loss of our Liberty and our enslavement under tyranny.

The Difference Between Collectivism and Liberty

If you are continually distracted, you can't know who you are. If you don't know who you are, you can never be free, and you will become whoever others want you to become. A nation where the majority of people don't know who they are is a nation of slaves. God exists in everyone, in all individuals everywhere. Due to this fact, regardless of which country or nation, the individual must remain free to choose his/her destiny, conjoined with Liberty that is protected, so that a fictitious "personhood" of a group representing the majority is never again allowed to crush Liberty. I say never again because during the COVID-19 pandemic this is what happened. Liberty was crushed because we allowed the will of the majority to override individual Liberty and to circumvent the Constitution.

A simple example is mask mandates. There are a good number of peer-reviewed studies that show that mask wearing did nothing to prevent the spread of COVID-19. There are some 170 peer-reviewed studies on masks, 78 of which have been consolidated into a published report by the Cochrane Collective that support this fact. [7,8,9]

The report concluded that wearing masks in public "probably makes little or no difference." Even though the Cochrane Collective Report was published in the midst of the COVID-19 pandemic and even though other peer-reviewed studies were published stating the same and, even though videos of people wearing masks (including the N95s) while spraying aerosols through the masks to show how easily they are penetrated by particles larger than the virus went viral on the Internet and, even though Anthony Fauci, in emails intercepted and published during the pandemic state that masks will not be effective in preventing infection from the virus (see next chapter in this book), the federal government, along with state and local governments refused to consider the science or the obvious. Furthermore, I know people who wore masks religiously who got Covid.

The question of the day became "If you're wearing a mask that you feel protects you, why do you insist that I wear one." When shopping in stores without wearing a mask, store managers chased me around the store waving masks in their hands in an attempt to get me to put one on. I refused and, more often than not, I was asked to leave the store, which I did. I also observed attacks on people who were either not wearing a mask or had their masks pulled down below their noses. In two of these situations, I witnessed mothers with babies in their arms being harassed and physically attacked because they weren't wearing masks, by those who were. I had to pull people off of these mothers in order to protect them. What I have just described is a perfect example of *collectivism* in action where the rights of the individual are violated by the majority.

"We hold these truths to be self-evident, that all men are created equal, that they are endowed by their Creator with certain unalienable Rights; that among these are Life, Liberty, and the pursuit of Happiness. That to secure these rights, Governments are instituted among men...."
        ~ *The United States Declaration of Independence*

Inalienable (spelled 'unalienable' in colonial times) means "not to be transferred to another." The purpose of the state is not to grant rights, but to secure them and protect them.

The discussion of Collectivism vs. Liberty in this section will prepare you to understand the presentations made in subsequent chapters of this book regarding the current push to destroy Liberty and establish collectivism (in the form of globalism) under one world government. In this section, the words 'government' and 'the state' are used interchangeably and mean the same thing.

1. Under constitutional law in America, government (local, state and federal) exists to secure and protect the rights of the individual. This means that, where governance is concerned, the authority to govern is granted by the people. Therefore, the government, by law, has no authority to do what you or I cannot do because the source of rights determines their nature. This is a foundational pillar of Liberty and constitutional law. The authority cannot exceed its source. Unfortunately, due to the ignorance and negligence of the citizenry, today most of the laws in the U.S., and even other nations, violate this fundamental principle. This must change.

2. With collectivism it is the exact opposite. The state reserves the right to do what we the people cannot do and/or have no right to do, exacted by laws passed by the government. This is the cornerstone of collectivism. It is also the trademark of tyranny.

3. Under Liberty, rights come from the people and governments are the servants of the people. With collectivism, rights are granted by the government and people are the servants of the collective (the government and the wealthy elite), for the greater good of the majority.

4. The problem with collectivism is this: if the government/state has the power to grant rights, it also has the power to take them away, and this is anti-Liberty. In a collectivist society, freedom is gradually eroded in this way.

5. All collectivist political systems embrace the view that rights are granted by the state (government). That includes Nazis, Socialists, Fascists, and Communists. The United Nations, a globalist organization founded on collectivism, in its Article Four of the UN Covenant on Economic, Social, and Cultural Rights states: "The States Parties to the present Covenant recognize that, in the enjoyment of those rights provided by the State ... the State may subject such rights only to such limitations as are determined by law."

So, again, if the state can grant rights, it can also take them away.
"..the State may subject such rights only to such limitations as are determined by law" means that when the state is ready to take rights away, all they have to do is to pass laws authorizing that to happen.

6. The Bill of Rights in the United States Constitution says "Congress shall make *no* law restricting freedom of speech, or religion, peaceful assembly, the right to bear arms, and so forth – not except as determined by law." The Bill of Rights is very clear in delineating laws that the U.S. Congress cannot pass. This is an example of Liberty designed to protect the individual who may be in the minority, from the will of the majority.

7. A just government derives its power from the people. This means the state cannot have any legitimate powers unless they are given it by its citizens. *Again, governments may do only those*

things that their citizens also have a right to do. If individuals don't have the right to perform a certain act, then they can't grant that power to their elected representatives. They can't delegate what they don't have. It makes no difference how many individuals there are. If none of them have a specified power to delegate, then millions of them don't have it either.

Let's go back to my mask story. People have the right to protect themselves from a virus in whatever means they choose, including wearing a facemask for their own protection. Individuals do not have the right to force other people to wear a mask. Therefore, individuals cannot delegate that right to the government, since it is a right no person possesses. And, in a free society founded on Liberty, (even if all the studies show that masks are effective in protecting a person against a contagion) government does not have the right to mandate that people wear masks because that right has not been given it by the people who do not possess that right either. So, the mask mandates that were strictly enforced during the COVID-19 state of emergency were, under the U.S. Constitution, illegal and anti-Liberty. *No matter where you live, neither individuals or government have the right to tell people what to put on or in their bodies.*

There is one exception and that is of businesses. Private enterprises (government is not a private enterprise) have the right, by law, to dictate to customers, the policies under which customers can do business with them. This includes policies for customers to enter retail establishments.

For example, during the declared pandemic, one of the local health food stores in the county in which I live posted a sign on the door that said "No entry without wearing a facemask. It's the law." The owner of the store did not know the difference between a law and a mandate. In this case, the Governor of the state of Ohio issued a comprehensive mask mandate. However, mandates are not laws. Laws are passed by legislatures, not by Governors. So, after bringing this fact to the attention of the storeowner, a group of us confronted him and told him that, if he insisted we wear masks in his store, we would stop shopping there. The owner immediately reversed the store mask mandate.

There was a similar situation with Walmart stores. When the Covid shots were distributed, the Walmarts in the county where I live adopted a policy that people had to show proof of Covid vaccination to enter the store. Boycotts were immediately organized, with picket lines at the entrances and exits of all Walmart stores in the county. Walmart reversed its policy due to the boycotts.

These are examples of using rights that every citizen has to force businesses to respect the rights of their customers.

8. Using this same example, under collectivism, the majority or 'group' has the right to take away the right of any individual not to wear a facemask, and has the right to allow the state to impose such tyranny.

9. As stated in his work, *The Chasm*, G. Edward Griffin tells us "When we hire police to protect our community, we are merely asking them to do what we, ourselves, have a right to do. Using physical force to protect our lives, liberty, and property is a legitimate function of the state, because that power is derived from the

people as individuals. It does not arise from the group."
[10]

10. During the COVID-19 plandemic, lockdowns and
stay-at-home orders were initiated in every state in
America and in many nations across the world. In the
U.S. these orders were made by decree by Governors of
each state. Businesses, churches and other places of
worship, government offices and just about any other
entity imaginable except for topless bars, strip clubs,
drug stores, gas stations and food markets were forced
to shut down.

In the state of Ohio where I currently live, as with most
of the other states in America, these orders were
enforced by police and, in some cases, the military. In
addition, in Ohio, the state health department setup
hotlines that were, in fact, 'snitch' lines and, in his daily
public news conferences, Governor DeWine encouraged
people to contact the state health department if they
observed anyone violating the lockdown and stay-at-
home orders. This included encouraging people to call
if they saw people not wearing masks or not social
distancing, and if they observed any gatherings of more
than 10 people in public areas or in people's homes.
Violations were met with fines and forced lockdowns,
along with ongoing surveillance. Some governors and
mayors threatened to jail people who did not comply.

This is an example of the group supremacy that is the
hallmark of collectivism. It is also an example of
tyranny. In the U.S., no individual has the right to
lockdown any entity and no individual has the right to
control the freedom of movement of another in any way
where there is no direct violation of persons or
property. This means that individual citizens, not
possessing that right, did not have the right to delegate

that power to the states and the states did not have the right, under any law, to mandate lockdowns and stay-at-home orders, nor to enforce such measures because these rights were not granted by the citizenry. These measures were not only illegal but tyrannical.

In Ohio, hundreds of lawsuits were brought against these lockdown orders. The lawsuits that were adjudicated in court were won by those who brought the lawsuits. Some of these cases involved restaurants that were deemed non-essential businesses and forced to close. Winning court cases allowed these businesses to reopen, but the truth is none of them had to obey the mandate since, under constitutional law, the mandates were unenforceable and void.

11. *When government claims to derive its authority from any source other than the people, this always leads to the destruction of Liberty.* Preventing people from frequenting places necessary to carryout their mundane existence may not seem to be a great threat to freedom, but once that behavior is established, it opens the door for more and more mandates until there is no more freedom.

12. So, again, if we accept that the government or any other group has the right to do things that individuals alone do not have the right to do, we are supporting the notion that rights are not intrinsic to the individual and that they, in fact, do originate with the group. Once we accept that, we accept tyranny. Under collectivism, government power is considered to be greater than the power of the citizens it governs. Collectivists believe that the source of those powers is not the individuals within a society, but society itself, the groups to which individuals belong.

13. With collectivism, the group is always more important than the individual. Furthermore, under collectivism, the group has rights of its own that supersede the rights of any person. This is why collectivists will always advocate for the individual and/or the individual's rights being sacrificed, if necessary, for the greater good of the larger number of people. The argument is that no one should object to the loss of Liberty or even the loss of life if it is for the greater good of society. This is the principle of group supremacy and the ultimate group, of course, is the government. Therefore, because the state is more important than individual citizens, it is acceptable to sacrifice their rights, if necessary, for the benefit of the state. *This premise is at the heart of all totalitarian systems built on the model of collectivism.*

14. The words 'group' or 'collective' are purposely abstract and left undefined. For example, government as a 'group' or a corporation as a 'group' often means that accountability and responsibility is shifted from individuals to the group – another trademark of collectivism. If something goes wrong the group can be blamed with little or no individual accountability. In fact, there are only groups of individuals. Therefore, only individuals exist and only individuals have rights. One group may have a smaller number of individuals than another. In this example, the individuals in the larger group do not have a higher priority or more rights than the individuals in the smaller group. In other words, rights are not derived from the power of numbers. They do not come from any group. They only exist as the sole possession of human beings. Therefore, there is no such thing as group supremacy, except under tyranny.

15. Furthermore, the notion of group supremacy does not exist to protect the group. When a government argues that individual rights must be sacrificed for the greater good of society, what the government is really saying is that the rights of some individuals will be sacrificed for the greater good of other individuals.

16. The 'moral imperative' of collectivism is always based on numbers. In this example, government may do anything so long as the number of people perceived to benefit is, supposedly, greater than the number of people whose rights are being violated. This is, in fact, an aberration. Under collectivism, the number of people actually benefitting is a very small percentage of the population governed. This can be easily understood by examining this principle of group benefit in countries like China and Russia. It can also be understood by examining the many peer-reviewed studies on the destructive impact of pandemic lockdowns on societies everywhere in the world. And, in the coming chapters, you will understand who that small group of individuals are who benefited at the expense of the rest of us.

17. In truth, sacrificing the rights of individuals for the benefit of the group is idiotic. Individuals are the essence of any group. So, sacrificing the rights of individuals means sacrificing the group, a person at a time. Also, the other person whose rights are being sacrificed, supposedly to protect yours, may be you tomorrow.

18. Collectivism thrives in a democracy. This is why the framers of the U.S. Constitution were *against* democracies and *for* the Republic that functions with the understanding that it exists to protect the God-given, inalienable rights of the individual. It's why you

will never find the word democracy in the U.S. Constitution. The framers of the U.S. Constitution were not against nations functioning democratically, meaning by the will of the people. However, they understood, correctly, that democracies are founded on the will of the majority being the law of the land. In other words, democracies support the growth of collectivism where rights are granted by the collective (the largest collective being the government) and are not intrinsic to individuals. And, in democracies, the government can also take away individual rights. *Indeed, the difference between a democracy and a republic is the difference between collectivism and liberty.*

Injustice has to be made visible in order to be cured. And there is no justice, no freedom, without massive action. When it comes to the reinstatement of our civil rights and liberties that are expressions of our God-given, unalienable rights, the complacency of today will always create the debt of enslavement tomorrow. If we lose our willingness and ability defend our rights under Liberty, we will lose those rights permanently. *Liberty has to be defended.*

In my experience, the ultimate purpose of Liberty under a Republic is to secure our right to pursue our lives in a way that we can come to know that happiness is a spiritual principle and spiritual state that is not dependent on anything or anyone outside ourselves – the pursuit of which must never be impeded in any way, under any circumstance, in any situation of our mundane existence, and not by any group or the government. Because, if we don't defend our right to this pursuit, the erosion of other individual rights will lead to this right being taken away from us – as is the case in countries like China and Russia. This is so because people's belief in and experience of God instills in them the experience that God is greater and higher than government or any group. Collectivism rails against this fact. *Therefore, defending Liberty is also the performance of Dharma, the act of loving the Truth more than mundane life itself.*

Chapter 2
The Growing Attack On Our Liberty
Pandemics

"The conscious and intelligent manipulation of the organized habits and opinions of the masses is an important element in democratic society. Those who manipulate this unseen mechanism of society constitute an invisible government that is the true ruling power of our country. We are governed, our minds molded, our tastes formed, our ideas suggested, largely by men we have never heard of."
~ *Edward Bernays,* From his book *Propaganda*

The topic entitled The Growing Attack On Our Liberty is divided into five chapters: *The Growing Attack On Our Liberty – Pandemics, The Growing Attack On Our Liberty – Digital IDs, The Growing Attack On Our Liberty – Central Bank Digital Currency (CBDC), The Growing Attack On Our Liberty – Censorship of Free Speech* and *The Growing Attack On Our Liberty – Environmental Social Governance (ESG)*. This chapter is the first of the five on this topic. In addition, for each chapter, there is posted a link to recommended additional reading and viewing. You can also find that information here: https://bhaktaschool.org/dharma-and-the-preservation-of-liberty/. (As of the publication of this book, all printed links are live. The Internet is fast moving. Some links may have been moved by the time you read this book.)

In reading this book, your perspective will change. Upon completion of your reading, you may even feel overwhelmed and somewhat despondent with regard to the sheer magnitude of the challenges we face in protecting our Liberty, God-given rights and bodily autonomy. You may be so overwhelmed that you don't know where to start or how to start. Each chapter has a list of action items, along with steps to engage them. For those of you who feel that there is far too much to address, I suggest you start with one or two actions that you have the ability to undertake now. Then you can pace yourself in the other steps you may want to engage, particularly after reading Chapter 8.

Liberty means that everyone has the right to determine his or her own path to happiness, free from undue government control. Our rights come from God, not from government and Liberty means that government exists to protect these God-given rights. Liberty also means that health freedom and bodily autonomy are protected. Public health orders are not a means to circumvent the First Amendment. There is no pandemic pause button on the U.S. Constitution. And, as the framers of the U.S. Constitution have stated, *Liberty means protecting the minority from the will of the majority.*

Whether intentional or not, there is a growing attack on our Liberty and well-being as part of a globalist agenda to create *one world government.* While the inner workings of this agenda are being kept from the general public everywhere, the intention for the implementation of this agenda is being openly espoused. In fact, there is a growing volume of evidence that shows that declared states of emergency have been and are being used to suspend human rights, civil liberties and the constitutions of nations. In light of the many facts exposed during the COVID-19 pandemic, one could argue that this is intentional.

In this chapter, I will provide you with information, commentary and evidence to support the growing attack on our Liberty using pandemics that increasing evidence shows are actually planned to expand socio-economic control over the masses. The evidence also points to this push for socio-economic control being perpetuated by a small group of wealthy elite who are unelected officials controlling vast amounts of financial assets and resources that they are using to buy governments. In fact, they comprise the *invisible government* that Edward Bernays refers to in the quote at the beginning of this chapter. Their aim is one world government. I will name some of these people in this chapter. These people are infected with the corruption of greed and maniacal egoism.

"The individual is handicapped by coming face-to-face with a conspiracy so monstrous he cannot believe it exists."
~ *J. Edgar Hoover, First Director of the FBI*

Mass Hysteria

My freedom does not end where your fear starts. Fear destroys intelligence. Therefore, acting out of fear also destroys clarity and breeds deluded thinking. It is extremely important that you not be an alarmist and that you not allow your life to be impacted by alarmists. Instead, become fully informed and get all the facts. This includes examining all sides of any debate on issues impacted by fear. During the last three years, at the onset of the COVID-19 pandemic, the public, along with medical professionals everywhere were not allowed to question the official narrative on the pandemic. Even now there are massive steps being taken to censor our ability to ask questions in order to be fully informed.

Mass Hysteria was the basis for the mask mandates, lockdowns, quarantines, social distancing and vaccine mandates over the last three years. After stating that we only needed three weeks "to flatten the curve," we were locked down for almost three years. As of this writing we are headed into the Fall flu season of 2023. There are reports of three additional variants of SARS-CoV-2 (Eris-EG.5, Pirola-BA.2.86 and JN1) circulating the globe. These variants are reported to be less infectious than previous variants, but may be more contagious. As of this writing there are only six reported cases of Eris worldwide and very few cases of Pirola and JN1. And yet, some schools and companies in the U.S. are already requiring masks and President Biden is claiming that there are new Covid shots that will be distributed in a month that every American should take.

At the same time, the CDC is claiming we don't yet know enough about these new variants. So, if we don't yet know enough about these new variants, how can there be new Covid shots that are being promised to address them!? In addition, Anthony Fauci, who has resigned his posts within the U.S. Federal Government, is now taking interviews in which he is recommending lockdowns.

And now it is Davos (World Economic Forum) week and the hysterical propaganda push from the globalists regarding "disease X" is in full swing. Almost every major news outlet in the world has run fear propaganda pieces about "disease X." The "experts" aren't actually named, the peer-reviewed papers supporting the thesis of "a deadly pathogen causing 20 times more deaths than COVID-19" or "killing 20 times more people than COVID-19" or "killing 50 million people" are non-existent. Yet these narratives are headline news in mainstream media. This noise will get louder in 2025, right after the U.S. Presidential election. View more about what is actually being planned here:

https://www.bitchute.com/video/bGanZUL7tZqp/ and here: https://rwmalonemd.substack.com/p/disease-x-and-the-corrupt-lancet.

The fact is, historically, viruses like SARS-CoV-2, the virus that causes COVID-19, are constantly circulating the globe. These viruses mutate quickly. The annual flu virus is one such virus. The Coronavirus that causes the common cold is another. Yet mask-wearing, lockdowns and vaccine mandates have never been required for addressing these viruses, not even in the case of the annual flu virus that kills millions of people each year. And by the time this book is published, there will be new strains of the virus. So why the mass hysteria over Covid? If we look closer, we find that there are other, hidden, and not so hidden agendas that are driving this mass hysteria – agendas that require fear in order to fully implement fraud – agendas that are also very much about money.

Nurse Erin Marie Olszewski joined the army at age 17 and was deployed to Iraq. She served on the frontlines. After returning from the war, she was employed as a nurse in various settings and then worked as a nurse at Elmhurst hospital in Queens, New York. During the early stages of the pandemic, Elmhurst hospital was the epicenter of hospitalizations for Covid in New York City, admitting and treating more Covid patients than any other hospital in New York.

While caring for Covid patients, Nurse Erin uncovered a huge amount of fraud in how Covid cases were being counted, along with widespread medical malpractice in how Covid patients were being treated in the emergency room and the ICU. Nurse Erin blew the whistle on Elmhurst hospital after wearing a wire and a hidden camera to document all of the abuses. You can view the undercover video that made headlines across the world here: https://21wire.tv/2020/06/11/undercover-nurse-

exposes-nycs-covid-epicenter-revealing-widespread-
medical-malpractice/

The Real Anthony Fauci

There has been a great deal of debate as to who
was charged with managing the COVID-19 pandemic
response, as well as who is responsible for the worst
public health response in the history of the world – the
COVID-19 pandemic response. With respect to both, Dr.
Anthony Fauci is the focus. Up until his recent
resignation, Anthony Fauci has run the National
Institute of Allergy and Infectious Diseases (NIAID) for
50 years. This means that, although he has "Dr." in
front of his name, he has been a government bureaucrat
for 50 years, during which time he has never treated a
single patient. This is an important point for you to
remember.

When you are in need of medical attention, do
you go to a government bureaucrat for diagnosis and
treatment? Or do you go to a competent medical
doctor with years of experience treating patients - a
doctor who has earned your trust by way of strong
credentials in treating you and other patients, a doctor
who is currently in practice? The truth is Anthony Fauci
has been at the center of controversy in several public
health emergency responses that include his bungling
of the HIV/AIDS epidemic. Because space is limited
here, for a detailed account of this and other Fauci
public health failures, I strongly recommend that you
read *Plague of Corruption* by Dr. Judy Mikovits and Kent
Heckenlively, JD, along with *Ending Plague; A Scholar's
Obligation In An Age of Corruption* by Dr. Francis W.
Ruscetti, Dr. Judy Mikovits and Kent Heckenlively, JD.
Drs. Mikovits and Ruscetti worked directly under Dr.

Anthony Fauci for many years and, eventually, blew the whistle on him.

During his 50 years at NIAID, Dr. Fauci formed corrupt relationships with Big Pharma and the U.S. Department of Defense (DOD), in direct opposition to his duty and responsibility to serve the public interest and protect public health.

Robert F. Kennedy Jr. ("Bobby") is a personal friend of mine and the godfather of two of my nieces. The son of Robert F. Kennedy, the former U.S. Attorney who was assassinated in 1968 while campaigning for President of the U.S., he is also an incredibly courageous environmental attorney who has gotten convictions against some of the biggest polluters in the history of the world. He is also the founder of Children's Health Defense and, as of this writing, is running for President of the United States. In his book, *The Real Anthony Fauci*, he states:

"Dr. Fauci's strategy for managing the COVID-19 pandemic was to suppress viral spread by mandatory masking, social distancing, quarantining the healthy (also known as lockdowns), while instructing COVID patients to return home and do nothing – receive no treatment whatsoever – until difficulties breathing sent them back to the hospital to submit to intravenous remdesivir and ventilation. This approach to ending an infectious disease contagion had no public health precedent and anemic scientific support. Predictably, it was grossly ineffective; America racked up the world's highest body counts. Medicines were available against COVID – inexpensive, safe medicines – that would have prevented hundreds of thousands of hospitalizations and saved as many lives if only we'd used them in this country. But Dr. Fauci and his Pharma collaborators deliberately suppressed those treatments in service to their single-minded objective – making America await salvation from their novel, multi-billion dollar vaccines. American's native idealism will make them reluctant to believe that their government's COVID policies were so grotesquely ill-conceived, so unfounded in science, so tethered to financial interests, that they caused hundreds of thousands of wholly unnecessary deaths. But, as you will see below, the evidence speaks for itself." [1]

Bobby continues to share:

"Dr. Fauci was clearly aware that his mask decrees were contrary to overwhelming science. In July 2020, after switching course to recommend national mask mandates, Dr. Fauci told Norah O'Donnell with *InStyle* magazine that his earlier dismissal of mask efficacy was correct "in the context of the time in which I said it," and that he intended to prevent a consumer run on masks that might jeopardize their availability for frontline responders. But Dr. Fauci's emails reveal that he was giving the same advice privately. Moreover, his detailed explanations to the public and to high-level health regulators indicate he genuinely believed that ordinary masks had little to no efficacy against viral infection. In a February 5, 2020 email, for example, he advised his putative former boss, President Obama's Health and Human Services Secretary, Sylvia Burwell, on the futility of masking the healthy. On February 17, he invoked the same rationale in an interview with USA Today:

A mask is much more appropriate for someone who is infected and you're trying to prevent them from infecting other people than it is in protecting you against infection. If you look at the masks that you buy in a drug store, the leakage around that doesn't really do much to protect you. Now, in the United States, there is absolutely no reason whatsoever to wear a mask. [2]

During a January 28 speech to HHS regulators, he explained the fruitlessness of masking asymptomatic people:

> The one thing historically people need to realize, that even if there is some symptomatic transition, in all the history of respiratory borne viruses of any type, asymptomatic transmission has never been the driver of outbreaks. The driver of outbreaks is always a symptomatic person. Even if there's a rare asymptomatic person that might transmit, an epidemic is not driven by asymptomatic carriers.

Consistent with Dr. Fauci's earlier statements, the peer-reviewed scientific literature has steadfastly refused to support masking the healthy as an effective barrier to viral spread, and Dr. Fauci offered a citation to justify his change of heart. A December 2020 comprehensive study of 10 million Wuhan residents confirmed Fauci's January 28, 2020 assertion that asymptomatic transmission of COVID-19 is infinitesimally rare. Furthermore, some 52 studies – all available on NIH's website – find that ordinary masking (using less than an N95 respirator) doesn't reduce viral infection rates, even – surprisingly – in institutional settings like hospitals and surgical theaters." [3]

In *The Real Anthony Fauci*, Bobby Kennedy continues:

"Dr. Fauci's mask deceptions were among several "noble lies" that, his critics complained, revealed a manipulative and deceptive disposition undesirable in an even-handed public health official. Dr. Fauci explained to the New York Times that he had upgraded his estimate of vaccine coverage needed to insure "herd immunity" from 70 percent in March to 80-90 percent in September not based on science, but rather in response to polling that indicated rising rates of vaccine acceptance. He regularly expressed his belief that post-infection immunity was highly likely (with occasional waffling on this topic) although he took the public position that natural immunity did not contribute to protecting the population. He supported COVID jabs for previously infected Americans, defying overwhelming scientific evidence that post-COVID inoculations were both unnecessary and dangerous." [4]

Years prior to the COVID-19 pandemic, Fauci appeared in an interview on C-SPAN to discuss the flu and other infectious diseases. Here is a brief transcript of the video recording:

C-SPAN Washington Journal Host:
She's had the flu for fourteen days, should she get a flu shot?

Dr. Anthony Fauci:
Well, no, if she got the flu for fourteen days, she's as protected as anybody can be because the best vaccination is to get infected yourself. If she really has the flu, if she really has the flu, she definitely doesn't need a flu vaccine. If she really has the flu.

C-SPAN Washington Journal Host:
She should not get it again this year?

Dr. Fauci:
No, she doesn't need it because the most potent vaccination is getting infected yourself.

You can view the video interview here: https://bhaktaschool.org/fauci-on-infection-and-vaccination/

Indeed, as you will read in this and other works that are recommended in this book, inoculation and vaccination are two different things. We have God-given immunity to even the worst of contagions in the incredible miracle of our immune systems. If you have a healthy immune system and you know how to keep it healthy and how to repair it by the many natural, non-toxic means available, you will always develop natural immunity to contagions that you may be infected with. That you become infected and develop natural immunity in this way is known as *inoculation*. Vaccination is also a form of inoculation by synthetic and sometimes harmful means.

In his handling of the COVID-19 pandemic, Dr. Fauci contradicted many supported scientific facts like the one indicated in the above interview transcript, to the detriment of Humanity.

Then, in early 2017, in a conference at Georgetown University, Dr. Fauci tells of a pandemic under President Trump:

Dr. Anthony Fauci:
I thought I would bring that perspective to the topic today, is the issue of pandemic preparedness. If there's one message that I want to leave with you today, based on my experience, and you'll see that in a moment, is that there is no question that there will be a challenge to the coming administration in the arena of infectious diseases, both chronic infectious disease, in the sense of already ongoing disease—and we have certainly a large burden of that— but also, there will be a surprise outbreak. And I hope by the end of my relatively short presentation, you'll understand why history, the history of the last 32 years that I've been the Director of NIAID, will tell the next administration that there's no doubt in anyone's mind that they will be faced with the challenges that their predecessors were faced with.

You can view the video of Fauci making the above statement here: https://bhaktaschool.org/fauci-predicting-pandemic/

So, three years before the COVID-19 pandemic, Dr. Fauci was telling people that it was about to occur. Does he have a crystal ball!? The only question remains what did he know and when did he know it?

Then, in a recent MSN publication, in an article written by *Dylan Housman* entitled *'Scientific And Public Health Failure': Fauci Admits COVID Shots Didn't Have A Chance Of Controlling The Pandemic,* we learned of the following:

"Dr. Anthony Fauci admitted in a recently published research paper that COVID-19 vaccines could not have been reasonably expected to get the pandemic under control....Fauci and other top government and healthcare officials repeatedly stressed during the pandemic that getting vaccinated would stop the spread of COVID-19 and was the most important step individuals could take to end the pandemic. However, in the paper published Jan. 11 in Cell Press, Fauci and two co-authors write that respiratory viruses like SARS-CoV-2 and the flu have never been well-contained by vaccines." [5]

And, in February of 2023, in an article written by Nate Ashworth for US Presidential News entitled *Fauci Now Admits Why Covid Vaccine Was Never Able to Slow the Spread* we learned the following:

"For months, perhaps even years, the public was endlessly told that the Covid-19 shot would prevent transmission and infection
of the Coronavirus. Just get the shot and the pandemic will end tomorrow, that's the precise message that was sent from public health bureaucracies, the federal government, and many state governments during the early months of 2021. The talking point from the White House became constantly lamenting Covid as a "pandemic of the unvaccinated." From a newly

published study, authored by Dr. Anthony Fauci, the nation's formerly highest-paid government employee, and top infectious disease doctor, it's clear that fighting respiratory viruses with a traditional vaccination model was a fool's errand from the start, and everyone was in on the joke. The full review, summarized by Cell, provides a deep look at specifically why anything called a "vaccination" will never be effective against a fast-mutating virus like the one that causes Covid-19..." [6]

"If people let the government decide what foods they eat and
what medicine they take, their bodies will soon be in as sorry
a state as are the souls who live under tyranny."
       ~ *Thomas Jefferson*

When Will We Learn?

History has taught us that, in crises such as these, the people making the decisions and calling the shots will never get
up in front of a camera to make public statements, and will never give an interview. When will we learn? People like Dr. Anthony Fauci and Bill Gates are mouthpieces for the people who are really pulling the strings. The reason, in this example, that Dr. Fauci flip-flopped on the science is because he was following a script given him by those behind the scenes who were calling the shots.

And, do you remember the news conferences held by every Governor in the United States in early January of 2020 proclaiming mask and social distancing mandates and lockdowns? Word-for-word their statements were exactly the same. In fact, if you viewed the news clip footage of these press conferences side-by-side, it is eerily comical to note how scripted these presentations were, and how all the scripts were exactly the same!

Unless we required hospitalization, we were told to stay home, mask up and social distance until a Covid shot was available. During this time, while waiting for the "vaccines," doctors on the frontlines who were effectively treating thousands of patients and saving lives with inexpensive, repurposed medications like Hydroxychloroquine, Ivermectin and Budesonide were censored and their medical licenses were suspended or revoked permanently. I know some of these doctors personally. At the same time, researchers whom I know were communicating with scientists in China who had performed studies showing that a combination of Vitamin D, C and Zinc given intravenously was preventing and healing infection of SARS-CoV-2. These studies were censored by the CDC in collaboration with all the Big Tech platforms and mainstream media.

In the state of Ohio where I live, 10 million doses of these repurposed medications were purchased by the state with our tax dollars, and then locked up in a warehouse while Governor Dewine searched for a buyer. While people suffered for lack of treatment while waiting for Covid shots to be developed and distributed under Operation Warp Speed, the remedy for SARS-CoV-2 infection was locked away from everyone while thousands of people died who could have been effectively treated.

It is a crime against Humanity to outlaw available treatments, whether experimental or not, when people are dying of a treatable disease. Read on as I now present to you evidence of what I have just stated in paragraphs above: that the COVID-19 pandemic and its "emergency public health response" was fully orchestrated by the U.S. Department of Defense and the CIA, in collaboration with the military industrial complex of other nations around the globe, as a bioterrorist weaponized military countermeasures response under martial law. This is why people like Dr. Anthony Fauci, Bill Gates, the Governors of the U.S. States, and their associates in the COVID-19 Pandemic response will never be brought to trial for their criminal activities during COVID.

Is Covid-19 A Bioweapon?

There is a long history of bioweapons development and testing that began, side-by-side with the nuclear arms race, at the start of WWII. The perpetrators were Germany, Japan and the United States. Of these, the U.S. has been the primary culprit in the development and testing of bioweapons, the testing of which has been done on American citizens and people of other nations. Professor Francis A. Boyle is a primary whistleblower with respect to bioweapons testing and development. As a result of his testimony, he was asked to draft what is now the U.S. Biological Weapons Antiterrorism Act of 1989 that was passed and signed into law. You can view a recorded interview of him about the history of bioweapons development here: https://live.childrenshealthdefense.org/chd-tv/shows/good-morning-chd/the-terrifying-bioweapons-arms-race-with-francis-boyle-phd/.
You should also read the book *The Wuhan Cover-Up: And the Terrifying Bioweapons Arms Race* by Robert F. Kennedy, Jr.

The pandemic that was officially announced in December of 2019 and officially announced as being over in May of 2023 was a planned event. The response to the release of SARS-CoV-2 on the world population was not a public health response. It was a military countermeasures response under martial law against a known pathogen, the experimentation on which dates back to 1965.

It is important for you to understand that, with military medical countermeasures, at least in the United States, the countermeasures used do not have to be safety tested (see the Sasha Latypova interview transcript later in this chapter). In addition, under any application of countermeasures in the United States, stakeholders and others who are carrying out the countermeasures are immune from any and all liability that may result from the application of the countermeasures – in this case the Covid shots.

I will now share with you five different sources (there are more) to substantiate the fact that SARS-CoV-2, the virus that causes COVID-19 was manufactured in a lab and then released on us, everywhere.

Covid-19 Was Biological Warfare On The Human Race

Dr. David E. Martin and his work in exposing the 2019-2023 Sars-Cov2 outbreak as a plandemic is the subject of the now renowned documentary *Plandemic 2: Indoctornation – How the Covid-19 Pandemic Was Planned Years Before the Outbreak by the Military and Intelligence Communities*. You can view the entire documentary here: https://plandemicseries.com/plandemic-2-indoctornation/. Dr. David E. Martin is the Founder and Chairman of M·CAM Inc., the international leader in innovation finance, trade, and intangible asset finance. He is the developer of the first innovation-based quantitative index of public equities and is the Managing Partner of the Purple Bridge Funds. He is the creator of the world's first quantitative public equity index – the CNBC IQ100 powered by M·CAM. Actively engaged in global ethical economic development, Dr. Martin's work includes financial engineering and investment, public speaking, writing and providing financial advisory services to the majority of countries in the world.   For many years he has also been following the money connected to coronavirus patents and the nefarious relationship between Big Pharma, the U.S. and British intelligence communities and governments around the world.

Speaking to the European Union Parliament about the Covid-19 plandemic, Dr. Martin stated the following:

"In 2005, this particular pathogen (Sars-Cov) was specifically labeled as a bioterrorism and bioweapon platform technology. Described as such— that's not my terminology that I'm applying to it. It was actually described as a bioweapons platform technology in 2005. And from 2005 onwards, it was actually a biowarfare enabling agent, it's official classification from 2005 forward. I don't know if that sounds like public health to you, does it? Biological warfare enabling technology. That feels like not public health; that feels like not medicine; that feels like a weapon, designed to take out humanity. That's what it feels like. And it feels like that because that's exactly what it is. We have been lured into believing that EcoHealth Alliance and the U.S. Defense Advanced Research Projects Agency (DARPA) and all of these organizations are what we should be pointing to, but we've been specifically requested to ignore the facts that over $10 billion dollars have been funneled through black operations, through the check of Anthony Fauci. And a side-by-side ledger where NIAID has a balance sheet, and next to it is a biodefense balance sheet, equivalent dollar-for-dollar matching, that no one in the media talks about, and it's been going on since 2005."

"Our gain of function moratorium, the moratorium that was supposed to freeze any efforts to do gain of function research, conveniently, in the fall of 2014, the University of North Carolina Chapel Hill received a letter from NIAID saying that while the gain of function moratorium on coronavirus in-vivo should be suspended, because their grants had already been funded, they received an exemption. Did you hear what I just said? A biological weapons lab facility at the University of North Carolina Chapel Hill received an exemption from the gain of function moratorium so that, by 2016, we could publish the journal article that said SARS coronavirus is poised for human emergence, in 2016."

"And what, you might ask, Dave, was the coronavirus poised for human emergence? It was WIV-1, Wuhan Institute of Virology Virus-1. Poised for human emergence in 2016 at the proceedings of the National Academy of Sciences, such that, by the time we get to 2017/2018, the following phrase entered into common parlance among the community: "There is going to be an accidental or intentional release of a respiratory pathogen." The operative word, obviously, in that phrase: the word "release." Does that sound like "leak"? Does that sound like a bat and a pangolin went into a bar in the Wuhan Market and hung out and had sex and lo and behold, we got SARS CoV-2? No.

"Accidental or intentional release of a respiratory pathogen" was the terminology used. And four times in April of 2019, seven months before the allegation of patient number one– four patent applications of Moderna were modified to include the term "accidental or intentional release of a respiratory pathogen" as the justification for making a vaccine for a thing that did not exist. If you have not done so, please make sure that you make reference in every investigation, to the premeditation nature of this. Because it was in September of 2019 that the world was informed that we were going to have an accidental or intentional release of a respiratory pathogen so that by September 2020, there would be a world-wide acceptance of a universal vaccine template."

"That's their words, right in front of you, on the screen. The intent was to get the world to accept a universal vaccine template, and the intent was to use coronavirus to get there. We have to read this into the record everywhere I go: *"Until an infectious disease crisis is very real, present, and at the emergency threshold, it is often largely ignored. To sustain the funding base beyond the crisis,"* he said, *"we need to increase the public understanding for the need for medical countermeasures, such as a pan-influenza or pan-coronavirus vaccine. A key driver is the media, and the economics will follow the hype. We need to use that hype to our advantage to get to the real issues. Investors will respond if they see profit at the end of the process."* [7] Sounds like public health? Sounds like the best of humanity?"

"No, ladies and gentlemen. This was premeditated domestic terrorism stated at the proceedings of the National Academy of Sciences in 2015, published in front of them. This is an act of biological and chemical warfare, perpetrated on the human race, and it was admitted to, in writing, that this was a financial heist and a financial fraud. "Investors will follow if they see profit at the end of the process." Let me conclude by making five very brief recommendations. Nature was hijacked. This whole story started in 1965 when we decided to hijack a natural model and decided to start manipulating it. Science was hijacked when the only questions that could be asked were questions authorized under the patent protection of the CDC, the FDA, the NIH, and their equivalent organizations around the world. We didn't have independent science; we had hijacked science. And unfortunately, there was no moral oversight, in violation of all of the codes that we stand for. There was no independent, financially disinterested independent review board ever impaneled around coronavirus; not once. Not once, not since 1965."

"We do not have a single independent IRB ever impaneled around coronavirus. So, morality was suspended for medical countermeasures, and ultimately, humanity was lost because we decided to allow it to happen. Our job today is to say: no more gain of function research— period. No more weaponization of nature— period. And most importantly, no more corporate patronage of science for their own self-interest unless they assume 100% product liability for every injury and every death that they maintain."

You can view Dr. Martin's entire presentation to the European Union Parliament here: https://rumble.com/v2qm8ne-dr.-david-martin-fact-covid-19-was-biological-warfare-on-the-human-race.html.
    In the documentary *Plandemic 2: Indoctornation*, Dr. David E. Martin provides a great deal of information and evidence to support his statements above. In his short and concise paper entitled, *The Criminal Conspiracy of Coronavirus*, Dr. Martin states:

"Every single Act, the declaration of the State of Emergency, the Emergency Use Authorization, the fraudulent face masks, the business closures, and the OSHA and CMS vaccine mandates are ALL admitted by the conspirators to be acts to coerce the population into taking a vaccine. They announced it in 2015, then prepared the pathogen in 2016, and laid out the terror campaign in September 2019. And now they profit from the death of Americans."

You can download the full, 4-page document here: https://covid19alternativeperspectives.files.wordpress.com/2021/11/the-criminal-conspiracy-of-coronavirus.pdf.

In addition, there are two videos connected to the above, regarding vaccine nanotechnology in the Covid shots and Transhumanism, that I encourage you to view for additional information and evidence. You can view those here: https://bhaktaschool.org/vaccine-nanotechnology/. Thanks to *Time to Free America* and *Stew Peters Productions* for presenting these.

Researcher Denis Rancourt has put together a team of analysts to research changes in all-cause mortality during the Covid-19 pandemic. The early findings are that the major increases in all-cause mortality did not occur until the Covid shots were distributed and taken by a majority of the world population. There was a spike in all-cause mortality that coincides with the uptake of the Covid shots. These findings are preliminary and the research team is continuing this project. However, it will be interesting to see if their detailed findings support the rising death toll of people who were inoculated with Covid shots during the pandemic. You can view a video of Denis Rancourt presenting their findings here: https://www.bitchute.com/video/U2kWRSAm3XGn/

Meanwhile, in a notice to the FDA the Florida State Surgeon General has called for a halt in the use of all Covid-19 mRNA vaccines due to findings regarding what's in the shots that are clearly indicative of DNA altering ingredients. You can view the article here:

https://www.floridahealth.gov/newsroom/2024/01/202
40103-halt-use-covid19-mrna-vaccines.pr.html. Dr.
Joseph Mercola has done an extensive analysis of
scientific findings as to the content of the Covid shots
that are of great concern. You can view his article here:
https://vachristian.org/scientist-issues-dire-warning-
about-covid-boosters-and-mrna-shots/

The Truth About Wuhan

Dr. Andrew Huff is a combat veteran,
technologist and infectious disease epidemiologist with
decades of experience in scientific research, national
security, and entrepreneurship. He was a senior
scientist and vice president with EcoHealth Alliance
(EHA) and was a senior member of the technical staff at
Sandia National Laboratories. He has held positions in
government, non-governmental organizations, industry
and academia. Dr. Andrew Huff is also one of the
primary whistleblowers regarding both the
release of the SARS-Cov-2 virus from the Wuhan
Institute of Virology (WIV) and the Gain of Function
(GoF) research performed on the virus under the United
States Dual Use Research of Concern (DURC).

The DURC allows for projects to be funded to
develop treatment for viruses while, at the same time,
allowing for research and development to take place to
develop viruses and other pathogens as bioweapons.
This allowed the GoF to be funded by the U.S. National
Institutes of Health (NIH) and the National Institute of
Allergy and Infectious Diseases with grants assigned by
Dr. Anthony Fauci. This funding was based largely on a
research article co-authored by Ralph Baric at the
University of North Carolina at Chapel Hill entitled
SARS-like WIV1-CoV poised for human emergence. You

can view the article here:
https://www.pnas.org/doi/10.1073/pnas.1517719113

Dr. Andrew Huff was interviewed by Del Bigtree on *The HighWire*. I strongly encourage you to view the interview here: https://thehighwire.com/ark-videos/ex-ecohealth-alliance-exec-turns-wuhan-whistleblower/. In his book *The Truth About Wuhan – How I Uncovered the Biggest Lie in History*, Dr. Huff tells us the following:

"This is the truth about Wuhan: there is no evidence that SARS-CoV-2 naturally emerged...Drs. Peter Daszak, Billy Karesh, Jon Epstein, Kevin Olivial and I were always socializing and strategizing with global key players at powerful companies and governments. Our objective was to create an alliance of companies, organizations and government officials that dominated the sources of funding and controlled the entire scientific discourse within the field of zoonotic emerging infectious diseases...This, in my opinion, was how EcoHealth Alliance was able to bypass the ban on dual use research of concern (DURC), the infectious disease research that can be used for peaceful or harmful purposes, in the United States, and that was likely part of why "Understanding the Risk of Bat Coronavirus Emergence" was funded when it was clearly GoF and DURC, and it could be reasonably argued that EHA set up China to fail. If you are a more powerful scientific organization and possess more advanced capabilities than one of your consortium partners or subcontractors, then it is in your organization's best interest to ensure that they are set up for success." [8]

In *The Truth About Wuhan*, we are given an exact copy of a section of the grant proposal submitted to NIH by both EHA and the WIV titled "Specific Aims," a proposal that was fully funded by NIH for GoF on bat-CoVs (coronaviruses derived from bats). In this section it specifically states:

Specific Aim 3: Testing predictions of CoV inter-species transmission. We will test our models of host range (i.e. [*sic*] emergence potential) experimentally using reverse genetics, pseudovirus and receptor binding assays, and virus infection experiments in cell culture and humanized mice. With the bat-CoVs that we've isolated or sequenced, and using live virus or pseudovirus infection in cells of different origin or expressing different receptor molecules, we will assess potential for each isolated virus and those with receptor binding site sequence, to spill over. We will do this by sequencing the spike (or other receptor binding/fusion) protein genes from all our bat-CoVs, creating mutants to identify how significantly each would need to evolve to use ACE2, CD26/DPP4 (MERS-CoV receptor) or other potential CoV receptors. We will then use receptor-mutant pseudovirus binding assays, in vitro studies in bat, primate human and other species' cell lines, and with humanized mice where particularly interesting viruses are identified phylogenetically, or isolated. [9]

The Medical/Military Industrial Complex

The truth is since approximately 1965 the U.S. government has collaborated with Big Pharma to produce vaccines as medical countermeasures by creating medical crises after crises to justify the purchase of biologics that are not safety tested, and then to mandate that these biologics, like Covid shots, be forced on society. To date, the CDC in the U.S. is the largest purchaser of these shots in the world.

In his book *The Truth About Wuhan*, Dr. Huff provides what he refers to as *The Real Covid Timeline*. The following are excerpts from that chapter.

"In 1995, a scientist at the University of North Carolina, Dr. Ralph Baric, made a series of discoveries during interspecies transfer experiments with coronavirus via serial passage (a gain of function technique). Then, in 2002, Baric's scientists introduced their mouse coronavirus into flasks that held a suspension of monkey cells, human cells, and pig testicle cells. Baric's team had discovered a way to create a full-length infectious clone of the entire mouse-hepatitis genome. They wrote that the "infectious construct" replicated itself like the real thing. They also determined how to perform the genetic assembly seamlessly, without any signs of human engineering. The result is that a person would not be able to determine if a virus had been fabricated in a laboratory or grown in nature. As previously discussed, Baric called this the no-see-um method and he asserted that it had "broad and largely unappreciated molecular biology applications." The method was named after a "very small biting insect that is occasionally found on North Carolina beaches."

"These methods, if applied to a virus like SARS-CoV-2, the agent that causes COVID-19, would make it difficult to discern whether an agent was human-engineered. In 2002, the BioIndustry Initiative's mission was to counter the threat of bioterrorism through targeted transformation of former Soviet biological weapons research and production capacities:

The U.S. Department of State BioIndustry Initiative (BII) is a nonproliferation program authorized in the Defense and Emergency Supplemental Appropriations Act for Fiscal Year 2002 (Public Law 107-117). The bill focuses on two objectives: (1) The reconfiguration of former Soviet biological weapons (BW) production facilities, their technology and expertise for peaceful uses; and (2) the engagement of Soviet Biological and Chemical Weapons scientists in collaborative R&D (research and development) projects to accelerate drug and vaccine development for highly infectious diseases.

This was a program run by the U.S. Department of State, which saw numerous American biologists and virologists visit former Soviet biowarfare facilities to examine the technology they had developed over the years and see if anything was suitable for patenting and repurposing for civilian use. Dr. Michael Callahan formerly served as the health director for USAID in Nigeria where he carried out research on deadly pathogens. In 2002, he was hired as the State Department's director for the Bureau of International Security and Nonproliferation to serve as "clinical director for Cooperative Threat Reduction [CTR] programs" at six former Soviet Union Biological Weapons facilities as part of the BII program. He was officially tasked with carrying out the state goals of the mission, which entailed the "reconfiguration of former biological weapons production facilities" in the former Soviet Union and the acceleration of "drug and vaccine production." Callahan would be put in charge of gain of function programs and for viral biological agents at these facilities."

"From 2002 through 2003, there was a large SARS outbreak, which frightened the globe and generated much interest in these new types of coronaviruses and the opportunities to conduct GoF research involving them. In fact, a patent war broke out over the intellectual property rights for the genetic material of the agent SARS-CoV-1....In my opinion, as the size and complexity of these well-intended and effective programs increased, they became too difficult for government officials to effectively manage. As it appears, at least in the case of the laboratory creation of SARS-CoV-2, the lack of effective program management may have been abused by some members of the U.S. government to outsource GoF research during the domestic pause on GoF research."

"In 2009, Michael Callahan's old employer USAID launched PREDICT, an early warning system for new and emerging diseases, in twenty countries. In 2009, Dennis Carroll, a former USAID director for the emerging threats division who had led the United States' response to Avian influenza (H5N1) in 2005, would go on to create PREDICT. USAID partnered with a non-profit called EcoHealth Alliance to carry out its nine-year effort to catalog hundreds of thousands of biological samples, "including over 10,000 bats." UC Davis was the prime contractor, and Metabiota and EHA received sub awards on the prime contract (a.k.a. the group was known as the PREDICT partners). Also, in 2009, the Wuhan Institute of Virology (WIV) in Wuhan, China began collaborating with EcoHealth Alliance on the USAID Emerging Pandemic Threat program on a project titled PREDICT. The PREDICT partners were USAID, UC Davis, Wildlife Conservation Society, EcoHealth Alliance, Metabiota, and the Smithsonian Institute and PREDICT and USAID are listed in the letters of support from the collaborators in China in the "Understanding the Risk of Bat Coronavirus Emergence" proposal. By identifying unknown viruses before they spilled over into humans – to "find them before they find us," as WIV virologist Shi Zhengli put it – researchers hoped to establish an early-warning system. <u>PREDICT worked in dozens of countries, but WIV was one of its linchpins, and Shi Zhengli became famous as China's 'Bat Woman.'</u>" [10]

In *The Truth About Wuhan*, Dr. Andrew Huff continues to elaborate in great detail the COVID timeline as it matches the GoF research and development of deadly pathogens like SARS-CoV-2 in the lab at WIV, subcontracted out and managed by EHA, and at UNC at Chapel Hill under the management of Dr. Ralph Baric. He goes on to state the fact that, at one point, EHA was approached by the CIA. This led to EHA forming a relationship with In-Q-Tel (IQT). [11] IQT is a Department of Defense and Central Intelligence Agency venture capital firm that invests in companies that make technology that is of a national security interest. Dr. Huff states that, eventually, the CIA and the U.S. Department of Defense were directly involved in managing GoF development on pathogens, including SARS-CoV-2, which was engineered in labs at WIV and UNC Chapel Hill under DURC for bioweapons development.

Dr. Huff goes on to state that he believes there were two releases of SARS-CoV-2 from WIV; the first being an accidental leak, and the second a willful release of the virus in the wet market in Wuhan to make it look like the emergence of a natural, wild virus. He also shares details of the SARS-CoV-2 cover-up that he calls the biggest cover-up in history. When you read Chapter 20 of this book, *I Am Over the Target*, to understand the facts of how the U.S. government spent millions of our taxpayer dollars to harass and attack Dr. Huff and his family, at times with deadly force, you will understand the lengths our government went to in order to silence this courageous whistleblower to keep the truth from us.

Is COVID-19 a Bioweapon?
A Scientific and Forensic Investigation

What is Gain-of-Function (GoF) research and how is it undertaken? GoF utilizes a method known as Reverse Transcription to reverse transcribe mRNA to DNA to make complimentary DNA using pathogens like murine leukemia virus and other viruses like HIV. This process is used to create a chimeric coronavirus. Chimeric comes from chimeras, creations made by combining the genetic code of one organism with that of another to make a new organism. [12] For a better understanding of how this works, you can also view my interview of Dr. Judy Mikovits here: https://bhaktaschool.org/greed-and-the-great-reset/. Simply put, GoF is reverse genetics, meaning this is a process effectively used to change genes, otherwise known as gene therapy.

The fact is, here in America, our government has used our taxpayer dollars to fund the research and development of a chimeric, gain-of-function, gene altering virus that it then tested by allowing it to be released on us. Dr. Richard M. Fleming was deposed on this matter and gave testimony to support his fact. You can view the full deposition here: http://vrijheid.wtf/video/covidbioweapon.mp4. This research and development was funded through NIH and NIAID through grants that were approved and managed by Dr. Anthony Fauci, a government bureaucrat who, in over 50 years has never treated a patient.

Dr. Richard M. Fleming is a Physicist, Internist, Cardiologist, Preventive & Nuclear Cardiologist, Certified in Positron Emission Tomography (PET). He is also a Juris Prudence Doctor of Law with degrees in Biology, Chemistry, and Psychology. In addition, he is a renowned research scientist, inventor and author. In 1994, Dr. Fleming presented to the American Heart Association his theory that cardiovascular disease was due to inflammation. What was theory in 1994 has become well known fact for decades and was highlighted in 2004, with a feature on ABC's 20/20 News. The Fleming Method patent (FMTVDM) covers ALL methods and devices able to measure metabolic and regional blood flow differences. This breakthrough made it possible to differentiate functionality of tissue, tissue types as well as non-tissue, and the measurement of treatment response using all isotopes, enhancing agents and devices capable of detecting and measuring isotopes. Dr. Fleming is also one of the preeminent researchers on COVID-19 and effective treatments for it.

In his book, *Is COVID-19 a Bioweapon? A Scientific and Forensic Investigation*, Dr. Richard M. Fleming states:

"Like many of you, I began to ask questions, and the answers I found led to more questions about the ultimate motives of the people involved. For patients becoming infected and those hospitalized, we had turned the practice of medicine and honest scientific investigation over to the government and those funded by the government, just as the German Medical Association and scientists of the day had turned it over to Adolf Hitler...Despite the Nuremburg Code of 1947 and the International Covenant on Civil and Political Rights (ICCPR) Treaty being implemented in an effort to prevent such atrocities being committed by people upon people ever again, we find ourselves in the same situation today – unethical experiments conducted by those in power upon those not in power. When the government is involved in experimentation on its citizens, it must use a combination of fear and hope to effectively control the people and manipulate them into submission." [13]

When Did It All Start?

Although the initial plan for GoF that is biopweapons research and development can be traced back to 1965, the funding for it formally began in 1999 when the US Department of Health and Human Services began formerly earmarking taxpayer dollars to fund infectious disease research. This research was focused on understanding how infectious disease can become more infectious over time by natural means. One of the original proposals for researching this came to be known as GoF. GoF quickly morphed from the study of naturally occurring organisms whose infectious ability becomes stronger over time to the development of the means to artificially (in a lab) make these contagions more infectious. As stated earlier in this chapter, the Dual Use Research of Concern (DURC) program was established to allow this to happen.

By 2000, Dr. Ralph Baric at UNC Chapel Hill (see earlier in this chapter) had successfully used reverse genetics to develop GoF coronaviruses. This research was funded by NIH (grant numbers A123946, GM63228, and AI26603. These viruses were patented in 2003. [14]

In his book *Is COVID-19 a Bioweapon?*, Dr. Fleming shares a statement made in a section of the patent document:

> This approach facilitates the reconstruction of genomes in Vitro for reintroduction into a living host, and allows the Selected mutagenesis and genetic manipulation of Sequences in Vitro prior to reassembly into a full length Genome molecule for reintroduction into the same or Differenthost (United States Patent No. US006593111B2). [15]

Then, Dr. Fleming provides the following information:

"In 2002 following the SARS-CoV-1 outbreak in China, Dr. Shi Zhengli, a.k.a Shi Zhengli-Li (the bat lady), and colleagues at the Wuhan Institute of Virology (WIV) began investigating how SARS-CoV-1 was transmitted. (*Note – this is just before the global outbreak of SARS-CoV-1 in 2003.) In particular, Zhengli was interested in how SARS-CoV-1 could be transmitted from person to person. (**Note – in a previous section of this chapter I provided you with evidence presented by Dr. David E. Martin that SARS-CoV-1 was also engineered in lab through GoF.)   To do this, she developed chimeric (Gain-of-Function) coronaviruses using human immunodeficiency virus-based pseudovirus systems with cell lines of people, civet cats, and horseshoe bats. In March 2004, HHS announced that it was going to create the National Science Advisory Board for Biosecurity (NSABB) to be managed by the National Institutes of Health (NIH).   A press release issued by then Secretary of HHS Thompson states the following:

> Our nation has been a world leader in life sciences research because of our emphasis on the importance of the free flow of scientific inquiry. **Yet, sadly, the very same tools developed to better the health and condition of humankind can also be used for its destruction.**

In 2005, Baric published a paper – omitting unpublished research (pg. 21 in Baric's paper) - declaring that he could alter the genome of coronaviruses, noting the "alteration of any part of the coronavirus genome." In 2006, using chimeric (Gain-of-Function) research, Chinese scientists reported their ability to combine parts of four different viruses into a single viral genome. This report raises a few serious questions in my mind.

First, why were these researchers combining parts of four dangerous viruses – specifically, hepatitis C virus (HCV), human immunodeficiency virus-1 (HIV-1), SARS-CoV-1 (identified as SARS-CoV-1 and not SARS-CoV), and SARS-CoV-2? Second, if as we've been told, SARS-CoV-2 didn't appear until 2019 and there were no identified naturally occurring SARS-CoV-2 reported between this 2006 publication and 2019, then doesn't this, at least, in part, suggest that SARS-CoV-2 is not naturally occurring but manmade? Third, if the answer to question number two is that the virus is manmade, going as far back as 2006, then doesn't this add credence to those who have cautioned that SARS-CoV-1 was a bioweapon and SARS-CoV-2 is an upgraded version of that bioweapon?" [16]

In his book *Is Covid-19 a Bioweapon?*, Dr. Fleming goes on to provide many details about other GoF RNA to DNA reverse transcription projects in the U.S., including the very first GoF project on the virus QB phage in 1974. He then continues to provide a great deal of evidence on U.S. funding of GoF by presenting details of the paper trail for this funding that used our taxpayer dollars to develop bioweapons that were eventually released on us, along with copies of the actual patents on the manmade chimeric viruses that were granted.

Dr. Fleming also provides detailed information about the SARS-CoV-2 spike protein, along with data that shows that the SARS-CoV-2 bioweapon was intentionally released on the world. This data includes images of slides of supporting evidence and a written transcript of an interview he conducted with Dr. Karaladine Graves and Virologist Dr. Li Meng Yan who speaks about her direct observations regarding the release of the SARS-CoV-2 bioweapon by the CCP.

The Covid-19 Covert Military Program

Sasha Latypova is a former pharmaceutical R&D executive. She worked in the industry for 25 years, and ultimately owned and managed several contract research organizations working on clinical trials for 60+pharma companies, including Pfizer, AstraZeneca, J&J, GSK, Novartis and many others. She worked for many years in cardiovascular safety assessments and interacted with the FDA and other regulatory agencies on these matters on behalf of her clients and as part of the FDA Cardiovascular Safety Research Consortium.

Her research has exposed how all Covid countermeasures, including the biological warfare agents marketed as "Covid-19 vaccines," were created, produced and distributed in a covert military program, where the pharma manufacturers worked as subcontractors to the military. What follows is a transcript of part of her interview conducted by The Epoch Times:

Sasha Latypova:
What we found is the whole representation of what is happening is a lie. It's basically the U.S. government is representing to the public that this is a health event, and a response to a health event. But in fact, what they are doing, this is a military operation. These so-called vaccines, they're not really vaccines. But these injections are being manufactured under defense contracts utilizing Defense Production Act, other transaction authority, and Emergency Use Authorization under public health emergency. So, when these things are used together, then good manufacturing practices do not apply to these products at all.

Jan Jekielek:
Even legally?

Sasha:
Even legally. There's this law on the books, 21 U.S.C. 360bbb (21 U.S. Code § 360bbb-3) [17,18] that says emergency use authorized countermeasures, under public health emergency, cannot constitute clinical investigation. So, clinical investigation is actually not possible for these countermeasures. And if clinical investigation is not possible, then you cannot have clinical trials, you cannot have informed consent, you cannot have clinical trial subjects, or clinical trial investigators.

So, utilizing the structure of Emergency Use Authorization, public health emergency, and other transaction authority, Defense Production Act, the government was able to commandeer pharmaceutical companies to produce these non-compliant injectable products and distribute them, calling them medicine, where in fact, it's not a medicine; it's an act of war.

They're using Defense Production Act in machinery, United States military; even internationally this is being distributed from this military to oversees militaries, not pharmaceutical distribution chains. So, they're using the military machinery to distribute these non-compliant products, including biologicals, chemicals, all kinds of ingredients we don't really understand very well, and call it public health and medicine.

Jan:
First of all, this sounds so fantastical, what you just said. Right? What? Really? That's crazy. Now, one thing I know for sure is not crazy, which is the fact that it's the military that did the distribution; that's official. That's actually public knowledge that was announced. I know people that were responsible for the distribution and they're very proud of doing the distribution because they felt it was the only structure in society that's able to deploy something like this fast enough. I have that on record. But what about these other parts, like that this is actually the U.S. government contracting these pharma companies to develop a countermeasure against what?

Sasha:
The countermeasure is a very important legal term, and I advise people to look it up. The countermeasure is a very fuzzy term, first of all. So, anything can be a countermeasure; a lock on the door is a

countermeasure against a break-in. So, calling something a countermeasure, you already remove the precision of the legal definitions of a pharmaceutical, for example. But we know already that it's not a pharmaceutical. It's not a conspiracy; definitely not, because the law that I just described, this 21 U.S.C. 360bbb, is cited by everyone, including the FDA in their documents, including by the manufacturers in their documents, by GAO reports that discuss this.

Recently, as you may know, Brook Jackson's False Claims Act case was dismissed. The judge, you can read the dismissal of this case. The judge agrees with what I just said. He agreed with the fact that Pfizer wasn't supposed to be compliant with good manufacturing practices, per contract with the Department of Defense; that they were producing countermeasures, that they were producing large scale manufacturing demonstration which is how these things were ordered from the government. He essentially describes this in a more sophisticated hundred-page document.

Jan:
Based on a contract.

Sasha:
Based on a contract that Pfizer produced. Pfizer produced their DOD contract, and since then, hundreds of Department of Defense contracts for Covid countermeasures were released through FOIA, although they're partially redacted. I read a lot of them, and they're all online. I've read the Pfizer and Moderna ones, and some other vaccines, and they're all essentially similar. They're utilizing the structure of ordering countermeasures, ordering prototypes; Department of Defense ordering it from the pharmaceutical manufacturers under Defense

Production Act, under other transaction authority. The good manufacturing practices are not part of it at all.

So, this product, by statute and by contract with Department of Defense, does not need to be compliant with good manufacturing practices. Another additional part of this whole scheme is this Public Health Emergency announcement. So, when Public Health Emergency happens, essentially, the executive branch of the government usurps the power from the legislative and judicial.

Public Health Emergency, by various illegal amendments and acts over a long period of time, has been created into this trigger that triggers this whole system where the HHS Secretary becomes like a de facto dictator. So, HHS Secretary is the sole person who can deploy these products in the United States. So, FDA need not be part of it.

In the law, it says that HHS Secretary, he or she, whoever that happens to be – it used to be Alex Azar who was under Trump, and now it's Xavier Becerra, they can determine whether these countermeasures can be deployed in the United States, based on available data, if available, it does not have to be available, and based on his own determination about current risk-benefit profile and future risk-benefit profile. Again, he can take advice of whoever he wants to take advice from, but the decision is up to him.

Jan:
That's very interesting because it's also counter intuitive. If it's a DOD operation, why is the HHS Secretary responsible for the deployment?

Sasha:
In the structure of Public Health Emergency, it's a militarized structure, so they merge. It's all executive branch. HHS and DOD become kind of one organization, and they also wrap FDA in.

Jan:
In terms of this operation.

Sasha:
In terms of this operation. The Public Health Emergency becomes that trigger for essentially invoking all these military-type of laws saying that now they're one organization. There's also inter-agency agreements that go into this where they determine confidentiality, they determine how they're going to make these countermeasures and so forth. The HHS Secretary deploys them, DOD orders them, they get funding through the DOD through the Biomedical Advanced Research and Development Authority (BARDA). BARDA is an HHS agency, so they're all intertwined. FDA kind of rubber stamps everything and pretends they're regulating these things, but they're impersonating regulators basically, because there's nothing in the law that says that FDA regulates countermeasures; they don't.

Jan:
You would think someone would want to know. Let's say, I've had a number of people on this show who have been pretty serious vaccine injuries, for example. One of the pieces of fallout from this scheme that you're describing is the idea that these people could be harmed is denied by society and certainly denied by the authorities; not 100%, there's admissions in the NIH, and so far, that's rare. Mostly they say there's no signal; mostly they say that this doesn't work; people are

diagnosed with anxiety and things like that. This seems to be linked to this idea that this is somehow not a health response. I don't know what your thoughts are on this?

Sasha:
I understand why the government denies it, clearly. I still can't wrap my head around denial of this happening by regular physicians. I know that there is a monetary structure that incentivizes this behavior, so there is definitely payments from Medicare and Medicaid to the doctors to vaccinate, bonuses for numbers of vaccinations administered, bonuses especially very high bonuses to vaccinate somebody who hasn't been vaccinated. There's a high price on the heads of people who haven't been vaccinated to get the injections in and to give boosters and so forth. There's huge monetary incentive there.

The entire structure is, essentially, the government extended its sovereign liability protection to everyone who complies with this system.   Throughout this whole structure of producing these injections, distributing them, injecting them, then denying the injury, there's a huge not only monetary compensation and incentive, but also liability protection through the PREP Act. That's explicit also in the DOD contracts with vaccine manufacturers. And not just vaccines, actually, it goes with the entire Covid countermeasures production, which includes vaccines, therapeutics, monoclonal antibodies, blood products, diagnostics, even masks and swabs and staffing and things of that nature.

All of them have this clause that says PREP Act liability exemption clause, which describes that if you were in compliance with all of this, then you would treat it as a covered person under this Act, and you are exempt from liability if you essentially followed the orders. And the last sentence of that clause says that this is both civil and military application; this product is both civil and military application.

By the way, the contracts are redacted. With most common redactions, there are two redactions: B-6 and B-4. B-6 has to do with if we reveal this information, it hurts U.S. foreign policy or U.S. foreign relations. B-4 is if we reveal this information, we reveal information about state-of-the-art technology in the U.S. weapon system.

I'd like somebody to answer this. I'm just listing a set of facts. You can make your own conclusions, but I'd like somebody to answer this question: Why and what is being put in these injections? What are people being injected with? Because we know there's huge amounts of deaths and injuries, but we can't address those injuries until we know what they were injected with. We still don't know that.

Jan:
I mean, ostensibly, it's a mRNA—synthetic mRNA in a lipid nanoparticle envelope that activates production of synthetic spike in the body to create an immune response; it definitely does that, but there's more to it. I guess that's what you're saying is that there's more to it than that?

Sasha:
Right. So, that's what's claimed. I know you just said it's claimed on the label of the product, but I've described before we know for sure they're not Good Manufacturing Practice compliant, which means they can't themselves, verify to themselves, that that's what they're making. Right? So, they are probably making

that in some instances, but there is also a whole bunch of other effects and varieties.

By the way, if a product is not Good Manufacturing Practices compliant, it's open to adulteration and falsification, whether on purpose or accidental. So, we have now a whole bunch of unknowns happening.

Jan:
I remember this scene where Dr. Renata Moon opened up the—I forget which one, but it was one of the mRNA vaccine's insert as Bobby Kennedy, Jr. says "the one place where the vaccine companies tell the truth." Right? And she opens it up and all that's on there is "intentionally left blank" or something close to that.

[transcription from video clip referred to above]

Dr. Renata Moon:
I unsealed the box that the entire thing came in and then I pulled this out, and this is what it looks like. I'd like to show this to you. It's blank on both sides.

Dr. David Gortler
Boom. There it is.

Dr. Moon:
It says "Intentionally Blank" on it.

Dr. Gortler
That's the data that pharmacists and physicians are basing on giving the injections outside of mainstream media recommendations. There it is, right there. Here's a good question: Why didn't they just print that on a piece of paper the size of a postage stamp? Why all the theater of folding it up into a great big piece of paper like that? Why?

Senator Ron Johnson:
That's what's passing for informed consent?

Dr. Moon:
Right. So, how am I to get informed consent to parents
when this is what I have? I have a government that's telling
me that I have to say "safe and effective," and if I don't, my
license is at threat. How am I to give informed consent to
patients? We're seeing an uptick in myocarditis; we're
seeing an uptick in adverse reactions; we have trusted these
regulatory agencies − I have, for my entire career up until
now. Something is extremely wrong.

[End of video clip - See the video clip of Dr. Renata Moon
speaking in Washington, D.C. about the Covid shot package
inserts here:
https://www.informedchoicewa.org/pediatricians-contract-
terminated-by-wsu-after-reporting-to-senate-roundtable-on-
covid-shot-harms/. If this video has been taken down or you
can't access it, use this link to view Dr. Renata's testimony as
part of the U.S. Senate congressional hearings conducted by
Senator Ron Johnson, *COVID-19 Vaccines: What They Are, How
They Work and Possible Causes of Injuries* here:
https://rumble.com/v1ze4d0-covid-19-vaccines-what-they-
are-how-they-work-and-possible-causes-of-injuri.html

The referenced testimony runs from 2:24:29-2:26:19 in the
video]

Shortly after giving the above testimony Dr. Moon was fired
from her tenured professorship position at Washington State
University]. [19]

Later in the Sasha Latypova interview there is an
exchange regarding mRNA biologics. Below is part of
that discussion from the interview.

Sasha:
It's very easy to subvert it, to change it, to introduce
other codes, to introduce other nefarious types of
pieces of code into it. And if you don't know what was
introduced, you don't have an assay to test for it. It's

completely open to adulteration and falsification. Correct, the technology has been in development since the 90s, but no products have come to the market out of it; no successful medical products because of all these problems I've described: the manufacturability of it; you can't really make it consistently in Good Manufacturing Practices compliant; and it's wide open for these falsifications and weaponization-type of approach. It's also documented in a lot of literature, including NIH textbooks, military reports, bioweapons technologies has very well documented this phenomenon. The use of it is indistinguishable between supposedly medicinal use that has never been demonstrated, and weaponized use that has been demonstrated.

That whole obsession with this technology seems extremely problematic to me; very questionable. Somebody again has to explain, how do you distinguish between weaponization use of this technology and what you claim is beneficial, medicinal use?

Jan:
Yeah, that's a great question. I just want to clarify when you were talking about the code, you're basically saying that the mRNA that goes into that technology that is then delivered via the way that the mRNA vaccines were delivered, that code is subject to change and you can introduce some other mRNA and you wouldn't even know to test for it if you didn't know what was put in there; and since the whole system is a black box, it's very hard to actually track and assay for it and so forth?

Sasha:
Yes—assay for it, verify it. In fact, it's been allowed by the regulators. Another thing I haven't discussed yet, I

think you've also covered it in your publication. At the end of 2020, there was a leak from European Medicines Agency and a bunch of documents were released. Pfizer manufacturing documents at the time of the approval and a bunch of emails between EMA staffers that were discussing this. In these documents, it was clear that at the end of 2020, the European Medicines Agency deemed Pfizer not Good Manufacturing Practice compliant. It was the number one objection from the regulators to their approval. And two, they found this issue of mRNA breaking down and creating broken pieces of mRNA, broken code.

At the time, Pfizer told them that the standard for approval should be 50% of mRNA should be consistent with the declared code, and the regulators went along with it. So, because the product was approved in Europe within weeks of this discussion that was released. So, 50% of mRNA should be consistent with the code that they declare for BNT162b2, and then the other 50% is unknown.

Jan:
Right. They lowered the standard.

Sasha:
They lowered the standard arbitrarily for themselves, and regulators somehow miraculously agreed with that nonsense, which means that 50% is undeclared. Fifty per cent can be practically any sequence; it could be any designer sequence you can make, and if you made a designer sequence and didn't tell anybody what it is, how are you going to make an assay to test for it? You can't.

You can view the entire interview with Sasha Latypova here:

https://www.theepochtimes.com/exposing-the-vaccine-military-machinery-behind-the-global-covid-19-response-sasha-latypova_5335644.html.

For more about this you can also view *DOD 'Vaccines': Lara Logan & Sasha Latypova Dec 21 on DOD "vaccine" Coverup /w FDA Theater* here: https://rumble.com/v22ijfs-lara-logan-and-sasha-latypova-on-dod-vaxx-coverup-w-fda-theater.html

SARS-CoV-2 Engineered and Released From a Lab

Dr. Li Meng-Yan is a virologist who received her medical degree from Xiangya Medical College of Central South University in China. In 2014, she completed a PhD in ophthalmology from Southern Medical University in Guangzhou. After this, she was a postdoctoral fellow at the University of Hong Kong (HKU) until 2020. She was affiliated with the State Key Laboratory of Virology, Wuhan Institute of Virology, Chinese Academy of Sciences, and the University of Chinese Academy of Sciences. Before the COVID-19 pandemic, Dr. Yan had served as a co-author on articles about Aquareoviruses and universal influenza vaccines.

After threats were made on her life, Dr. Li Meng-Yan fled China after blowing the whistle on the CCP's coverup of the fact that SARS-CoV-2 is a manmade, GOF virus that was designed as a bioweapon and escaped from the Wuhan Institute of Virology. She has been interviewed by a number of journalists, including Tucker Carlson. A transcript of a short portion of her Tucker Carlson interview appears below.

Tucker Carlson:
Give us, for a non-scientific audience, a summary of why you believe this virus came from a lab in Wuhan, please.

Dr. Li-Meng Yan:
Okay. Briefly, from my first report, I can present solid scientific evidence to our audience that this virus, Covid-19, Sars-Cov-2 virus, actually is not from nature. It is a man-made virus created in the lab, based on the China military discover and owned the very unique bat coronavirus which cannot affect people, but after the modification becomes a very harmful virus now. So, I have evidence to show why they can do it, what they have done, how did they do it.

Carlson:
So, what you're saying is much more sinister, even than we've suggested on this show, than Tom Cotton, than almost anyone's suggesting. You're saying that the Chinese government manufactured this virus, if I'm hearing you correctly. That's what you're saying?

Dr. Yan:
Yes, exactly, based on the virus genome is basically like our fingerprint. So, you can see the very unusual characters in their genome which, conveniently, based on the other evidence they left during the modification, we can see finally this is exactly the one that comes from their own special bat coronavirus that then targets humans.

Carlson:
What you're alleging is shocking more even than I anticipated when we invited you on.

You can view a more recent Fox News interview of Dr. Li Meng-Yan here: COVID-19 an 'intentional release' from Wuhan lab: Dr Li-Meng Yan.
https://www.foxnews.com/video/6314583376112

The Select Subcommittee On the Coronavirus Pandemic Hearing

The U.S. Congress has convened a select subcommittee on the origins of the SARS-CoV-2 outbreak. This is the Select Subcommittee On the Coronavirus Pandemic in which hearings are now being conducted. Below is a transcript of a portion of the opening of that hearing regarding the Proximal Origins report that insists that the SARS-CoV-2 outbreak came from nature and not from a lab.

Dr. Brad Wenstrup (Committee Chairman):
This is not an attack on science, it's not an attack on peer-review, and it's not an attack on an individual. We're examining whether government officials, regardless of who they are, unfairly and perhaps biasedly, tipped the scales toward a preferred origin theory. We're examining any conflicts of interest, biases, or suppression of scientific discourse regarding the origins of COVID-19. We're examining the science of Proximal Origin because, while I believe it's not solely a scientific question, the science behind the origins is vital.

In one word, we're examining the scientific methodology applied to the origins question. In my mind at this point, I view the processes to be flawed. If we're to do better in the future, we must make every effort to mend our flaws. And overall, we're examining whether scientific integrity was disregarded in favor of political expediency, maybe to conceal or diminish the government's relationship with the Wuhan Institute of Virology; or perhaps its funding of risky gain-of-function coronavirus research; or maybe, to avoid blaming China for any complicity, intended or otherwise, in a pandemic that has killed more than one million Americans and has had a crushing effect on all of humankind.

In the earliest stages of the pandemic, scientists and public health authorities raced to understand this novel coronavirus, called novel for good reason— to understand how it spread, who was at risk, its origins, and most importantly, how to prevent loss of life. As work advanced gradually on most of these fronts, the origins question stalled. Did it come from a natural spillover, transferred from a bat to an intermediate source to a human? Or was it the result of a laboratory or research-related accident? In other words, did it come from a lab? Honestly, we may never know with 100% certainty the origins of COVID-19, especially without full, legitimate cooperation and transparency from all involved.

However, we do know some things for certain: that the drafting, coordination, and publication of Proximal Origin and downplaying the lab leak was "antithetical to science." Not my words. That's what Dr. Redfield, the former CDC Director and renowned virologist, testified to our Select Subcommittee in March. He testified that "..science never selects a single narrative... We foster... debate. And we're confident that with debate, science will eventually get to the truth."

Did we do that? That wasn't the case with Proximal Origin. Dr. Anderson, testifying today, wrote that the authors' "main work over the past couple of weeks had been focused on trying to disprove any type of lab theory."

While it's true that the scientific method consists of raising a hypothesis and then testing that hypothesis, often through falsifiability, it's not true nor appropriate to make definitive conclusions based on a falsification process riddled with assumptions. Assumptions are not science.

To be clear: the goal of science is to prove and disprove, regardless. It would be seemingly misleading to assume that Proximal Origin proved or disproved anything it sought to test. Its conclusion is flawed, as it relies on unsupported assumptions, including guessing what a hypothetical scientist would do in hypothetical experiments.

The facts are that the authors' of Proximal Origin ultimately took a one-sided, educated guess. They guessed that in the previous three years, science would discover a furin cleavage site in a SARS-related virus or viruses, and didn't. They guessed that maybe the WIV, the Wuhan Institute of Virology, wasn't working with pangolin viruses, and they were wrong, as related by ODNI, the Office of the Director of National Intelligence.

Perhaps most troubling, it appears that the authors' views on a potential lab leak changed abruptly after the February 1st conference call with Drs. Fauci and Collins. The authors continued their pursuit to disprove the lab leak theory and fully support the nature theory, employing faulty assumptions and willfully ignoring circumstantial evidence that tended to support a lab leak hypothesis. Why? Why? They also tended to act more akin to politicians than scientists.

Dr. Rambaut, Dr. Fauci Dr. Collins, all expressed concerns that the lab leak theory, if verified, would have significant international political implications, particularly for China. Dr. Fauci also wrote that downplaying a lab leak "would... limit the chance of new biosafety discussions that would unnecessarily obstruct future attempts of virus culturing..." These are quotes. Why try to avoid biosafety discussion when people are dying? Science should be clear, even when politics are not. On April 16, Dr. Collins expressed dismay that Proximal Origin didn't fully squash the lab leak theory and asked Dr. Fauci if there was anything more they could do to put it down.

You can view the video footage of the entire hearing here: https://www.c-span.org/video/?529219-1/hearing-origins-covid-19.

Just after taking the oath of office, President Biden was repeatedly asked on several occasions to comment on the origins of SARS-CoV-2 and reports stating that the virus was likely released from a lab at the Wuhan Institute of Virology. Biden refused to comment. In some cases, when questions were posed about WIV, Biden looked at reporters in disgust and walked away.

On July 17, 2023, the Department of Health and Human Services issued a memorandum to suspend and propose debarment of the Wuhan Institute of Virology from participating in any U.S. government procurement and nonprocurement programs. The memorandum makes repeated reference to NIH, NIAID and EcoHealth Alliance. Here is an excerpt of the memorandum:

ACTION REFERRAL MEMORANDUM

"On behalf of the United States Department of Health and Human Services (HHS), I hereby suspend and propose the debarment of Wuhan Institute of Virology, Chinese Academy of Sciences Capital Construction

WIV from participating in United States Federal
Government procurement and nonprocurement
programs. This action is initiated pursuant to 2 C.F.R.
Part 180. HHS adopted and gave regulatory effect to 2
C.F.R. Part 180 at 2 C.F.R. Subpart 376.10. The
suspension and proposed debarment for WIV is based
on information from the following:

1) a September 29, 2022, Referral of Information (ROI),
from the National Institutes of Health (NIH), Office of
Policy for Extramural Research Administration (OPERA)
concerning WIV;

2) the October 1, 2013, NIH Grants Policy Statement
(NIH GPS) for Fiscal Years 2013- 2014;

3) a May 27, 2014, Notice of Award (NoA) for Grant
Number 1R01AI110964-01, awarded

4) a May 28, 2016, letter from NIAID to EcoHealth;

5) a June 8, 2016, letter from EcoHealth to NIAID;

6) a July 7, 2016, letter from NIAID to EcoHealth;

7) a November 30, 2016, Revised NoA for Grant Number
5R01AI110964-03, awarded by NIAID to EcoHealth;

8) a May 26, 2017, NoA for Grant Number
5R01AI110964-04, awarded by NIAID to EcoHealth;

9) HHS Framework for Guiding Funding Decisions about
Proposed Research Involving Enhanced Potential
Pandemic Pathogens (HHS P3CO Framework), published
on December 19, 2017;

10) a June 18, 2018, NoA for Grant Number
5R01AI110964-05, awarded by NIAID to EcoHealth;

11) a July 24, 2019, NoA for Grant Number
2R01AI110964-06, awarded by NIAID to EcoHealth;

12) an April 19, 2020, letter from the NIH to EcoHealth;

13) an April 24, 2020, letter from the NIH to EcoHealth;

14) a May 22, 2020, letter from the law firm of , to the
NIH;

15) a July 8, 2020, letter from the NIH to EcoHealth;

16) a July 23, 2021, letter from the NIH to EcoHealth;

17) an October 20, 2021, letter from the NIH to

EcoHealth;

18) an October 26, 2021, letter from EcoHealth to the NIH;

19) Year 4 Research Performance Progress Report (RPPR), for Grant Number 5R01AI110964-05;

20) Year 5 Interim-Research Performance Progress Report (I-RPPR) for Grant Number R01AI110964-05;

21) a November 5, 2021, letter from the NIH to EcoHealth;

22) a November 18, 2021, letter from EcoHealth to the NIH;

23) a January 6, 2022, letter from the NIH to EcoHealth;

24) a January 21, 2022, letter from EcoHealth to the NIH;

25) an August 19, 2022, letter from the NIH to EcoHealth; and

26) a January 25, 2023, HHS Office Of Inspector General (OIG) Audit Report Number A- 05-21- Effectively Monitor Awards And Subawards, Resulting In Missed Opportunities To The information summarized below indicates that WIV lacks the present responsibility to participate in United States Federal Government procurement and nonprocurement programs. The information from this record provides cause for the suspension under 2 C.F.R. § 180.700(b) and (c) for the debarment cause provided in 2 C.F.R. § 180.800(d) Any other cause of so serious or compelling a nature that it affects your present responsibility HHS believes there is adequate evidence in the record for this debarment cause and that immediate action is necessary to protect the public interest."

You can read the full memorandum here: *US Government Suspends Funding to Wuhan Lab Over Risky Experiments*
https://www.documentcloud.org/documents/23881768-hhs-memorandum-on-wuhan-laboratory-funding.

In my mind, this is, at the very least, an admission of complicity on the part of the U.S. Federal Government in the COVID-19 plandemic that cost the world millions of lives, with millions more left sick with long-haul Covid and millions more permanently injured from Covid jabs that were never properly safety tested and were not required to be Good Manufacturing Practice compliant. Clinical trials for the Covid shots were not required because the shots were procured by the U.S. Department of Defense under the Defense Production Act. In other words, an untested biologic was mandated and distributed worldwide, and we are the guinea pigs.

Also, there is population control element to all of this which is now being investigated by the Sovereignty Coalition (more about the coalition later in this book). Concerns over the use of Covid shots as part of a Eugenics plot began when Bill Gates gave a TED talk in which he stated that there is a necessity to reduce the world's population by 10-15% in the coming years. Then Gates presented a list of ways in which to do so, and vaccines are on that list. You can view the video clip of this section of his presentation here that starts at 5 minutes and 45 seconds in to the video: https://bhaktaschool.org/died-suddenly/.

The Next Pandemic Has Already Been Planned

On October 18, 2019, exactly two months before the Covid-19 Pandemic was declared, The Johns Hopkins Center for Health Security in partnership with the World Economic Forum and the Bill and Melinda Gates Foundation performed a pandemic tabletop exercise in New York City. The video footage was immediately posted on YouTube.   The exercise illustrated the pandemic preparedness efforts needed to diminish the large-scale economic and societal consequences of a severe pandemic. You can view selected moments from the Event 201 here: https://www.youtube.com/watch?v=AoLw-Q8X174

The exercise is now widely considered to have been a foreshadowing of the Covid-19 Pandemic designed to create panic to prepare people for accepting Covid-19 lockdowns and other unconstitutional mandates. It is during declared states of emergency that it becomes easiest for government and the wealthy elite to violate our constitutional and human rights and civil liberties. In fact, in many cases, this is why these states of emergency are created in the first place.

The next pandemic is already being planned. *The SPARS Pandemic – 2025-2028. A futuristic Scenario for Public Health Risk Communications.* That subtitle should read, "A futuristic Scenario for How to Control the Narrative and All Messaging for Public Health Risk Communications." This is a medical countermeasures (MCM) document that begins in very much the same way that Event 201 does – by claiming that the scenario depicted in the document is fictional. It is a setup for "disease X."

Under a subheading that states "Unbridled Global Access to Information Coupled With Social Fragmentation and Self-affirming Worldviews," the 'scenario purpose' is stated.

"The following narrative comprises a futuristic scenario that illustrates communication dilemmas concerning medical countermeasures (MCMs) that could plausibly emerge in the not-so-distant future. Its purpose is to prompt users, both individually and in discussion with others, to imagine the dynamic and oftentimes conflicted circumstances in which communication around emergency MCM development, distribution, and uptake takes place. While engaged with a rigorous simulated health emergency, scenario readers have the opportunity to mentally "rehearse" responses while also weighing the implications of their actions."

Mentally rehearse responses to a medical/health emergency that does not exist?! This document also voices concerns about diversity in media that make it difficult to control the narrative.

In this document, the 'fictional' scenario begins with an outbreak of a virus in St. Paul, Minnesota – hence the name St. Paul Acute Respiratory Syndrome Coronavirus or SPARS-CoV, named after the city in which the outbreak first occurs. The narrative then unfolds pointing to a global pandemic of SPARS-CoV. In response to the pandemic, a drug called Kalocivir is immediately developed and distributed for treatment of symptoms, while a vaccine is being rushed to development. Kalocivir. It sounds eerily similar to Remdesivir, the drug touted in the Covid-19 pandemic as being the only treatment for Covid, outside of the Covid shots.

The document goes on to narrate that there are side effects to Kalocivir, but that the benefits outweigh the side effects – and then goes on to suggest how health agencies can diminish the overwhelming reports of Kalocivir side effects by minimizing those reports online and promoting the safety and effectiveness of the drug in a way that drowns out the complaints. In this regard, there are specific references to addressing the voices of the 'anti-vaccinators,' the anti-Kalocivir movement and the natural medicine movement online. In a section entitled 'The Grass Is Always Greener (On the Other Side)' there is also a reference to new antiviral drugs being used in other countries instead of a vaccine, and that these antivirals have been ruled out in the U.S. in favor of waiting on a vaccine named Corovax.

The document then focuses on how the narrative can be managed to promote the use of Kalocivir and Corovax. In the entire 89 pages of this document is there any reference to how credentialed frontline doctors who have been treating patients for many years are treating the virus? No! Is there any reference to necessary communication between highly credentialed virologists, researchers and epidemiologists around the globe who would interface with government health agencies to compare notes and discuss other available forms of effective treatment for SPARS? No! There is not even a single reference to government health agencies working together to determine how many other alternative and effective treatments could be repurposed to treat SPARS.

In other words, this document being circulated by the John Hopkins Center for Health Security proposes a strategy not for finding as many viable treatments as possible but only for how to control the narrative online and elsewhere, ahead of a rollout of a vaccine. These people have learned nothing from the failed worldwide response to Covid-19.

You can read and download the full document here: https://centerforhealthsecurity.org/sites/default/files/2022-12/spars-pandemic-scenario.pdf

Remember the year – 2025. As you read further you will understand the significance of the year 2025 with respect to coordinated plans to globalize MCMs and Digital IDs under a control grid run by unelected officials and the wealthy elite.

The Intentional Suppression of Effective, Inexpensive Alternative Treatments for Covid-19

When is a pandemic a plandemic? A pandemic is a plandemic when millions of people are allowed to die from a contagion while waiting for an injectable biologic, when viable, inexpensive, effective repurposed medications are readily available as a prophylaxis to the contagion, as effective treatment to cure infection and as effective treatment for those who are hospitalized so that they can quickly go home cured.

This is exactly what happened with COVID-19. We were told that if we got sick with the virus, we should go home, wear a mask and isolate until a 'vaccine' was available. In the early stages of the plandemic, there were highly credentialed frontline doctors who were treating patients infected with SARS-CoV-2 and saving lives using well-known, FDA-approved medications that have been used in the medical field for, at least, 30-60 years prior to the plandemic. Most of these doctors had their medical licenses threatened or permanently revoked for doing what they were trained to do – saving lives and curing patients. Some of these doctors I know personally and I have interviewed several of them for online podcasts and conferences. Chief among them are:

Vladmimir Zev Zelenko, MD
Peter A. McCullough, MD
Meryl Nass, MD
Pierre Kory, MD
Paul Marik, MD
Simone Gold, MD
Robert Malone, MD
Dr. Judy Mikovits

Sherry Tenpenny, DO
Rashid Buttar, MD
Trisha Bhatt, MD
Harvey Risch, MD
Kevin Wheelan, MD

Then there are the doctors and researchers who are also professors at Universities. These professors put together research teams of virologists and epidemiologists to study and provide alternative treatments for COVID-19. They were also vilified and threatened for successfully treating the virus with these inexpensive, effective FDA-approved medications. Some of these professors are:

Professor Didier Raoult
Professor Joseph Varon, MD
Professor Gianfranco Umberto Meduri, MD
Professor Jose Iglesias, MD

The treatments that were used in various combinations to successfully cure people of SARS-CoV-2 infection include:

Hydroxychloroquine
Azithromycin
Ivermectin
Budesonide
Ozone therapy
Nebulized Peroxide
Nasal Interferon
Nitric oxide nasal spray
Iodine
Vitamins C and D and zinc, whether oral or intravenous
Methylprednisolone (a corticosteroid)
Monoclonal Antibodies

Hydroxychloroquine, Azithromycin and Ivermectin have been used to successfully treat other Coronaviruses such as SARS-CoV-1, MERS, HCov-229E, HCov-NL63, HCov-OC43 and HCov-HKU1.

In the book *The Courage to Face COVID-19* by John Leake and Peter A. McCullough, MD, MPH, we are told the following:

"Research teams in China were reporting favorable results from treating Covid patients with hydroxychloroquine – a drug that had been FDA-approved since 1955 for malaria prophylaxis, as well as for the treatment of lupus and rheumatoid arthritis. In India, the state medical councils recommended that front line medical workers take the drug as prophylaxis. 'The only thing I'm seeing in the literature is the antimalarial hydroxychloroquine," McCullough replied. 'I think we should take the Indian medical council's recommendation and give it a try.' And so, he and Dr. Wheelan decided to conduct a clinical trial of Hydroxychloroquine." [20]

This became one of the first successful trials for using Hydroxychloroquine to treat COVID-19.

A world-renowned microbiologist named Didier Raoult has been on the leading edge of researching, testing and applying effective treatments for viruses. SARS-CoV-1 and SARS-CoV-2 are about 85%-90% the same and there is evidence that SARS-CoV-1 was also manufactured as a bioweapon (see *The Truth About Wuhan* earlier in this chapter). In 2003, Professor Raoult monitored the outbreak of SARS-CoV-1 in China and studied the literature on anti-viral properties of chloroquine and hydroxychloroquine to fight the virus. In 2007, he published a paper offering evidence of hydroxychloroquine as a weapon against future infectious diseases. In 2018, he reported that azithromycin was a potent treatment for cells infected with Zika virus.

"When SARS-CoV-2 broke out in 2020, again emanating from China, he wanted to know how Chinese doctors were treating the disease. In February, he saw reports from multiple Chinese research teams stating that chloroquine and hydroxychloroquine were reducing disease severity and accelerating clearance of the virus. The People's Hospital of Wuhan University posted a notice on its website that none of the 178 patients admitted so far had lupus, suggesting the Hydroxychloroquine they were taking to treat lupus may have prophylaxis value against COVID-19. On February 19, a pharmacology research team in Qingdao, China published a report in English that on February 17, the State Council of China held a news briefing in which it announced that chloroquine phosphate had demonstrated marked efficacy and acceptable safety in treating COVID-19. After positive in vitro studies, several clinical trials were conducted to test chloroquine and hydroxychloroquine for the treatment of COVID-19." [21]

"For Professor Raoult, this report was cause for jubilation. Facing a pandemic that could inflict untold suffering and death on mankind, it appeared that a well-known, safe, cheap, and easy to manufacture drug was effective at treating it. Wanting to share this good news, on February 25 he posted a video on YouTube titled *Coronavirus: Game Over!* "It's excellent news – this is probably the easiest respiratory infection to treat of all," Raoult said. He then formulated his own treatment protocol. He chose hydroxychloroquine because it is less toxic than its analogue chloroquine. He combined it with azithromycin because of the anti-viral effect he'd observed in using it against the Zika virus, and for its value against secondary bacterial infections. As for the safety profile of these drugs, they'd been around for decades, with billions of doses taken and well-tolerated. Both hydroxychloroquine and azithromycin are on the World Health Organization's Model List of Essential Medicines." [22]

In March of the same year, Professor Raoult announced that he would test and treat anyone who came to his hospital. People came in droves. There were so many that his staff had to erect tents outside to examine and treat sick patients. Each was treated with his combination therapy. A clinical study was then performed to evaluate the impact of hydroxychloroquine on respiratory viral loads.

By day 6, only 6 of the 14 patients receiving hydroxychloroquine tested positive. All 6 patients treated with a combination of hydroxychloroquine and azithromycin had cleared the virus. By day 6, 14 of the 16 control patients who were not treated with this combination continued to test positive for the virus. [23] These results made a strong case for using this combination to treat patients with COVID-19, while continuing to perform larger trials. Professor Raoult published the results of this study in the *International Journal of Antimicrobial Agents*. With a pandemic raging and many people dying, the expectation was that medical professionals, scientists and researchers would be, at least, optimistic about the study – enough to begin trying these medications with their own patients. Instead, there was a study done of 96,000 patients, hailed by some as the definitive study, showing the drug hydroxychloroquine was most certainly dangerous and ineffective, and that it killed 30% more people than those who didn't take it. However, within days, that study was retracted, with the editor of one of the two most respected medical journals in the Western world conceding the study was "a monumental fraud." [24]

There is a saying that no good deed goes unpunished. That certainly applies here. Professor Raoult's efforts showing the promise of these combined, repurposed medications that were eventually proved to be efficacious in the treatment of COVID-19 were met with steps to suppress the validity of this treatment.

On the heels of this falsified study designed to discredit the many frontline doctors who were treating their patients with the above list of FDA-approved, effective and inexpensive medications, I decided to run an online Covid conference. In this two-and-a-half hour live conference several frontline doctors and researchers were interviewed. In addition to talking about how they used inexpensive, effective, off-label FDA-approved medications to cure COVID-19, they also speak about how these treatments were suppressed by government and mainstream media. I strongly encourage you to view the recording of this conference here: https://bhaktaschool.org/covid-conference/

In addition, to further understand how these life-saving, alternative medications were suppressed while we were told to wait for Covid shots that were not properly safety tested and that proved dangerous and life-threatening, go to this web page https://bhaktaschool.org/covid-alternative-therapies/ for a wealth of additional information and data on this topic.

Dr. Paul Marik, Dr. Mary Bowden and Dr. Robert Apter are three medical professionals whose medical licenses were revoked for prescribing Ivermectin for the treatment of COVID-19. The three filed a lawsuit against the FDA in this matter that is now on appeal. As of this writing, an attorney for the FDA has just announced that doctors can now prescribe Ivermectin for COVID-19. A day after this announcement, the FDA countered that announcement by restating that Ivermectin has not been approved to treat COVID-19. Dr. Mary Bowden is leading a group of doctors who have brought a lawsuit against the FDA that is now pending.

Understand the Mindset of Our Adversaries

Big government and the wealthy elite really do believe that the rest of us are sheep who can be easily manipulated to any outcome they deem fit. They also believe that people have to be forced to change their behavior by dictatorial and even tyrannical means. Although far from the only example, Professor David Halpern's public statement is a perfect example. Professor David Halpern heads up the Behavioral Insights Team (the "Nudge Unit"). The Nudge Unit exists to provide the UK government with "frictionless access to behavioral expertise." Halpern's unit developed slogans such as "hands, face, space," to increase citizen compliance with Covid-19 restrictions and regulations. In fact, this agency exists to brainwash people into present and future compliance with government mandates that severely restrict freedom.

In a recent interview, Professor Halpern stated, "Citizens will comply with future lockdowns, obedience can be 'switched back on." Professor David Halpern believes citizens will comply with future lockdown restrictions after having "practiced the drill." Halpern told The Telegraph that since the Covid-19 pandemic allowed the citizens of the United Kingdom to "practice" wearing facemasks and following lockdown restrictions, the country "could redo it" in the future. Halpern told The Telegraph that the people of the

United Kingdom would comply with future "stay at home" orders since they already "kind of know what the drill is." Although Halpern believes that fear-based messaging is not usually effective, he argued that it can be used in extreme situations, such as a worldwide pandemic. "There are times when you do need to cut through... particularly if you think people are wrongly calibrated," he said.

Halpern described the tasks his unit was responsible for in his interview with *The Telegraph*, demonstrating how his unit was able to reinforce new behaviors on the United Kingdom's population. You can read the full article here: https://americanmilitarynews.com/2023/07/citizens-will-comply-with-future-lockdowns-obedience-can-be-switched-back-on-uk-official-says/. Also, I urge you to download and read *FLAGGED. How the Global Government is Tracking, Fingerprinting, and Controlling the Unvaxxed* so that you understand what is at stake with respect to global government taking more steps to control our bodies. You can download the eBook here: https://bhaktaschool.org/pdfdownload.php?file=eBook-FLAGGED.pdf

As I stated earlier in this chapter, the response to the release of SARS-CoV-2 on the world population *was not* a public health response. It was a military countermeasures response under martial law against a known pathogen, the experimentation on which dates back to 1965. In order to control and restrict our behavior, government needs to form a nefarious relationship with Big Business and, increasingly, Big Tech. As you will begin to understand in the next chapter, this relationship is, by design, the linchpin for the rollout of Digital IDs that will include digital vaccine passports, digital surveillance of all bodily functions with chips under the skin and central bank digital currencies (CBDCs). This is all part of a global data mining project designed to place socio-economic control of the masses in the hands of despots.

What to Do About It

We face a lot of challenges to our God-given rights and Liberty. Here are some proposed solutions to the challenges discussed in this chapter.

1. **No more Bioweapons**. All bioweapons research and development must be outlawed. This means the Dual Use Research of Concern (DURC) policy must be rescinded and medical countermeasures must be Good Manufacturing Practice Compliant so that they are required to go through clinical trials.

The reversal of DURC policy and the outlawing of bioweapons research in the United States can be accomplished by the U.S. Congress passing legislation for this purpose. If the Congress won't do it, then the States can pass laws on these measures.

For either or both of these to happen, we the people must act to pressure our elected officials to enact these laws. Pay close attention to the final chapter in this book, *How to Preserve Our Liberty*, for a detailed, step-by-step plan for how to get our elected officials to act on these measures.

2. **Return to the original National Childhood Vaccine Injury Act of 1986.** I am not an anti-vaxxer. I am pro-safety and I am for health/medical freedom and the right to choose, based on fully-informed consent. And I have been vaccinated growing up. However, *The National Childhood Vaccine Injury Act of 1986*, in its current form, is not the original bill passed into law by the U.S. Congress in 1986. The original bill did not

provide blanket immunity from liability for vaccine manufacturers and did not provide any liability protection for design flaws in vaccines. The bill was then gutted with a series of amendments (see Chapter 7, Barbara Loe Fisher). The bill in its current, amended form prevents any person who is injured by a vaccine from suing the manufacturer. This law means that vaccine manufacturers are not liable for any injury arising from the use of their product. *This is insane and must be changed.*

The existence of this law set the stage for what we are experiencing in the development of vaccine nanotechnology that is designed to alter cellular DNA and embed circuitry in our cells in order to hook us up to the Cloud like common computer devices (see earlier in this chapter). Vaccines are now a device for Transhumanism and Big Pharma can put anything they want in these vaccines without the knowledge of the public or government. We can be used as guinea pigs and, no matter how high the body count, until this bill is reverted to its original form, there is nothing we or the government can do about it. This bill gives Big Pharma a license to alter the human species, to maim and to kill.

At the time the bill was first introduced, Big Pharma complained that it had too many lawsuits being brought against vaccine manufacturers due to injury caused by vaccines. Pharma threatened to stop making vaccines altogether unless the Congress provided vaccine manufacturers with immunity from all liability. The argument on the part of the vaccine manufacturers was this: In the U.S., the States and the Federal Government *mandate* that children be vaccinated on the CDC childhood vaccination schedule in order to be able to attend school. There are also mandates for travel in and out of the country. The vaccine manufacturers were being sued left and right for injuries from vaccines that government mandates. *It's due to government vaccine mandates that vaccine manufacturers demanded liability protection.*

So, in order to protect the profits of the vaccine manufacturers, instead of requiring Pharma to make better vaccines, the U.S. Congress amended this law to prevent you from suing the manufacturer of the product that has injured you or killed a loved one. *In turn, this has enabled government to continue mandating vaccines.* For a complete understanding of the development of the 1986 Act, view this excellent interview with Barbara Loe Fisher here: https://thehighwire.com/ark-videos/1986-the-untold-story/. Vaccine mandates are the challenge to our Liberty. There should be no vaccine mandates.

Since the passage of this law, the number of vaccines approved for both the childhood and adult vaccine schedules has more than tripled from 15-18 vaccines to 72 vaccines. Furthermore, vaccine injury has skyrocketed since the bill was amended. And, as of the date of this writing, Pharma is required to do little and, in some cases, no safety testing before gaining approval from the FDA. This latest development is due to regulatory capture of our government health agencies by Big Pharma, a point that will be further discussed on this list. For a very good docuseries on the history of vaccines and vaccine injury, go here: https://go.thetruthaboutvaccines.com/ttav/?a_bid=c2b8 d87c&a_aid=5903de82cac79

We can pressure our elected officials in Congress to remove the amendments to the original version of The National Childhood Vaccine Injury Act of 1986. The Act, in its current form, has not properly addressed vaccine safety and efficacy and has reduced the quality of health care in the U.S. by infecting the medical field with the notion of 'one size fits all' treatments. Any good medical professional will tell you that's a recipe for disaster.

Furthermore, Big Pharma makes far too much money on vaccines (billions of dollars per year). They would never ever stop making them simply because they no longer have liability protection. Instead, they would make safer, better vaccines. Congress has acknowledged that "vaccines are unavoidably unsafe" and the Supreme Court has stated that vaccines have "unavoidable adverse side effects." [25]

3. **Support H.R.7551 - LIABLE Act.** If passed, this bill will require that Big Pharma be completely liable for all injuries and deaths resulting from its Covid-19 vaccines. Go here to read the bill:
https://www.congress.gov/bill/118th-congress/house-bill/7551/text
and go here to sign the petition and to contact your Congressional representatives to urge them to vote 'Yes' on the bill.
https://standforhealthfreedom.com/actions/liable/

4. **The state of Louisiana is about to pass a bill that will outlaw the implementation of any pandemic treaty measures** by the WHO, UN and WEF in the state of Louisiana. Send the link to the copy of this bill to your state legislative representatives demanding that they adopt a similar bill in your state.
https://legiscan.com/LA/text/SB133/2024?utm_source=substack&utm_medium=email

5. **Decentralize public health care**. Any centralized agency within the federal government tasked with disease control and prevention will always be highly susceptible to corruption, both by big government and big business (i.e. Big Pharma). And any such agency will, eventually, become a political arm of big government. This translates to public health responses becoming more about political ideology than science. We've seen this historically. Public health responses in the U.S. that have been coordinated by the CDC, NIH and NIAID have, for the most part, been complete failures and this is why, from the HIV public health response to the response to COVID-19, we have been consistently subjected to epidemic public health responses that have failed to properly address the contagion by way of early outpatient treatment to prevent growing illness and hospitalization.

Therefore, we must demand that the U.S. Congress greatly reduce the size and scope of the CDC that, although well-intentioned from the start, has become a political organization that has relentlessly failed the American people. Medical collectives like the Cochrane Collective, America's Frontline Doctors and the Covid-19 Critical Care Alliance (formerly FLCCC) can be developed in each state. These collectives can be made up of highly credentialed frontline doctors and researchers in each state. They can be non-profit organizations that receive their funding from the State and private donors, with no funding from the Federal Government so that their activities cannot be dictated or restricted by the Federal Government.

In the event of a public health emergency, and/or to address other, ongoing public health issues and responses, the CDC would be required by law to interface with each state medical collective to discuss, gather and share information and data regarding effective treatments being deployed on the frontlines, along with the degree of their success. This would ensure that real-time treatment data is coming directly from medical professionals who are successfully treating patients on the frontlines, rather than from government bureaucrats who are not treating patients and, in addition, are under political pressure to make medical decisions based on ideology rather than science – medical decisions that are not in the best interest of public health.

As doctors and researchers who are no longer actively engaged in treating patients or actively engaged in research requested by practicing physicians are identified in these collectives, they could be rotated out to provide room for incoming medical professionals with current practices on the frontlines of treating disease. There would be a published directory of the collectives in each state made available to the public and all medical professionals.

6. **Outlaw the falsification of death certificates and numbers of people infected during a public health emergency.** One of the greatest evils of the COVID-19 plandemic was the falsification of primary cause of death on death certificates to inflate the numbers of deaths attributed to COVID-19. This was mandated first by the World Health Organization (WHO): "The World Health Organisation has told governments to code deaths to Covid even if the virus was not identified in an autopsy and even if it was not medically correct."
[26]

Following the lead of the WHO, directives were then issued by State health departments, other public health agencies and State medical boards advising doctors to record the primary cause of death as COVID-19 for anyone who was infected with the SARS-CoV-2 virus at the time of his/her death, even if the person had an underlying condition that was the actual cause of death. [27,28]

So, as an example, if a person who got into a car accident and was admitted to the ICU because he/she was dying of injuries related to the accident, but tested positive for COVID and then died of the accident injuries, the primary cause of death was listed as COVID-19. Every death certificate has a secondary cause of death section on the death certificate. And, in this example, that's where COVID-19 should have been indicated. Why would medical boards and health departments do this? Money. With respect to people who died *with*

COVID-19 and not of COVID-19, hospitals and doctors connected to hospitals were given a monetary incentive to declare the primary cause of death as COVID-19. If the patient was covered by Medicare or Medicaid, dependent upon whether or not the patient was on a ventilator at the time of death, that payout for listing COVID-19 as the primary cause of death was a range of $19,000-$49,000 per patient.

To better understand this, you can view an interview of whistleblower Dr. Scott Jensen here: The Truth About COVID-19 Death Certificates | Dr. Scott Jensen
https://www.youtube.com/watch?v=PHxj_Luclxs
Also, you can view a video of a death certificate clerk speaking about how death certificates are supposed to be filed and with what criteria – in connection to the inaccurate reporting stated above. See it here:
https://www.youtube.com/watch?v=7McVsC2mm_w

Another evil that must be addressed is the fact that hospitals and State health departments falsified the reported numbers of people infected with COVID-19 to increase the total number of people reported to be infected with the virus. This was done because, during a declared public health emergency, our billions of our taxpayer dollars are allocated to hospitals and State health departments by the U.S. Federal Government for emergency relief. So, again, the falsification of these numbers is about money.

Either the States or the U.S. Congress can pass a law that subjects hospitals, medical boards, health departments, other health agencies and doctors to a fine of $100,000 plus 5 years imprisonment for each instance of falsifying a death certificate or numbers of people infected during any declared public health emergency. This is the answer to this evil.

7. **Demand proper safety testing of vaccines, even in a public health emergency.** As stated earlier in this chapter, there are many off-label, inexpensive and effective FDA-approved medications that can be quickly repurposed to treat a contagion in a public health emergency. Many of these medications have been used to treat contagions of different kinds in past epidemics and pandemics. These are the treatments that should be rolled out first in any public health emergency. *It is a medical fact that vaccines do not prevent the spread of viruses.* Viruses are known to quickly mutate faster than any vaccine can provide relief for. And by the time boosters and new vaccines are manufactured and distributed, viruses have mutated again. So, existing repurposed medications are the foundation for treatment that supports natural immunity to mutating viruses.

New, injectable biologics like vaccines should then be properly safety tested meeting the standard of a minimum of 5-8 years of safety testing. Given the fact that the PREDICT program and USAID have partnered with other nations in the collection of practically every known and unknown contagion on the planet, *there are plenty of existing lab samples with which to begin testing vaccines against in clinical trials that can be started long before any outbreak.* Even so, vaccines during a public health emergency are only useful in treating those who are severely immune system compromised, those with underlying co-morbidities and those over age 65, in order to prevent hospitalizations and relieve symptoms. The above can be ensured by the passage of health/medical freedom laws and laws regarding treatment options and approaches. These laws can be passed by the States and the U.S. Congress, by way of pressure on our elected officials.

In the State of Ohio, I worked with a team of citizens to write citizens bills that were introduced to the Ohio State Legislature and, at present, are being considered by Ohio lawmakers. In Ohio, we are also introducing a medical right to refuse amendment to the Ohio State Constitution that we hope will be ready to vote on by 2024 in a public ballot referendum. These actions can be replicated in any state. To view the Ohio State Medical Right to Refuse initiative, go here: https://www.medicalright2refuse.com/

8. **No vaccine passports**. The proposed vaccine passports that are being rolled out in other countries such as Israel, Canada and the European Union are part of a scheme to introduce digital IDs all over the globe. Also, the only reason to have a digital vaccine passport system is to enforce vaccine mandates by stripping us of the right to choose, based on fully-informed consent.

During the COVID-19 plandemic, people who refused the Covid shots were denied employment, denied enrollment in schools and denied entry to shops, other businesses and sporting/entertainment venues. In addition, people were denied medical, religious and philosophical exemptions to inoculation by Covid shots.

If allowed into our society, vaccine passports, by design, will create a two-tiered society of people who can move about freely and people who cannot. Furthermore, vaccine passports are not about public health. The intention behind them is to create a massive control grid, based on a social credit system linked to digital IDs and central bank digital currency. This challenge, including what to do about it, is covered at length in the next chapter.

9. **Regulatory capture**. There is a revolving door between Big Pharma and the FDA, CDC, NIH and NIAID. This is also true of Big Agra and the USDA. The people appointed to head up these government agencies are almost always people who have held senior positions in Big Pharma and Big Agra. This means federal government agencies that are vital to the uncorrupted service of the citizenry have become completely corrupt in service to large corporate conglomerates and the wealth elite who run them. For example, more than half of the FDA's budget for operations comes from licensing fees paid by pharmaceutical companies. This puts tremendous pressure on the FDA to license drugs that may not have undergone proper safety trials or may have shown the potential for serious harm during safety trials.

The same is true for the U.S. Department of Agriculture (USDA) whose operational budget relies on payments from the very food manufacturing/distribution companies it is charged with regulating. Another example is that the CDC is the biggest buyer of vaccines on the planet, using our tax dollars to do so. This represents a huge conflict of interest on the part of America's leading health agency that is tasked with monitoring and managing disease control and prevention using *all* available science, medical data and treatment options. This is why the CDC routinely overlooks FDA-approved, effective and inexpensive treatment options for disease in favor of pushing a 'one size fits all' agenda using vaccines that often are not properly safety tested.

The answer is that the heads of the Department of Health and Human Services (DHHS), the CDC, the FDA, the NIH, NIAID and USDA should be elected officials, rather than being appointed bureaucrats. Making this change to rein in the administrative state can be accomplished by an amendment to the U.S. Constitution proposed by two thirds of the U.S. Congress or proposed by a Convention of States that is then ratified by three fourths of the several states. (See Article V of the U.S. Constitution)

10. **No Extended States of Emergency**. During the COVID-19 plandemic, the state of emergency lasted three years. Lockdowns, mask mandates and restricted travel were imposed for almost the entire 3-year period. This is outrageous and unnecessary. In addition, most states in the U.S. have a provision in their State constitutions that clearly say that any state of emergency can only be declared by a two-thirds vote of the State legislature. This is the case in the State of Ohio where I currently reside. What this means is that, in Ohio (as in many other states), the Governor suspended the state Constitution in order to impose

lockdowns and other public health mandates. This is illegal and unconstitutional.

In the State of Ohio we had constitutional attorneys who took the Governor and State health department to court and obtained decisions that reversed the lockdown orders that were imposed on restaurants, parks, churches and small businesses. In Ohio, as in most other states, there was a published list of 'non-essential' businesses that were ordered to lock down. Under threat of county sheriffs and police, most of these businesses and organizations closed and many of them never reopened due to the financial hardship caused by the lockdowns. At the same time, churches and spiritual centers were declared non-essential and ordered to lockdown while topless bars and nude entertainment establishments were allowed to remain open. In addition, all schools were shut down and classes had to be attended online.

In the State of Ohio, a group of us who were meeting with State legislators twice each week during lockdown pressured State legislators to enforce our State constitution which says that states of emergency can only be declared by a two-thirds vote of the General Assembly. This means that, legally, no one in the state of Ohio was obliged to obey the Governor's lockdown orders. The Governor's response to this fact was to threaten, in a written document that was distributed throughout the state, that he was prepared to rollout the Ohio State National Guard to enforce lockdowns, mask mandates and mandated vaccination.

So, we had to pressure the State legislature to pass a law. The Governor announced that he would veto the bill, so we got it passed with enough votes to override the veto. Sub SB 22 is now law in the state of Ohio.

The law states that the Governor and/or the State health department can only declare a state of emergency for a period of 60 days. If the Governor or State health department requests it, the public health emergency can be extended for another 30 days by a vote of two thirds of the General Assembly. This law also provides for a cap on any declared state of emergency of 90 days. In addition, the Ohio State legislature can rescind any declared state of emergency by a concurrent resolution. The legislature can also rescind any such order by concurrent resolution if it is determined that the Governor or State health department has attempted to cover up the origins of a disease on which a public health emergency has been declared.

You can view the entire bill that was passed into law here: Sub SB 22 Ohio https://search-prod.lis.state.oh.us/solarapi/v1/general_assembly_134/bills/sb22/EN/05/sb22_05_EN?format=pdf. It is up to every citizen to read and understand your State constitution to ensure that your government officials are not violating your constitutional rights, especially during declared states of emergency. And if your constitutional rights are being violated, you can do as we did in Ohio by pressuring your lawmakers to force the executive branch of your State government to abide by your State constitution and pass any additional law necessary to ensure that's what happens.

I also encourage you to watch the video recording of the 2023 Florida Summit on COVID: "Food, Family & Medical Freedom!" here: https://www.theepochtimes.com/epochtv/live-11-11-9am-2023-florida-summit-on-covid-food-family-medical-freedom-5521816.

You can also watch Dr. Ryan Cole's update on COVID here
https://www.theepochtimes.com/epochtv/dr-ryan-cole-gives-update-on-covid-calls-for-return-to-real-health-and-wellness-5528787

11. **Religious liberty cannot be suspended during a state of emergency.** The freedom to gather and to worship God in whatever way one chooses is a constitutional right and a human right that must never be suspended during states of emergency. The right to gather for this purpose must be protected at all times.

This is a matter of each of us maintaining sustained contact with our elected officials to ensure that they are always taking action to uphold our religious freedoms. For those elected officials who are not doing so, we can and should vote them out of office.

12. **The Constitution cannot be suspended during a declared state of emergency.** Nowhere in any State constitution or the U.S. Constitution does it state that the constitution can be suspended during declared states of emergency. And yet, in most states in America, during the COVID-19 Plandemic, our constitutional rights were violated over and over again with enforced lockdowns, mask mandates and vaccine mandates.

I have addressed actions that can be taken, in part, in number 8 above. In addition, there are bills being considered in various states and the U.S. Congress to outlaw vaccine mandates and vaccine passports. These bills require your support to be passed into law. I discuss this in detail in Chapters 4, 5, 6, 7 and 8.

13. **Health Freedom Amendment to the U.S. Constitution and State Constitutions.** I have addressed this in number 5 above.

"Unless we put medical freedom into the Constitution, the time will come when medicine will organize into an undercover dictatorship to restrict the art of healing to one class of men and deny equal privileges to others; the Constitution of the Republic should make a Special privilege for medical freedoms as well as religious freedoms."

> ~ *Dr. Benjamin Rush, signatory to the Declaration of Independence*

This quote certainly indicates what happened during the COVID-19 Plandemic and also speaks to what is taking place with regulatory capture of our government agencies by Big Pharma. As well-stated by Dr. Benjamin Rush, we need a health/medical freedom amendment to the U.S. Constitution. This can best be accomplished by gathering enough signatures in the several states to place a health/medical freedom amendment on a ballot referendum within each state. It can also be accomplished through an amendment to the U.S. Constitution that is passed by a Convention of States. You can learn more about the Convention of States here https://conventionofstates.com/.

14. **Eliminate all conflicts of interest.** Appointing a Big Pharma upper management executive to run the FDA is a huge conflict of interest. For years the U.S. Federal government has hired people right out of Big Pharma to run the FDA. This is also true of appointments made to run agencies like NIH and NIAID. There is a revolving door between Big Agra and the USDA, and between the U.S. Central Bank, a private corporation (called the U.S. Federal Reserve) and the Department of the Treasury. We must demand of our elected officials to put a stop

to this practice. This can be accomplished by pressuring the U.S. Congress to pass legislation that forbids these conflicts of interest that represent outright government corruption.

In addition, Big Pharma has successfully engaged in regulatory capture of every agency within the U.S. government tasked with regulating Big Pharma, and every agency tasked with public health. The people appointed to run these agencies own patents on contagions. Then they purchase stock in Big Pharma and promote vaccines and other biologics, that have not been properly safety tested before going to market, as the only answer to addressing the contagions they hold a patent on. This is how the science that these appointees are charged with upholding and supporting gets corrupted in political ideology for the sake of greed.

So, for example, the people who run these agencies are engaged in a direct conflict of interest when, as supposed experts, they promote mask mandates, lockdowns and vaccine mandates because they own the patents on the viruses for which vaccines are being developed. Every time these people call for such mandates, their stock price goes up. This practice promotes the Big Pharma business model of creating a problem that they then present what they deem to be the only answer to the problem. This is organized crime and we must push for legislation that prevents the people who run these government agencies from owning patents on contagions, as well as, prosecuting them for insider trading on their stocks.

Additional information and data relevant to this chapter can be found here: https://bhaktaschool.org/dharma-and-the-preservation-of-liberty/

Chapter 3
Natural Immunity

I studied Eastern and Oriental Medicine and graduated with degrees in both from the Kushi Institute. I then had a practice in New York City for more than 15 years. In that time, I interfaced with many medical doctors and researchers. Over the years I have developed relationships with a good number of medical professionals, including virologists and epidemiologists, some of whom I have interviewed in various podcasts. During the COVID-19 pandemic, I remained in contact with several frontline doctors who were treating thousands of Covid patients. I also maintained contact with 175 treating medical professionals who participated in the *White Coat Summit* as part of *America's Frontline Doctors*. You can view videos of all sessions of the 2023 White Coat Summit here: https://www.whitecoatsummit.com/videos/2023

Your immune system is a miracle. To understand this miracle, it's important that you have a basic knowledge of how your immune system works and what natural immunity is. In addition, if you are in good health, your immune system will prevent any pathogen from creating illness and disease in your body. And, if you are not in good health or suffer from an immune system that is compromised due to underlying health conditions, you can strengthen your immune system without the use of toxic, pharmaceutical drugs. You can optimize your immune system against any virus, bacteria or other pathogen, whether wild or man-made. A healthy immune system is vital to your well-being and essential for disease prevention.

What Are the Branches of the Human Immune System?

The primary branches of the immune system are:

- The Gut Microbiome
- The Brain
- The Lymphatic System
- The Bone Marrow
- Skin

<u>Your Gut Microbiome</u>

Your Gut Microbiome is a central pillar of your immune system. It protects you against foreign invaders and also secretes vitamins, minerals and micronutrients that upregulate your immunity while optimizing your overall health. We are all asymptomatic carriers of bacteria and viruses that become part of the natural flora in the gut. This supports the ability of our immune system to adapt and become stronger as we are exposed to new pathogens like wild viruses that are constantly circulating in the environment.

Gut Microbiome secretions are part of how our bodies expose our immune system to new pathogens so that the immune system can quickly create protections against them. This is why, for people who are in general good health, it is important to be exposed to bacteria, as well as, the flu virus and coronaviruses like SARS-CoV. Each time you are infected, your immune system develops protections against future infection. This includes protection against mutations/variants. In fact, it can be said that new wild bacteria and viruses circulate in our environment precisely so that we can develop natural immunity to them. This is known as natural immunization.

Many of the mother cells in our body, known as stem cells, are manufactured in your gut. Stem cells are essential to vibrant health because they are responsible for regenerating all of the other 50 billion plus cells in your body in every 24-hour period. Without healthy stem cells, you would age very quickly and your lifespan would be very short. Stem cells are also responsible for upregulating your immune system.

Leaky Gut is a disease that downregulates your immune system, weakening immune system response and setting the stage for autoimmune reactions and diseases on the autoimmune spectrum. So, to keep your immune system healthy it is necessary to maintain a healthy Gut Microbiome and, if you have leaky gut, you have to address it right away so that you don't become immune compromised.

Also, soil is rich in healthy bacteria and nutrients that are good for your health. Exposure to dirt strengthens the immune system and exposes the body to probiotics from the soil that you automatically assimilate by breathing when you are digging in soil. For example, this is why it's so important to take walks on trails in nature and to do some gardening in your yard.

Your Brain

Your brain is responsible for converting thoughts in your mind into signaling that your cells can process to function optimally. Part of that signaling is what causes the healthy reproduction of stem cells. If you have a healthy mindset and you have conquered your restless mind in order to keep your mind quiet and free of worry, anxiety and fear, your brain will be able to engage in optimal cell signaling for the healthy reproduction of your stem cells and all your other cells.

However if, for example, you are caught up in fear and the fight/flight mechanism that so many people were caught up in during the Covid pandemic, your brain is going to send signals down the vagus nerve to your gut, which will downregulate healthy stem cell production. This, in turn, will weaken your immune system and, over time, will cause you to become immune compromised. This is called stress and suffering stress is a leading factor in poor health and a compromised immune system. So, it's really important to engage in practices like Meditation and Chanting with the aim of making your restless mind quiet and keeping it quiet, as this has a direct impact on your immune system, and your spiritual journey, as well.

Your Lymphatic System

Your lymphatic system provides an important layer of protection from things like gram-negative bacteria and viruses that don't belong in your body. Your lymphatic system is also responsible for maintaining healthy fluid levels in your body, absorbing excess fat from the digestive tract and removing cellular waste from the digestive tract. It also drains excess fluid from your cells, tissues and organs.

Your lymphatic system also removes the 'garbage' from your body by way of removing waste from the lymph that has been filtered through the lymph nodes, and by removing waste from the bloodstream. A lymphatic system that does not function properly downregulates the immune system. An optimally functioning lymphatic system supports healthy immune system response.

Your Bone Marrow

Maintaining optimal bone health is essential for a properly functioning immune system. The bone marrow is the spongy tissue inside our bones that produces our blood cells. Red blood cells, platelets, white blood cells and lymphocytes are all produced inside the bone marrow. Other cells important to immunity like myeloid derivatives and dendritic cells are also produced in the bone marrow.

In the group of white blood cells that are produced to fight infection, T-cells such as T-killer cells (natural killer cells) and B cells are also manufactured in the bone marrow. Your bone marrow is called upon to manufacture these cells to fight off infection and pathogens that are circulating in your body.

As we age, our bone marrow begins to deteriorate and losses its ability to secrete the blood cells necessary to fight infection and heal from disease. This is why, with age, it is necessary to take immune system supplements and herbs that support bone health with age. Healthy bone marrow is an absolute necessity for a strong immune system that supports natural immunity.

Your Skin

Your skin is actually a microbiome, commonly known as the Skin Microbiome, and it is also a branch of your immune system. Your skin seals you from the rest of the outside world. Your skin protects you from bacteria and other contagions that are not supposed to enter your body. There are anti-microbial peptides on your skin that help facilitate this. If you were to examine your skin under a microscope, you would find that there are trillions of microbes on your skin, including 1 million organisms such as bacteria, viruses and parasites over each square centimeter of skin.

In addition, your skin contains many antibiotics. It contains defensins and cathelicidins that regulate inflammation and aide in healing wounds. You also have toll-like receptors on your skin that recognize foreign invaders, as well as healthy germs, bacteria and viruses (yes, there are viruses that are good for you). Your skin uses these to invigorate itself to increase the healthy life of your skin. Your skin secretes its natural antibiotics through sweat glands, sebaceous glands, apocrine glands and hair follicles. Each of these contains unique microbiota. For these reasons, it is important to keep your skin healthy and vibrant.

You can learn more about Natural Immunity by watching a video on the basics of the immune system and its function here : https://bhaktaschool.org/how-to-develop-and-sustain-a-strong-immune-system/. In addition, there is an effective method for boosting your immune system against contagions like viruses, including COVID-19. You can view a video of how to use the method yourself here: https://bhaktaschool.org/boost-your-immune-system-against-any-virus/. This is part of the Nambudripad Allergy Elimination Techniques (NAET). To learn more about NAET go here: https://www.naet.com/en-US

In addition, homeopathy provides a very good means of strengthening your immune system against any contagion. Homeopathy uses nosodes that are diluted forms of pathogens like viruses and bacteria that have been rendered completely inactive. However, the energetic component of the pathogen remains intact. Then the inert pathogen is poured on to sugar pills that are taken orally. Homeopathy can be used to prevent infection from pathogens as well. This is known as homeoprophylaxis. Homeopathy is widely used all over the world and has been used extensively in countries like India and Asia to treat millions of people during epidemics of all kinds.

Natural immunity is your first and foremost line of defense against all contagions, including viruses (whether wild or man-made). If you are healthy and you are not immune system compromised, natural immunity is far greater than immunization by vaccination.

Herd Immunity

During the COVID-19 declared pandemic there was a lot of talk about herd immunity. Herd immunity occurs when a critical mass of the population achieves immunity from a contagion (like a virus) and is able to transfer that immunity to other infected people in the population. Here's how it works:

1. A large portion of the healthy people in a population are infected with (in this example) a virus. Their healthy immune systems begin to secrete *neutralizing antibodies* to the virus.

2. These neutralizing antibodies attach themselves to the viral molecule, thereby creating a new molecule that has the neutralizing antibody attached to it.

3. Those infected people with the new molecule containing neutralizing antibodies to the virus come into contact with other people and infect them with the new molecule. Those infected with the new molecule get an upgrade to their immune systems to fight off the virus and become immune to it. Those with weaker immune systems, when infected with the new molecule, inherit a viral molecule that has been neutralized, and

this strengthens their immune systems against that virus and its variants/mutations.

Herd immunity can also be accomplished through vaccination if the vaccines have been properly safety tested (a minimum of 5-8 years of safety trials that include human trials), and if they have been proved to prevent infection and transmission. This means the vaccines must be proven to cause the secretion of *neutralizing antibodies*. Many vaccines, including the Covid shots, do not cause the secretion of neutralizing antibodies, instead only causing secretion of binding and non-neutralizing antibodies. Due to the lack of proper safety testing of most vaccines and, in particular, the Covid and Flu shots which do not prevent infection or transmission, history has shown that natural herd immunity is superior to herd immunity by vaccination.

There are situations in which certain groups of people in a population may need to be vaccinated. This group includes elderly people, people with one or more comorbidities and people with compromised immune systems. In such cases, the intention of vaccination is to keep these people out of the hospital, and to help them manage symptoms of infection. Even in such cases, the vaccines need to be properly safety tested over a minimum period of 5-8 years and they must actually be vaccines and not gene therapy.

Huge Conflicts of Interest And Corruption

The U.S. Center for Disease Control and Prevention (CDC) is a corrupt Federal agency that has been captured and is controlled by Big Pharma. Due to this fact, they do Pharma's bidding. Any center for *disease control* and *prevention* should be focused, first and foremost on lifestyle recommendations for maintaining optimal health, along with promoting education and protocols for natural immunity. Instead, the CDC is almost entirely focused on vaccination to address all illnesses and diseases. There exists thousands of years of knowledge about the effects of natural immunity—meaning the human body's natural ability to make antibodies for diseases which it has recovered from. Despite this mechanism being recognized since at least 430 B.C., the CDC insisted during the COVID pandemic that everyone had to take these so-called vaccines—including the naturally immune.

What basis did the CDC have for making this claim? Incredibly, as they now admit in the new Freedom of Information Act disclosure, they had no basis other than the say-so of a bunch of authors who were sponsored by companies that manufacture the said vaccines. It is a scandal of epic proportions. Yet once again mainstream media is silent. You can read the full article about the CDCs response to the FOIA here: https://www.theepochtimes.com/epochtv/new-foia-document-reveals-cdc-did-not-have-data-prior-to-vaccine-recommendation-for-the-naturally-immune-truth-over-news-5530242

The CDC is the largest purchaser of vaccines in the world. It is also complicit in covering up vaccine injury and the probability that many vaccines cause serious, lifelong injury and even death. In fact, as of this writing, the CDC is refusing to release their updated data on post-vaccination heart inflammation (myocarditis or pericarditis). You can read a report on this here: https://www.theepochtimes.com/epochtv/cdc-makes-disturbing-vaccine-move-facts-matter-5498309

Brian Hooker, PhD is the chief scientific officer at Children's Health Defense. He is the author of over seventy peer-reviewed scientific publications, including twenty-five papers covering the epidemiology of vaccine injury. During the Covid pandemic I interviewed Dr. Hooker regarding CDC fraud and his contact with CDC whistle blower William Thompson, PhD. You can view the full interview here: https://bhaktaschool.org/brian-hooker-interview-on-cdc-fraud/. This interview is very telling about the fraudulent manner in which the CDC operates and the lengths to which the CDC goes to cover up its fraud.

It is incredibly important for you to hear from people who have extensive experience dealing with the CDC and working inside the CDC so that you understand why you need to be very cautious in following any recommendations the CDC gives, without first examining how the CDC came to those recommendations. This includes the Advisory Committee On Immunization Practices (ACIP) that makes decisions about both the child and adult vaccination schedules, decisions that impact all CDC vaccination recommendations to doctors and the public at large.

The problem is this: ACIP is not an independent organization. The CDC manages ACIP. This means that the CDC manages the organization that has been set up to advise it and tells that organization how the CDC should be advised. To understand fully what I mean you can view a short clip of an ACIP meeting to see the utter stupidity with which they vote to make their recommendations to the CDC. You will also see what the WHO says behind closed doors about vaccine safety, while they tell us that vaccines are safe and effective. View that here: https://bhaktaschool.org/acip/

Pfizer Marketing Executive Caught On Video Tape Talking About Unsafe Covid Shots and Gain-of-Function

Project Veritas set up an undercover video in which it sent one of its journalists who was wearing a hidden video camera to discuss the Pfizer BioNTech Covid shots with Pfizer's senior marketing executive J.T. Walker. This was arranged as a date with the Project Veritas investigative reporter and Mr. Walker.

In the videotaped discussion at a restaurant that went viral on the internet, J.T. Walker talks about the lack of safety studies for the Covid shots and also discusses the fact that Pfizer is engaged in mutating viruses in its labs (Gain-of-Function/GoF) to address the manufacture of new shots. The reason this revelation is important is that it has long been suspected that Big Pharma is engaged in creating injuries and illnesses, by way of its products, that it has already manufactured a treatment for. Pharma makes some $50 billion a year on sales of its vaccines, and then makes more than $500 billion each year on the medications it sells to treat the injuries from the vaccines.

Mr. Walker also states that Pfizer has no idea of how much harm the Covid shots can do to people, but that Pfizer knew of the potential harms before distribution and never divulged those potential harms. You can view that video here: https://bhaktaschool.org/pfizer-exposed/

Then, later in the same conversation that was taped undercover, Mr. Walker admits that there are issues with the Covid shots harming women who take them when pregnant and that Pfizer knew about the harmful impact of its Covid shots on pregnant women before distributing the shots. You can view the full video of that part of the converation here: https://bhaktaschool.org/pfizer-exposed/

In addition, evidence has been revealed that shows that Biden knew about the potential harms from the Covid shots and covered that up. You can view the video about that here: New-Found Emails Prove Biden White House Hid COVID Vaccine Harms from the Public https://www.bitchute.com/video/Jtg0WI1d53D4/ Rasmussen Reports conducted a recent poll that shows that 24% of Americans know someone who died after getting a Covid shot. The same poll shows that forty-two percent (42%) say that, if there was a major class-action lawsuit against pharmaceutical companies for vaccine side effects, they would be likely to join the lawsuit. You can view the article here: https://www.rasmussenreports.com/public_content/poli tics/public_surveys/killer_jab_24_say_someone_they_kn ow_died_from_covid_19_vaccine

Vaccinated Vs. Unvaccinated

In America, vaccine manufacturers are not liable for any harm done to you by their product. This means that, if you are injured by a vaccine, you cannot sue the manufacturer of the vaccine. This includes all Covid shots that are actually not vaccines, but rather gene therapy biologics. In order to be compensated for vaccine injury, you have to apply to the DHHS Vaccine Injury Compensation Program (VICP). I offer further details about this in the next chapter.

As I've stated earlier, I am not anti-vax. I am pro-safety and I have been vaccinated growing up. Furthermore, if a vaccine has been subjected to long-term safety studies and proved to be safe and effective with little or no side effects, I will be the first one to stand in line to take it. However, the way to settle the debate on vaccine safety is to examine studies that show what is actually in vaccines that can harm you, *and to also conduct studies that compare the health of the vaccinated with the health of the unvaccinated over extended periods of time.*

One of the most outrageous things about the CDC is that, in the entire history of vaccines and in the entire history of the childhood and adult vaccination schedules, the CDC has never conducted studies comparing the health of the vaccinated vs. the unvaccinated. This supports the existing evidence that the CDC has become nothing more than an arm of Big Pharma. However, these studies have been done and, before taking any vaccine, I strongly encourage you to examine these studies so that you and your family are fully informed before consenting to take any vaccine.

The first compilation of studies that you need to read is *Miller's Review of Critical Vaccine Studies* by Neil Z. Miller (ISBN 978-188121740-4). This book is a compilation of 400 scientific papers summarized for parents and researchers and it has become a go to manual for many medical professionals. Neil Miller has done an excellent job of investigating and determining the harmful ingredients (in many cases cancer causing) contained in most of the vaccines on the childhood vaccination schedule and many that are on the adult vaccination schedule.

Next, a large, comprehensive study comparing the vaccinated vs. the unvaccinated over a period of 10.5 years was conducted by Dr. Paul Thomas and James Lyons-Weiler, PhD ("Dr. Jack"). Dr. Jack is a personal friend of mine and we have spoken on panels together. Dr. Paul Thomas is a pediatrician who conducted a large practice of over 15,000 patients for many years in the state of Oregon. After publishing this comprehensive study, under pressure from Big Pharma, Dr. Thomas's medical license was permanently revoked. He cannot reapply. *This study remains one of the most comprehensive in showing that unvaccinated children are healthier and require fewer office visits than those who are vaccinated.*

You can view the entire interview I conducted about this study with Dr. Jack using the link below. It is presented in two parts. We agreed that Dr. Thomas would not appear in the interview because, at the time of the interview, his medical license was still under review for suspension/revocation after the release of this study.
https://bhaktaschool.org/greed-and-the-great-reset/ (scroll down the page)

In addition, Robert F. Kennedy Jr. and Dr. Brian Hooker have written an excellent book, *Vax-Unvax – Let the Science Speak*, in which they provide the conclusions of over 100 peer-reviewed studies comparing the health conditions of the vaccinated with the unvaccinated. These studies appear in the open, peer-reviewed scientific literature. Here is a summary of their findings:

1. The results of these studies consistently confirm that vaccinated children were not as healthy as their unvaccinated peers. [1]

2. Although the CDC childhood and adult vaccination schedules are recommendations, most schools require the shots on the schedule before children can attend classes. In addition, some employers require that some of the jabs on the adult vaccination schedule be taken as a qualification for employment. This requirement became even more common during the COVID-19 Pandemic when many employers required their employees to get the Covid shots to keep their jobs. When I was a child, there were only three shots on the childhood vaccination schedule. Today, children whose parents allow them to be vaccinated on the CDC childhood vaccination schedule receive a minimum of seventy-three shots, twenty-eight of which are administered by their first birthday. [2] This means children now receive multiple shots in a single session.

3. By their own admission, the CDC and ACIP have never conducted a single study to determine the safety of giving children multiple shots in a single session. (See the video link to this admission in the previous section above.)

4. When vetting vaccines to become fully informed before giving your consent, it's important to ask yourself the question "Vaccinate at what cost to my health?" Do the benefits *greatly outweigh* the risks? And what are the potential, long-term adverse events that could occur? Medical authorities credit vaccines on the childhood vaccination schedule with eradicating several deadly infectious diseases but these same authorities have little interest in studying the short-term and long-term effects of vaccination. [3] Many of these vaccines impact health in the long-term in a way that that does not become evident for years. In an interview conducted in 1999, Anthony Fauci, former director of the National Institute of Allergy and

Infectious Diseases, acknowledged that there are many severe injuries that are not diagnosed until years after vaccination and that, if vaccines are rushed to approval, "then you find out that it takes twelve years for all hell to break loose, and then what have you done?" [4]

4. In 2011, the Institute of Medicine (IOM), now the National Academy of Medicine, established a committee to evaluate 158 vaccine adverse events that reports of injury linked to eight different vaccines. The IOM determined that evidence "convincingly reported" or "favored acceptance" of a causal relationship with administration of the vaccine for eighteen adverse events. It was also determined that the relationship between vaccination and five adverse events favored rejecting the vaccines altogether. [5]

5. The IOM committee also considered 135 out of the 158 adverse events related to vaccination and stated that, with respect to a causal relationship between these adverse events and vaccination, the evidence was "inadequate to accept or reject." This contradicts the CDC's adamant and constant assertions that vaccines are safe and effective, and that they don't cause autism. For almost 90% of the vaccine adverse events, the CDC has never conducted studies to determine a causal relationship between those events and vaccination. This means the CDC cannot know whether the vaccines cause harm and cannot say that they don't. [6]

6. In 2013 the National Vaccine Program Office managed by DHHS commissioned another IOM update to the earlier findings. The committee found that "few studies have comprehensively assessed the association between the entire immunization schedule or variations in the overall schedule and categories of health outcomes, and no study has directly examined health

outcomes and stakeholder concerns in precisely the way that the committee was charged to address in its statement of task. Studies designed to examine the long-term effects of the cumulative number of vaccines or other aspects of the immunization schedule have not been conducted." [7]

7. The lack of safety studies was so concerning that the IOM also recommended "that the Department of Health and Human Services incorporate study of the safety of the overall childhood immunization schedule into its processes for setting priorities for research, recognizing stakeholder concerns, and establishing the priorities on the basis of epidemiological evidence, biological plausibility, and feasibility." The IOM also recommended that the CDC use retrospective analysis to study the overall health effects of the vaccination schedule, using the Vaccine Safety Datalink (VSD). To date, the CDC has yet to respond to the IOM committee's recommendations with any meaningful studies on the impact of the vaccination schedule on overall health. [8]

8. COVID-19 shots have been distributed in the U.S. for 30 months. The rate of vaccine injury from these shots is very high. In this period, the COVID-19 shots have caused 97% of all adverse events reported to the CDC's Vaccine Adverse Events Reporting System (VAERS). [9] In addition, most vaccine-injured people don't even know that VAERS exists. It is estimated that only 1% of all vaccine injuries are reported to VAERS. So, vaccine injury is not rare but, likely, extensive when the gross underreporting is considered.

9. The CDC has emphatically stated that injury from vaccines is one in a million. However, the CDC funded the Lazarus study and then later abandoned the study

because the Lazarus study found that, among a population of 375,000 people who were given a total of 1.4 million vaccines, the rate of adverse events for vaccination is 1 in 38. For each person, that's a 1 in 10 chance of having an adverse reaction to a vaccine. Even given this, their own study, the CDC, along with the FDA, refuse to study health outcomes in the vaccinated vs. the unvaccinated. [10]

10. There are various ways that can be utilized to consistently study the health impact of vaccines on children and adults. This includes retrospective studies that are very effective. And yet the CDC has never performed a single comparison study between the vaccinated and the unvaccinated.

Vax-Unvax Study Outcomes
Robert F. Kennedy Jr.-Brian Hooker, PhD

Here is a sampling of the study outcomes presented in their book, *Vax-Unvax. Let the Science Speak*, for the vaccinated vs. the unvaccinated.

Odds Ratios of Chronic Disease for
Vaccinated vs. Unvaccinated Children [11]

- Vaccinated children have 30 times greater odds of developing Allergic Rhinitis as compared to unvaccinated children.

- Vaccinated children have 3.9 times greater odds of developing allergies of any kind as compared to unvaccinated children.

- Vaccinated children have 4.2 times greater odds of developing ADHD as compared to unvaccinated children.

- Vaccinated children have 4.2 times greater odds of developing Autism as compared to unvaccinated children.

- Vaccinated children have 2.9 times greater odds of developing Eczema as compared to unvaccinated children.

- Vaccinated children have 5.2 times greater odds of developing a Learning Disability as compared to unvaccinated children.

- Vaccinated children have 3.7 times greater odds of developing a Neurodevelopmental Disorder as compared to unvaccinated children.

Rates of Infections Reported In
Vaccinated vs. Unvaccinated Children [12]

- Rates of Pneumonia in vaccinated children are 6.4% vs. 1.2% in unvaccinated children.

- Rates of ear infections in vaccinated children are 19.8% vs. 5.8% in unvaccinated children.

Odds of Neurodevelopmental Disorders
For Unvaccinated vs. Vaccinated, Including
Premature and Full-Term Birth [13]

- Vaccinated children were diagnosed with 2.7 times greater odds of a neurodevelopmental disability (NDD) than unvaccinated children.

- Vaccinated children born prematurely were diagnosed with 14.5 times greater odds of a neurodevelopmental disorder when compared to a reference group of unvaccinated children born at full-term.

Odds Ratios of Other Disorders In
Vaccinated Versus Unvaccinated Children [14]

- The odds of vaccinated children experiencing developmental delays are 2.18 times greater than that of unvaccinated children.

- The odds of vaccinated children developing Asthma are 4.49 times greater than that of unvaccinated children.

- The odds of vaccinated children getting ear infections is 2.13 times greater than that of unvaccinated children.

Odds Ratios of Gastrointestinal Disorders In
Vaccinated Versus Unvaccinated Children [15]

- The odds of vaccinated children developing gastrointestinal disorders are 2.48 times greater than that of unvaccinated children.

Odds Ratios For Obtaining a Diagnosis For
A Variety of Disorders In Vaccinated Versus
Unvaccinated Children – Hooker/Miller [16]

- The odds of vaccinated children getting a diagnosis of severe allergies are 4.3 times greater than for unvaccinated children.

- The odds of vaccinated children being diagnosed with gastrointestinal disorders are 13.8 times greater than for unvaccinated children.

- The odds of vaccinated children getting a diagnosis of Asthma are 17.6 times greater than for unvaccinated children.

- The odds of vaccinated children being diagnosed with Autism are 5.0 times greater than for unvaccinated children.

- The odds of vaccinated children obtaining a diagnosis of ADHD are 20.8 times greater than for unvaccinated children.

- The odds of vaccinated children being diagnosed with chronic ear infections are 27.8 times greater than for unvaccinated children.

Odds Ratios For Asthma Accounting for Vaccination and Breastfeeding Status [17]

- Unvaccinated children who are not breastfed have a 5.4 times greater odds of contracting Asthma than unvaccinated children who are breastfed.

- Vaccinated children who are breastfed have 10.7 times greater odds of contracting Asthma.

- Vaccinated children who are not breastfed have a 23.8 times greater chance of contracting Asthma.

Ratio of Office Visits Between Vaccinated And Unvaccinated Children [18]

- Vaccinated children have 4.59 times more doctor's office visits for fever than unvaccinated children.

- Vaccinated children have 1.65 times more doctor's office visits for ear infections than unvaccinated children.

- Vaccinated children visit the doctor for conjunctivitis 1.3 times more than unvaccinated children.

- Vaccinated children visit the doctor for Asthma 1.54 times more than unvaccinated children.

- Vaccinated children have 1.71 times more doctor's office visits for breathing issues than unvaccinated children.

- Vaccinated children have 3.62 times more doctor's office visits for anemia than unvaccinated children.

- Vaccinated children have 2.79 times more doctor's office visits for Eczema than unvaccinated children.

- Vaccinated children visit the doctor for behavioral issues 3.18 times more than unvaccinated children.

- Vaccinated children visit the doctor for gastroenteritis 2.79 times more than unvaccinated children.

- Vaccinated children visit the doctor for weight/eating disorders 1.60 times more than unvaccinated children.

- Vaccinated children have 2.68 times more office visits for respiratory infections than unvaccinated children.

This is a small sampling of the studies. Again, I encourage you to read the entire book.

Judy Mikovits, PhD

Dr. Mikovits earned a BA in Chemistry from University of Virginia in 1980 and a PhD in Biochemistry and Molecular Biology from George Washington University in 1992. In her forty-year quest to understand the causes, prevention and treatment of chronic diseases, she has co-authored seminal papers culminating in at least a decade of research in each of four fields: Immunology, natural products chemistry, epigenetics, and HIV/AIDs drug development.

In 2009, Dr. Mikovits led the team that first isolated and characterized a new family of human disease-associated retroviruses, XMRVs. Dr. Mikovits has co-authored more than 50 peer reviewed publications and book chapters, and holds a patent for Combination Therapy for Prostate Cancer using Botanical Compositions and Casodex. Dr. Mikovits is a New York Times best-selling author of the books *Plague, Plague of Corruption, Ending Plague* and *The Truth About Masks*.

I interviewed Dr. Judy Mikovits who, for many years, worked under Drs. Anthony Fauci and Francis Collins in U.S. laboratories managed by NIH and NIAID. She has comprehensive, first-hand knowledge of what's actually in the Covid shots and other shots. I interviewed her on this topic and you can find this comprehensive interview, in two parts, here (scroll down the page): https://bhaktaschool.org/greed-and-the-great-reset/. You can also visit a web site for more of her research and insight on Big Pharma, vaccines and the corruption of public/private partnerships in the history of vaccination. View that here: https://totalityofevidence.com/dr-judy-mikovits/and here: https://totalityofevidence.com/.

Fully-Informed Consent and the Right to Refuse Vaccination

I work out at a local gym four days each and every week. Over the years I have become friends with several people who I see regularly in the gym. Five of those people have been vaccinated for Covid. They tell me they did so either due to it being a requirement to visit a family member in a hospital, or as a requirement for remaining employed or going to school. All five have told me that, in addition to getting sick right after getting the shots, since getting the jabs, they are weaker, have far less energy and are not able to do the full workout they once did.

You have a duty to yourself and your loved ones to protect your right to health freedom, by way of fully informed consent and freedom of choice. With respect to the jabs, *informed consent means the right to refuse vaccination, based on being fully informed, without being discriminated against for doing so.* This is the area in which Big Pharma, by bribing government, continues a worldwide campaign to force vaccines on us, regardless of what is in them that is known to cause injury and chronic health conditions that, in many cases are permanent, and sometimes result in death.

In fact, they can (and do) put anything they want into the vaccines and you would never know it. In the manufacture of vaccines today, there are no safety standards with third party, peer-review that is not connected to conflicts of interest. There is no requirement on the part of Big Pharma to prove the efficacy of the vaccines, along with safety standards that are enforced *by a third party with no conflicts of interest.* This is because vaccine manufacturers have been permanently indemnified from all liability (you can't sue them due to injury from their product, even when their own internal documents show that they knew about the dangers and did nothing to remove them).

So, they have absolutely no incentive to spend a few pennies more per shot to make the vaccines safe. In addition, Big Pharma has a long history of putting profits before people. This is all the more reason why our right to fully informed consent, along with the right to refuse without being discriminated against, must be protected. This right is already being stripped away by State and Federal Government. The increase in the removal of all exemptions to the annual flu shot is one example of this. I will be the first to stand in line for a vaccine:

• If, in the development of a vaccine, the vaccine undergoes double-blind saline placebo safety testing (the standard for medical science that is not currently applied to vaccines) that is monitored and certified by third parties with no conflict of interest and proved to be safe in the proper animal trials (3-8 years minimum), followed by voluntary human trials.

• If the vaccine does not alter the human genome, making cell function reliant upon further vaccination and medication.

In early April 2023, microbiologist Kevin McKernan detailed finding massive DNA contamination in Pfizer's and Moderna's bivalent COVID booster shots. The highest level of DNA contamination found was 30%, meaning nearly one-third of the content of the shot was plasmid DNA, the presence of which dramatically increases the likelihood of DNA integration and cancer. An in-vitro experiment found that the modified RNA in the Pfizer jab has the ability to enter human liver cells and reverse transcribe into DNA in as little as six hours post-exposure. The lipid nanoparticles that the mRNA and DNA contaminants are encased in facilitate getting the DNA inside the cell. Once it's in the cytoplasm, bits of DNA can enter the nucleus by random chance.

Mice injected with the COVID mRNA shot passed on their acquired immune traits — both good and bad — to offspring, which not only suggests that the mRNA can enter the nucleus of the cell, but also that it can be permanently integrated into chromosomal DNA and have intergenerational effects. Pfizer's bivalent jab has also been found to contain Simian Virus 40 (SV40) promoter, an oncogenic piece of the virus' DNA known to drive very aggressive gene expression. Combined with pieces of DNA, the presence of SV40 promoter makes the risk of cancer all the more likely. The SV40 promoter is a sequence used in gene therapy to drive DNA into the nucleus of cells. If the shots aren't supposed to alter the human genome, why do they contain bits of DNA and an SV40 promoter that can drive that DNA into the nucleus? To view video-taped testimony about these facts, go here: https://healthrightsma.org/kevin-mckernan/

• If the vaccine is manufactured without any carcinogenic adjuvants that are currently used in all vaccines, that are known to edit the human genome permanently and downregulate immune system function.

• If reliable, third-party, peer-reviewed studies are produced and presented to the public that show that vaccinated people are healthier than those who are not vaccinated. To date, and with a recent CDC admission, government agencies including the CDC have never performed such studies.

The citizenry must have the freedom to demand answers to safety and human rights concerns over vaccines, medications, public health policy and planned mandates designed to change our way of life without our consent.   We must have the freedom to do so without being labeled and persecuted as anti-government, anti-medicine, anti-public safety and anti-vaccines.

Fully informed consent and freedom of choice must become the law of the land once again. Every person must be allowed to weigh the risks against the benefits of any vaccine or other medication, based on accurate information and whether or not safety standards have been met with third party oversight that is not mired in conflicts of interest. The preservation of our right to refuse must be protected. To support you in protecting this right a Vaccine Assessment Guide has been created. You can download the document here: https://bhaktaschool.org/pdfdownload.php?file=Vaccine -Assessment-Guide.pdf

What To Do About It

1. One of the major challenges with respect to fully informed consent for vaccines and other medications

and medical procedures is that many people do not take the steps to become fully informed. Instead, they trust their doctor, their nurse, the CDC, government and others to tell them what is safe and effective. The fact is it's your body, not theirs. So, you need to absolutely know what you're putting into your body and whether or not the benefits *greatly outweigh* the risks.

2. **Most doctors blindly follow government health department and government health agency recommendations, along with whatever Big Pharma tells them.** In fact, most of the classes taught in medical school are taught by Big Pharma representatives and doctors on the Pharma payroll. In addition, due to their patient workload schedule, most doctors do not take the time to fully research vaccines and medications they use to treat patients. They are provided with half-page summaries and that is what they read, if they have the time. Although it is true that some doctors are operating on the experience they have had with using vaccines and other medications to effectively treat their patients, that doesn't mean the same treatment will work for you.

Your doctor is your paid consultant and this is how you should be treating that relationship. This means you should always ask your doctor about his/her knowledge of the benefits versus the risks of any vaccine or other medication the doctor is recommending for treatment. Then, you should also perform your own due diligence on the recommended treatment by reading the package inserts for the medications online, and by reviewing the medication or vaccine information at the manufacturer's web site. And, if your doctor gets upset with you for asking a lot of questions and further researching a recommended form of treatment that your doctor is telling you to undergo, you need a new doctor.

In addition, you should also google the name of the vaccine or other medication and place "side effects and injury" behind the name for your search. This will bring up any medical articles and other documentation on the medication that will help you decide whether the benefits greatly outweigh the risk. Understand that many widely used medications contain carcinogens.

Many synthetic medications are also immunosuppressants. Since medications are often repurposed for the treatment of multiple illnesses and diseases, unless you have to undergo an organ transplant or similar procedure, you should be sure that any medication recommended to you for treatment is not an immunosuppressant.

In addition, most of the vaccines on the childhood and adult vaccination schedules suppress and/or change the natural function of the immune system. Many of the vaccines on the childhood and adult vaccination schedule (including the annual flu shot) are live, attenuated vaccines that combine some of the pathogen you are vaccinating against with adjuvants like thimerosal (a mercury-based compound) and aluminum. These are added as preservatives and also intended to evoke an immune response.

The majority of vaccines inhibit T-cell and NK cell (natural killer cells) response. This downregulates your innate immune system, which is your first line of defense. This is done to upregulate your adaptive immune system to force it to secrete antibodies. However, vaccines are not required to secrete the most important antibody – the neutralizing antibody.

Instead, a vaccine is deemed effective as long as it can be shown that the vaccine elicited an antibody response of any kind. Most vaccines only elicit a binding and non-binding antibody response that is not enough to prevent transmission or infection. This will only help manage symptoms, at best. And, with downregulated innate immunity, the immune system has great difficulty creating lasting immunity to future exposure of the pathogen and any variants. In addition, many vaccines on the child and adult vaccination schedules contain aborted fetal tissue, along with animal tissue.

Covid shots are even worse because they have, in fact, been shown to be gene therapy. The Covid shots are designed with MODrNA which means modified RNA that injects itself into DNA to modify DNA function altogether. This is a very dangerous proposition and really bad for your health. It is why there are now millions of cases of vaccine injury from the Covid shots. And there will, likely, be millions more cases. The long-term prognosis for these jabs is cancer and heart disease.

So, this is what you need to keep in mind regarding your fully informed consent before taking any vaccine or other medication.

3. **Most people treat their cars better than they do their bodies.** It is incredibly important that you have a basic understanding of your body's biology, along with how your cells function. Because, if you don't fix the cell, you will never get well and stay well. A great online course has been created for this purpose and I encourage you to enroll in it. You can view all of the information about the course here:

https://bhaktaschool.org/holistic-health-well-being-ohio/

4. In America, positions of leadership and decision-making in the FDA and CDC are filled in a revolving door between these agencies and Big Pharma. This is regulatory capture at its finest. As a result, there are so many conflicts of interest in upper management and the heads of these agencies that they have become corrupt. This can only be resolved to support real public health that includes fully informed consent if: 1. The heads of these agencies are professionals with strong credentials in the fields of food and medicine who have never worked inside Big Pharma and have no ties to Big Pharma; or 2. A change is made to laws governing the executive branch so that the heads of these agencies are elected by the citizenry. Right now they are appointed by the President.

5. One of the greatest challenges to public health protocols and improved medical treatment is the fact that doctors and other medical professionals are not allowed to even question the official narrative regarding a medical approach or public health response. We saw this kind of idiocy expand during the COVID-19 Pandemic.

However, this has been an ongoing challenge in the treatment of diseases like cancer where doctors who have tested and effectively treated with relatively inexpensive and alternative methods and approaches not within the mainstream of Big Pharma's narrative on medical interventions for cancer have been publicly vilified and have had their medical licenses suspended or permanently revoked – all because they discovered an inexpensive and more effective treatment for cancer. I know some of these doctors personally. For a better understanding of this I encourage you to read *The Secret History of the War On Cancer* by Devra Davis, PhD, MPH. You can also go here to sign up for the encore presentation of *The Truth About Cancer* docuseries with Ty and Charlene Bollinger: https://go.thetruthaboutcancer.com/agq-encore/.

Any censorship of opposing views, opposing research and opposing outcomes that are not in alignment with the official government and mainstream media narrative must be outlawed. This is the only way we can return to healthy science that is based on open scientific debate and the assessment of treatment and outcomes based on facts, rather than political ideology and narrative. In addition, the revocation of medical licenses in situations where the practitioner has successfully treated patients in a way that is not traditional and not aligned with the Big Pharma approach must be outlawed.

6. In Collier County Florida, commissioners voted to establish the Southwest Florida county as a "Bill of Rights Sanctuary County" in response to the Federal Government's COVID-19 response and other overreaches. You can read the full article here: https://flvoicenews.com/commissioners-make-collier-county-a-bill-of-rights-sanctuary-in-response-to-federal-overreach/

Download the document here and send a copy to your local county commissioner, demanding that they adopt a similar measure in your county.
file:///Users/SystemManager/Downloads/Snapshot-86673.pdf

Additional information and data relevant to this chapter can be found here: https://bhaktaschool.org/dharma-and-the-preservation-of-liberty/

Chapter 4
The Growing Attack On
Our Liberty - Digital IDs

"Vaccine passports are a normal, justifiable, and proportionate response to the threat posed by the COVID-19 pandemic. Or so we are told. The passports are no different from other mandated health and safety requirements, such as seat belts or laws that prevent people from smoking on airplanes. Or so we are told. They merely represent upgraded digitized versions of paper vaccine certificates that have been around for a long time. Or so we are told. None of these claims are true, but they give the comforting impression that nothing much will change as the passports are rolled out and come into effect. Nothing, in fact, could be further *from* the truth."

~ *Nick Corbishley*, from his book, *Scanned*

The truth is that, right now, the stakes could not be higher. As far as our Liberty and rights are concerned, this is the last hill left that we must protect. *This is our last stand.* Government rollouts of digital IDs that will include digital vaccine passports and digital health certificates containing all of our health information will restrict access to basic services, greatly increase travel restrictions, and impact our ability to work. Even if we comply, we will be exposed to levels of government and corporate surveillance, data mining and behavioral controls the likes of which have never been seen before in the history of the world.

Imagine a society in which you have to "prove

your personhood" in almost every activity you engage in during the course of your daily, mundane activities. Imagine a society in which all your identification information is stored digitally in a database that is monitored and accessed by state and federal government, your local health department and health agencies within the Federal Government and retail/wholesale corporations. Your response would probably be, "Well, we have that already." And, in one way, this is true – except that, currently, you volunteer your information on a need to know basis.

Now imagine that, connected to your digital ID is data about your vitals, including weight, height, nationality/ethnicity, marital status, level of education completed including any degrees you have earned, skin color, eye color, hair color, blood pressure, blood glucose levels and constant surveillance of all your biological functions via a chip implanted under your skin, all current medical conditions, all completed blood tests ordered by your doctor, along with records of any medical treatments you are undergoing and who is treating you, along with records of traffic violations, criminal records (even if expunged), records of eye exams and dental exams, your driver's license and passport information, your credit card records and banking records, and your entire purchase history of everything you have bought, and also everything you have ever sold.

Now add to all this complete control of whether or not you are able to access your bank account and spend your money, along with caps on how much you can spend in any given week (this has already been implemented in the EU) – because the only money you have is a central bank digital currency that can be switched on and off by government and central banks.

This is what digital IDs, digital health certificates and digital vaccine passports are designed to do. And the worst part is that what I have just described has already been rolled out to some degree in several nations across the globe. As stated earlier, the trading of truth for convenience is at the heart of coercing the masses to comply with digital IDs. They are and will continue to be promoted as a means of increasing convenience because the masses are used to trading truth and freedom for such conveniences.

I am convinced that this is because most people are not fully informed as to the grave threats of technologies like digital IDs, particularly in the hands of the greedy, maniacal wealthy elite and big government bureaucrats. It is the reason I am writing this book. If the majority of people on the planet understood the threat to freedom and liberty posed by the rollout of digital IDs, they would take to the streets in protest and oust their elected officials for being negligent in protecting their freedom and liberty.

"They invade our private lives through surveillance, they extract from our lives, rendering what they extract as behavioral data and then they claim those behavioral data as their property."
  ~ *Shoshana Zuboff, professor emerita, Harvard University*

A Global Social Credit Scoring System

In *Covid-19: The Great Reset* by Klaus Schwab (leader of the World Economic Forum (WEF)) and Thierry Malleret, a 4th Industrial Revolution (4IR) is proposed, based on ongoing, globalist strategy planning by the WEF, the United Nations and the Bilderberg Group. These organizations are attempting to secure one world government of unelected officials, based on a massive push to establish *globalism* – a centralized form of governance by the wealthy elite.

This is being accomplished, in part, by the regulatory capture of agencies and departments within world governments by corporate conglomerates like Big Pharma and Big Agra, along with central bankers. The other big part of globalism is the redistribution of monetary wealth from the middle class to the wealthy elite and their government cronies. And the basis of all socialism and a primary component of globalism is this wealth redistribution.

This occurs through policies that are set by, for example, the U.S. Federal Government, the U.S. Federal Reserve, the United States Agency for International Development (USAID), the Council On Foreign Relations (CFR), the WHO and the United Nations Development Program (UNDP). The inner circle of influence for these agencies and organizations/companies is the WEF, the Bilderberg Group and the Club of Rome.

The centerpiece of it all is a fully functioning social credit scoring system that is now being modeled after the social credit scoring system in China that is now about 80% implemented. The Chinese social credit scoring system was first rolled out on an opt-in basis to Chinese businesses. From there, it has been offered on an opt-in basis to all residents of China. Because many of the Chinese citizenry and businesses have chosen to opt-in, the CCP plans to make mandatory and fully implement a nationwide social credit system by 2030. 2030 is also the target date for the rollout of digital IDs globally that are intended to include vaccine passports.

The Center for Human Rights & Global Justice at the NYU School of Law has published an excellent primer entitled *Paving a Digital Road to Hell?* You are strongly encouraged to read it and you can download the entire document for free here:

https://chrgj.org/wp-
content/uploads/2022/06/Report_Paving-a-Digital-
Road-to-Hell.pdf

In this report the following is stated:

"Unlike traditional systems of civil registration, such as
birth registration, this new model of economic identity
commonly sidesteps difficult questions about the legal
status of those it registers.

Many consider rapid and widescale deployment of such
digital ID systems to be dangerous. Evidence is
emerging from many countries around the world about
actual and potential, often severe and large-scale,
human rights violations linked to this model of digital
ID. Such systems may exacerbate pre-existing forms of
exclusion and discrimination in public and private
services. The use of new technologies may lead to new
forms of harm, including biometric exclusion,
discrimination, and the many harms associated with
surveillance capitalism. Meanwhile, the promised
benefits of such systems have not been convincingly
proven. These dangerous digital ID systems may lead
to 'pain without gain.'

Our experience, both in implementing the mandate of a
UN independent expert and at the Center for Human
Rights and Global Justice at New York University School
of Law, has allowed us to collaborate with many
experts and practitioners viewing these systems from
different vantage points. Members of our project team
have been directly involved in global policy discussions
around digital ID, including public consultations and
events with the World Bank and its Identification for
Development (ID4D) Initiative as well as with other

international organizations, governments, foundations, and private technology vendors.

We have jointly organized workshops with civil society organizations (CSOs) to discuss the implications of digital ID systems for human rights across the African continent. We have discussed related concerns with experts through our Transformer States conversation and blog series, and have taught about these subjects in law school courses. In addition, we have partnered with national human rights organizations to research and challenge specific digital ID systems.

We found that many of the experts and practitioners we engaged with shared our deep concerns around the dangers of digital ID systems for human rights. First, many of the systems studied and assessed have been linked to actual and prospective, serious and large-scale violations of human rights. Work from CSOs, academic researchers, journalists, and other experts have demonstrated that these violations often follow comparable patterns across different countries. Second, similarities in legal and technological design and implementation are not coincidental, but rather are linked to efforts by a global network of digital ID promoters. This is because governments often rely on the same small group of international organizations, foundations, and technology vendors for strategic, conceptual, practical, and financial support to design or upgrade their national digital ID systems.

Third, apart from the work of a handful of highly motivated non-profit organizations, there is often a disconnect between the work of global human rights organizations and local activists around national digital ID systems. This has meant that efforts to resist harmful systems have remained siloed and often pay less attention to global dynamics. Fourth and finally, systematic efforts to gather evidence of the impacts of digital ID systems are still underdeveloped, apart from some notable exceptions. While burdens are disproportionately placed on the human rights movement—or ecosystem—to ascertain the 'facts on the ground' for systems promoted by global proponents like the World Bank, there is still a great deal of work that must be done to document precise human rights impacts.

In light of these concerns and considerations, we believe that there is an urgent need to reframe research and contestation of digital ID systems as a global matter. Since many initiatives are shaped and supported by a global network of powerful proponents, the only way to effectively counter this confluence of interests and ideas, and to change outcomes, is through an equally global effort by the entire human rights ecosystem. This includes not only organizations and individual experts working on digital rights, but also those working on poverty and social and economic rights, social justice, economic development, and many others within the broader ecosystem.

Digital ID systems will, in many ways, determine the shape and form of digital governments and societies of the future. These are not marginal issues that should only be discussed and contested by those with technical expertise on biometrics or database design, but fundamental concerns that should be on the agenda of any individual or institution working on human rights and development." [1]

On pages 51-52 the following is stated:

"In 2018, former ID4D Working Group coordinator Mariana Dahan offered a report in which she stated: "But then something terrible happened, something unplanned. In a stream of high-profile security and privacy breaches...the world realized that we are on the cusp of something critical for our humanity. The risks of creation of an Orwellian system too obvious to be ignored."

Why the Push For Digital IDs?

As I stated earlier in this book, the wealthy elite and their government cronies want full socio-economic control of the masses. This is a matter of greed and maniacal egoism. Digital IDs, if fully implemented, will mean *full compliance* on the part of every person on the planet, for all government mandates and public/private partnership projects and strategies that are developed (like those being promoted by the WEF) – in order to control the masses using digital technology that will be managed by Artificial Intelligence (AI).

The implementation of this plan depends on the expansion of centralized Big Government. And, as we have seen historically, centralized Big Government always leads to tyranny. And yet, the notion of the expansion of centralized Big Government is becoming more and more popular with advances in digital IDs. This also means an increase in taxes across the board that will primarily impact the middle class. *The foundation for all socialism is the redistribution of monetary wealth from the middle class to the wealthy elite and government bureaucrats.* This takes place through taxation.

In *Covid-19: The Great Reset*, in the section entitled "1.3.3. The Return of big government," the WEF authors state the following:

"The COVID-19 pandemic has made government important again. Not just powerful again (look at those once mighty companies begging for help), but also vital again: It matters enormously whether your country has a good health service, competent bureaucrats and sound finances. Good government is the difference between living and dying." One of the great lessons of the past five years in Europe and America is this: acute crises contribute to boosting the power of the state. It's always been the case and there is no reason why it should be different with the COVID-19 pandemic. ...the responses to major crises have always further consolidated the power of the state, starting with taxation: 'an inherent and essential attribute of sovereignty belonging as a *matter of right* to every independent government.' A few examples illustrating the point strongly suggest that this time, as in the past, taxation will increase. As in the past, the social rationale and political justification underlying the increases will be based upon the narrative of 'countries at war' (only this time against an invisible enemy)....Today the situation is fundamentally different; in the intervening decades (in the Western world) the role of the state has shrunk considerably. This is a situation that is set to change...Already and almost overnight, the coronavirus succeeded in altering perceptions about the complex and delicate balance between the private and public realms in favor of the latter. It has revealed that social insurance is efficient and that offloading an ever-greater deal of responsibilities (like health and education) to individuals and markets may not be in the best interest of society....Looking to the future, governments will most likely, but with different degrees of intensity, decide that it's in the best interest of society to rewrite some of the rules of the game and permanently increase their role." [2]

So, here the WEF is advocating for bigger centralized government in all areas of society, by way of reducing the power of the individual. This is entirely the opposite of the clear intention of the framers of the U.S. Constitution and reeks of the collectivism (socialism/communism/fascism) that forms the foundation for governance in countries like China and Russia. In fact, the most recent annual meeting of the WEF was held, not in Davos where it has always been held, but in China.

In this meeting, Klaus Schwab praised the CCP for their governance and rule of law over the Chinese citizenry, something very telling about the intentions of the WEF, given that China enforces tyrannical rule over its people in the form of an overt dictatorship – a dictatorship funded, in part, by the harvesting and sale of organs taken out of Chinese dissidents who were executed for speaking out against their government.

The WEF has been promoting the following as part of its narrative, posted at the WEF web site:

"You'll own nothing and you will be happy. Whatever you want you will rent and it will be delivered to you by drone. The U.S. won't be the world's leading superpower. A handful of countries will dominate."

The World Council For Health has produced a policy document entitled *Unregulated Digitalization on Health and Democracy*. You can download the full document here: https://worldcouncilforhealth.org/wp-content/uploads/2023/08/Unregulated-Digitalization.pdf. In it they state the following:

"The Fourth Industrial Revolution presents a significant challenge to democracy and human rights. Totalitarian mechanisms such as China's Social Credit System are made possible by digital technology and surveillance. Without a critical analysis and correction of course, the digital transformation and Fourth Industrial Revolution are moving us into that dire direction where every aspect of a person's life is harvested, analyzed, traded and controlled by powerful private entities and governments. Some government and corporate actors have come to regard individuals as hackable animals, a term coined by World Economic Forum ideologue Yuval Harari. This means that these actors believe that they can hack people like machines, causing them to do anything (whether in the economic, political, ideological, social or cultural realm) by manipulating them via propaganda, psychographic messaging and other tools. Any form of private data is an asset for them to build a 360 degree view of a person that can then be used towards that end. [3]

Coercion and Compliance

Historically, we have seen Big Tech and government make promises of *privacy, inclusion and increased convenience*. These are the standard "buzz words" used to coerce us into complying. For example, at its advent, Facebook promised total privacy across its platform with no account/personal information shared except that which the account holder chooses to share. Then after being exposed for selling all Facebook and Instagram user account data and post information to businesses wanting to pitch their products/services to Facebook users (this is how Facebook makes its money), Mark Zuckerberg, the CEO of Facebook and its parent company, Meta, stated openly in interviews that there is no such thing as privacy on the Internet.

Google (owned by Alphabet) followed suit in selling YouTube user account data to businesses and then made a similar statement. With YouTube advertising at an all-time high, YouTube is at the forefront of mining data on your behavior, right down to monitoring how long it takes you to unpause a video you've been playing when you've hit play and stepped away from your device.

The fact is, since the advent of the Internet, in addition to selling advertising, Big Tech companies have been collecting, quantifying and selling user data to the public and private sectors. This data is collected every time you use a web browser. When you open a web browser and begin surfing the web, cookies are embedded into the browser. These cookies gather information on every aspect of your Internet use and browsing history. That data is shared by the owners of the web sites you visit and the company whose web browser you are using.

Third party cookies have been used to hack computers and mobile devices. In order to avoid this type of surveillance, you have to delete cookies, your browsing history and cache from your web browser after each session, and this is a very good practice for reducing the amount of surveillance you are exposed to.

The point here is digital surveillance of the public and the collection, management, use and sale of the data from that surveillance has been going on for as long as there has been an Internet. Indeed, this is why it is also known as the World Wide Web and coincides with the plan for the Internet of Things (IoT). [4] The plan for IoT is one in which all devices in your home and office, including your appliances and any electric cars you own will be connected to the Internet, meaning that they will require an Internet connection to operate. *Digital IDs are part of the IoT plan and will*

*take this surveillance to an entirely new and dangerous
level, due to the amount of control over our daily existence
this will give to Big Tech and centralized Big government.*

The United Nations has established a panel
designed to drive global cooperation for digital IDs by
2030. The first of the UN Secretary-General's High-
level Panels on Digital Cooperation was led by Melinda
Gates from the Bill & Melinda Gates Foundation
(according to the bio, Melinda "helped develop many of
the company's multimedia products" during her time at
Microsoft) and tech billionaire Jack Ma from the Chinese
Ali Baba Group. Jack Ma is also the creator of China's
social credit scoring system. So, already you know this
digital cooperation push is all about surveillance and
control of the masses. Even as many tech experts have
warned of a "totalitarian Nightmare," the UN is
launching a Bill Gates-funded global digital ID program.
You can read bout that here:
https://needtoknow.news/2023/12/un-launches-gates-
funded-global-digital-id-program-as-experts-warn-of-
totalitarian-nightmare/.

This group of arch-Technocrats is deciding the
future of humankind connected to total digitalization of
everything in our lives. All of this is being designed to
connect to cell phones that, in their world, will be
required for daily, basic existence. What you will hear
from these people are narratives based on notions of a
digital divide that has created digital inequality,
particularly for women everywhere, and also youth in
underdeveloped nations. You will hear them tout the
necessity for digital IDs in order for women have to
have a seat at the table as the creators of society. One
of their complaints is that women don't have the same
access to capital/finances as men do, and that digital
IDs are necessary for female equality.

They use words like "inclusiveness" and "leave
nobody behind" – beneficial on their face value. But,

because their main focus is to get women onto the control grid first, you will hear them talk about increased income for women through a digital ID superstructure, along with "fair globalization" and "globalization for all" because "there's nothing wrong with globalization." They want to "use AI to make machines like people" and they want limited regulation and have even openly stated, "Don't worry too much about safety and privacy."

The one word you will never hear them utter is LIBERTY. You can view an interview about UN Secretary-General's High-level Panel on Digital Cooperation with UN Secretary-General António Guterres, Melinda Gates and Jack Ma here: https://www.activistpost.com/2023/06/uns-vision-of-the-future-an-apex-body-and-digital-id-to-rule-us-all.html. The International Monetary Fund (IMF) has already released a Digital Currency Handbook for the world's central banks. You can read bout that here: https://www.theepochtimes.com/article/imf-releases-digital-currency-handbook-for-worlds-central-banks-5532716.

The push for worldwide digital cooperation to launch digital IDs comes with assistance from the Young Global Leaders of the WEF, along with generous contributions from the World Economic Forum's Center for the Fourth Industrial Revolution. These are collectivist organizations that seek to destroy Liberty.

As I said earlier, a key part of the coercion campaign is the focus on convenience. How many people have dreaded having to go into the local motor vehicle office to process a registration, renew a driver's license or transfer a deed of ownership? Just the thought of having to wait on a long line (take a number and have a seat) or the thought of having to arrive 30-60 minutes before the office opens to grab a spot on a line outside the door can be a nagging endeavor. So, part of the coercion campaign to move people on to full digital IDs is to start with digital drivers' licenses.

"These three states — California, Michigan and Iowa — are joining Arizona, Colorado, Louisiana, Mississippi, Georgia, Hawaii, Ohio, Utah, and Maryland in offering biometric digital drivers' licenses. The digital IDs will likely require biometric/ biological identification such as a face scan, eyeball scan or palm scan that can be stored and shared. California, Michigan, and Iowa are all taking steps to implement digital IDs. California is testing, Iowa is launching, and Michigan is considering legislation related to mobile driver's licenses. These states are planning to join Arizona, Colorado, Louisiana, Mississippi, Georgia, Hawaii, Ohio, Utah, and Maryland in offering mDLs."

"New digital driver's licenses will allow residents to virtually perform services that otherwise would have required an in-person trip to the DMV," says Ajay Amlani, President and head of Americas, iProov in a comment emailed to Biometric Update. Michigan is proposing a bill that would allow the Secretary of State to issue digital IDs in addition to their traditional physical counterparts, according to a local outlet. If passed, mDLs would become official IDs, equivalent to physical licenses. They would be valid for state government services, banking, police stops, and ID checks for age. Some raise concerns about whether an ID can be accessed on a lost or stolen phone. Others raise concerns that deepfakes and other cyberattacks can circumvent biometric authentication." [5]

Maybe you are old enough to remember LP records that were played with a needle on a phonograph, or the television sets that had VHF and UHF antennas to grab broadcasts. CDs have replaced LPs and they don't make LPs anymore. Your father's television set was made obsolete with the advent of the Internet. Today you have to have an Internet connection, an online account and a digital device to view/listen to broadcasts of any kind. If we allow ourselves to be coerced into compliance, physical driver's licenses will go the same route as LPs and free standing TVs.

iProov and LimitediProov is the world leader in biometric face verification. Their product enables banks, government agencies and other organizations to verify that an online individual is who they claim to be. They claim that this helps prevent identity theft and other cybercrime, while also making online services easier to access. [6] *The issue is biometrics.* Face and eyeball scans are the stuff of high security entry and access in agencies like the CIA, NSA, MI5, MI6, KGB and Mossad.

These scans are designed to store other biometric data, including body temperature and brain wave patterns. And it is a very easy leap to program these scans to include health data such as blood test results, illnesses/diseases that a person is being treated for, heart rate, oxygen levels, blood glucose levels and vaccination history. In fact, these digital scanning systems can be programmed to scan whatever is taking place under the skin, as well as the monitoring, storage and sharing of that data. The intention for digital ID systems is that they be *interoperable.* You will see this word in all of the data on digital ID development. Interoperability means that, given the fact that nations across the globe will design and implement their own digital IDs, the varying digital ID systems will be programmed to talk to each other worldwide. This will pave the way for government and businesses of any country to be able to access all digital IDs of everyone on the planet.

Amazon, the largest online retailer in the world, has just rolled out Amazon One. At select retail stores (such as Whole Foods Market) that are owned and managed in the Amazon network of offline businesses you are now able to pay with your palm print. Once you've signed up for Amazon One your palm print is linked to your existing Amazon online account that has your credit card on file. Amazon One customers simply wave their palm in front of a scanner and the purchase is charged to the customer's Amazon online account. [7] "One scan does it all."

In the U.S., if you are charged with a crime, you are fingerprinted upon arrest. But, if you are not convicted of the crime, your fingerprints are removed from the FBI database after two years. It's only if you are convicted that they remain in the FBI database for life. With Amazon One, Amazon corp. and its affiliates have your palm print for life. Of course, they don't state or guarantee what will happen with your palm print on file if you decide to close your Amazon online account.

In another recent development, Microsoft has patented a system that will allow the user of a computer, laptop or mobile device to receive a cryptocurrency 'award' (presumably the cryptocurrency developed and owned by Bill Gates) when sensors installed in the user's computer recognize certain body movements and activity. The patent abstract summary states the following:

"Human body activity associated with a task provided to a user may be used in a mining process of a cryptocurrency system. A server may provide a task to a device of a user which is communicatively coupled to the server. A sensor communicatively coupled to or comprised in the device of the user may sense body activity of the user. Body activity data may be generated based on the sensed body activity of the user. The cryptocurrency system communicatively coupled to the device of the user may verify if the body activity data satisfies one or more conditions set by the cryptocurrency system, and award cryptocurrency to the user whose body activity data is verified." [8]

So, the question is, do you trust Bill Gates with the data gathered from surveilling your body activity through your computer? How else will that data be used?

Nick Corbishley is a writer, journalist, teacher and translator based in Barcelona. Formerly a senior contributing editor at the San Francisco-based economics and finance news site Wolf Street, he is currently a regular contributor to the US financial news and analysis blog *Naked Capitalism*, where he writes about financial, economic and political trends and developments in Europe and Latin America. In his book, *Scanned – Why Vaccine Passports and Digital IDs Will Mean the End of Privacy and Personal Freedom*, referencing pandemics, Nick Corbishley tells us:

"That opportunity could not be clearer: to use global health challenges as a pretext for implementing digital identity programs around the world, which is precisely what is happening right now. While digital identity may offer certain benefits for citizens, including greater ease in verifying one's identity as well as the convenience of having all your digital records stored in one place, it also poses huge dangers. The biggest danger of all is that governments and companies will have much greater ability to track and control populations, impose behaviors, and influence politics. The worldwide rollout of vaccine passports/digital IDs represents nothing less than the redrawing of the social contract – a fact the World Economic Forum admitted in its 2018 report, *Identity in a Digital World: A New*

Chapter in the Social Contract: Government, the private sector and civil society communities from the World Economic Forum network have identified six priority areas for collaboration to help shape digital identities of the future:

> *1. Moving the emphasis beyond identity for all to identities that deliver user value*
> *2. Creating metrics and accountability for good identity*
> *3. Building new governance models for digital identity ecosystems*
> *4. Promoting stewardship of good identity*
> *5. Encouraging partnerships around best practices and interoperability where appropriate*
> *6. Innovating with technologies and models and building a library of successful pilots*

> *As the International Organization for Public-Private Cooperation, the World Economic Forum offers a platform for such collaboration that advances the practice of "good" identities and maximizes value to individuals.*

At the WEF's Annual Meeting in Davos 2018, senior representative of businesses, governments, and civil society made a commitment to advance towards a "good" future for digital identity. In the months following, those stakeholders identified an initial set of five requirements that a "good" identity should satisfy, which the WEF shared in its *Identity in a Digital World* report. For a digital ID to be good, it must:

1. Be fit for purpose, by offering "a reliable way for individuals to build trust in who they claim to be, to exercise their rights and freedoms and/or in their eligibility to carry out digital transactions."

2. Be secure – protecting individuals, organizations, devices, and infrastructure from identity theft, unauthorized data sharing, and human rights violations.

3. Be useful, meaning it "offers access to a wide range of useful services and interactions and is easy to establish and use."

4. Offer choice. A digital ID can be empowering for users, the report claims, allowing them to control "what data they share for which interaction, with whom, and for how long." This is most likely an empty promise. After all, how much control and ownership do we have over reams of digital data we generate today?

5. Be inclusive. This is a popular buzzword, often used to describe things that are anything but. For example, the cashless economy is often marketed as a means of promoting "financial inclusion," when it does the exact opposite. Those who stand to benefit most from a cashless economy are in the more comfortable classes, who by and large are computer literate and already use digital money for most of their transactions, while those most dependent on cash – the poor and the elderly – will suddenly find life a lot more difficult.

So, who would benefit most from the system of mandatory digital IDs? The most likely answer to that question is the WEF's most important stakeholders: the world's most powerful corporations, biggest financial institutions, and the wealthiest individuals. In other words, Davos Man and Davos Woman." [9]

The Office of Homeland Security and The Patriot Act

In order for centralized Big government to succeed, two primary things must take place. First, the citizenry must be surveiled and they must know that they are being surveiled. Second, free speech must be censored. Both are taking place right now, even in nations like the United States that pride themselves on being Republics that are governed democratically. I will address the growing censorship of free speech in Chapter 7. Digital IDs are, in part, designed to increase surveillance of the public while, at the same time, censoring free speech. Historically, these are methods that ensure compliance to government dictatorial demands.

Dr. Naomi Wolf is a bestselling author, columnist, and professor; she is a graduate of Yale University and received a doctorate from Oxford. She is cofounder and CEO of DailyClout.io, a successful civic tech company. She was a Rhodes scholar, and was an advisor to the Clinton re-election campaign and to Vice President Al Gore. In her book *The End of America – Letter of Warning to a Young Patriot – A Citizen's Call to Action*, Dr. Wolf shares the following:

"According to the ACLU's Barry Steinhardt, you should assume, if you are an activist, that your email may be monitored and your phone calls tracked. He says that if your communications reach a certain level of interest to the government, a human being may be tasked to read and listen in on what you are saying, and you won't know about it. The White House surveillance program (this is a program established by President G.W. Bush under the Patriot Act) is triggered by certain key words and names. (The sophisticated Stasi listening station on Brocken Mountain, which monitored ordinary citizens' calls between East and West Germany, was also programmed to record conversations when a certain name or word came up.) Even though you pose no terrorist threat to the state, there is a reason you can be placed under surveillance now. Tyrants place populations under surveillance because this is the prime means of control. The Gestapo, the NKVD, the KGB, the Stasi, and the Chinese Politburo all requisitioned private data such as medical, banking, and library records; now, with the Internet, Chinese authorities track citizens' computer use. One reason dictators demand access to such private data is that this scrutiny breaks down citizens' sense of being able to act freely against those in power. Such intrusions also erode citizens' loyalties to civil and professional groups and redirect their primary loyalty to the state." [10]

On October 8, 2001, in response to the September 11, 2001 attacks on the United States, the Office of Homeland Security was established by the Bush Administration. [11] On October 26, 2001 the U.S. Patriot Act was passed and signed into law. [12] This was a necessary response to the attacks on the World Trade Center, the Pentagon and Flight 93 that killed more than 3,000 people. At that time, we were told that the Office of Homeland Security was temporary, and that it would be dismantled when the threat posed by the 9/11 attacks no longer existed.

Twenty-two years later, the Office of Homeland Security still exists and has expanded its activities, many of which are executed in direct violation of the U.S. Constitution. These violations are carried out "in the interest of national security" and, therefore, are covered up to the point where even the U.S. Congress is denied access to information on those activities.

Upon establishing the Office of Homeland Security, President Bush initiated Operation TIPS. Operation TIPS, where the last part is an acronym for the Terrorism Information and Prevention System, was a domestic intelligence-gathering program designed by President George W. Bush to have United States citizens report suspicious activity. You can read about Operation TIPS here: https://www.wikiwand.com/en/Operation_TIPS. The program's website implied that US workers who had access to private citizens' homes, such as many cable installers and telephone repair workers, would be reporting on what was in people's homes if it were deemed "suspicious." The initial start of the program was to be August 2002 and would have included one million workers in ten US cities, to be expanded from there.

Operation TIPS came under intense scrutiny in July 2002 when the Washington Post alleged in an editorial that the program was vaguely defined, and investigative political journalist Ritt Goldstein observed in Australia's *Sydney Morning Herald* that TIPS would provide America with a higher percentage of 'citizen spies' than the former East Germany had under the notorious Stasi secret police. Goldstein later observed that he broke news of Operation TIPS on March 10 in Spain's second largest daily, *El Mundo*, but that he struggled until July before finding a major English language paper which would print the story.

In the days immediately following Goldstein's revelation, publications such as the libertarian magazine *Reason*, and then the *Boston Globe*, emphasized the Stasi analogy, widely highlighting Operation TIPS' shortcomings. TIPS was subsequently cancelled after concerns over civil liberties violations. Operation TIPS was accused of doing an "end run" around the United States Constitution, and the original wording of the website was subsequently changed. President Bush's then-Attorney General John Ashcroft denied that private residences would be surveiled by private citizens operating as government spies. Mr. Ashcroft nonetheless defended the program, equivocating on whether the reports by citizens on fellow citizens would be maintained in government databases. While saying that the information would not be in a central database as part of Operation TIPS, he maintained that the information would still be kept in databases by various law enforcement agencies.

The databases were an explicit concern of various civil liberties groups (on both the left and the right) who felt that such databases could include false information about citizens with no way for those citizens to know that such information was compiled about them, nor any way for them to correct the information, nor any way for them to confront their accusers.

The United States Postal Service, after at first seeming supportive of the program, later resisted its personnel being included in this program, reasoning that if mail carriers became perceived as law enforcement personnel that they would be placed in danger at a level for which they could not reasonably be expected to be prepared, and that the downside of the program hence vastly outweighed any good that it could accomplish. The National Association of Letter Carriers, a postal labor union, was especially outspoken in its opposition. [13]

There was an initial attempt by the U.S. Congress to pass a bill outlawing the program. This move was based on concerns that the program was very similar to J. Edgar Hoover's abuse of power in misusing the FBI during the 1960s when Hoover set up programs that spied on U.S. citizens who were engaged in public protests against the government. This initial attempt failed.

Operation TIPS was officially cancelled when the Homeland Security Act was passed by Congress in November 2002. Section 880 explicitly prohibited the program. On June 30, 2008, the *Denver Post* reported that 181 individuals, including police officers, paramedics, firefighters, utility workers, and railroad employees had been trained as Terrorism Liaison Officers to report suspicious information which could be signs of terrorist activity. The article also stated that TLOs were already active in six other states and the District of Columbia.

Based on outrage over Operation TIPS and similar activities, The Patriot Act was modified in 2015 but still contains many of its original provisions. The fact is we don't know to what degree The Patriot Act is still being executed by the Federal Government. What is obvious is that, if digital IDs are established, activities conducted under The Patriot Act will make programs like Operation TIPS look like child's play.

The Iron Triangle

In China the CCP enforces three types of government surveillance. This is known as "the iron triangle." This comprises a residence permit that limits where people live; a secret personnel file that is a record of your sins in the government's eyes, along with political liabilities a person has incurred; and the work unit that supervises every aspect of the lives of the citizenry. The secret personnel file is called *dangan*. It looks like a manila envelope and there is one for every person living in China. The *dangan* is transported around the country through a special postal system. If a person transgresses against the government or CCP, a note is placed in that person's *dangan*. These notes haunt the Chinese citizenry wherever they go and impact a person's ability to earn a living, to move to a new home and to leave the country.

The *dangan* has been implemented in the U.S. There are now three forms of surveillance initiated in 2005 and 2006. New York Times reporters James Risen and Eric Lichtblau exposed an *email* and *phone monitoring* program that was operating without any warrants being issued. [14] It was also revealed that U.S. treasury agents, under the management of the CIA, were *reviewing millions of private bank transactions* without court-ordered warrants or subpoenas.

We don't know if these programs still exist. What is certain is that programs like these are good reasons to ensure that digital IDs never become a reality, as such programs will be simple to establish and nearly impossible to expose if digital IDs are implemented.

Digital Health Certificates and Vaccine Passports

Before we examine digital health certificates and vaccine passports there are some points I want to make, as an introduction to this section.

1. **In America, vaccine manufacturers are not liable for any harm done to you by their product.** This means that, if you are injured by a vaccine, you cannot sue the manufacturer of the vaccine. This includes all Covid shots that are actually not vaccines, but rather gene therapy biologics.

2. **In the U.S., if you are injured by a vaccine, you have to apply to have your case heard in vaccine court** where an administrative law judge who is actually an attorney representing the Department of Health and Human Services (HHS) gets to decide whether or not you will be compensated for your injury. HHS is charged with running the Vaccine Injury Compensation Program (VICP). The average awarded claim is $450,000, *based on your having to negotiate a settlement with HHS in*

which HHS has not concluded, based upon review of the evidence, that the alleged vaccine(s) caused the alleged injury. In other words, in order to obtain a settlement for your vaccine injury, you have to agree with the HHS assessment that the vaccine did not cause the injury. Indeed, this makes vaccine court a 'kangaroo court.'

I know several vaccine injured patients and the doctors who have attempted to treat their injury who attest to this fact. Out of the average awarded claim of $450,000 comes your attorney fees which can run as high as 70% of the award. What's left is never enough to address the medical care necessitated by the injury. If you don't want to take your case to vaccine court, your only other option is a Tort vaccine injury case. This is a civil suit that would have to be brought against HHS. Tort cases can take 5-7 years to try. Whether you win or not, the legal expenses of a Tort case can bankrupt you.

3. **The Covid shots do not prevent infection or transmission, nor are they designed to do so. It's the same for the annual flu shot.** After holding press conferences in which he lied to Americans about the shots preventing infection, and after getting the jab and the booster shots, President Biden announced that he got Covid again. [15] The first lady, Jill Biden also got Covid after being inoculated and boosted [16] In fact, there are millions of people who have gotten Covid after getting the shots.

4. **It is impossible to effectively vaccinate for viruses, Corona viruses included.** These viruses mutate very quickly and wild, naturally-occuring viruses circulate the globe year round. This is why a vaccine has never been manufactured for the common cold that is caused by wild, naturally-occuring Corona viruses like 229E,

NL63, OC43, and HKU1. In addition, seasonal upticks in endemic respiratory viruses like COVID-19 are normal and no cause for alarm. Vaccination targeted at viruses, at best, can only help to prevent hospitalization for those with underlying comorbidities and those who are immune system compromised.

5. **mRNA vaccine technology is not stable and there is mounting evidence that the risks of mRNA vaccines in general outweigh the benefits.** [17,18] Even one of the co-inventors of mRNA vaccines, Dr. Robert Malone, has expressed his doubts about the use of mRNA vaccines for treating Corona viruses.

6. **Peer-reviewed studies now show that up to 74% of post Covid shot deaths are caused by the shots themselves.** [19,20,21,22]

7. **The truth is vaccine manufacturers can put anything they want into their vaccines, including ingredients that they are not presently required to reveal for FDA approval.** Therefore, it stands to reason that it is imperative that we find out what's in the shots we are fed under the childhood and adult vaccination schedule. It also stands to reason that studies should be conducted comparing the vaccinated to the unvaccinated to determine which group has overall better health and protection against infectious diseases.

Fortunately for us, there are many scientific, peer-reviewed studies on vaccines, and studies comparing the vaccinated to the unvaccinated have also been done. The reason you may not have heard about these is because most of the doctors involved in conducting these studies have had their medical licenses suspended or permanently revoked by state medical boards, at the request of Big Pharma. Some of these doctors I know personally. See Chapter 3 for a review of these studies.

As I've stated earlier in this book, I am not an anti-vaxxer. I am pro-safety and I am for health/medical freedom and the right to choose, based on fully-informed consent. And I have been vaccinated growing up. However, there is no question about the fact that many vaccines being used today have risks that greatly outweigh the benefits, and are, historically, dangerous to one's health. The CDC has been repeatedly complicit in covering up data that reveals many diseases caused by vaccines. To understand this and vet the information for yourself, you can view an excellent documentary entitled *Vaxxed: From Coverup to Catastrophe* here: https://bhaktaschool.org/vaxxed-1/

Make sure that you are fully-informed before you even consider vaccination.

8. **Digital health certificates will create two-tiered societies segregating people who comply with globalist health mandates from people who don't.** [23,24] To date, there is not a single statistic that shows that digital health certificates actually protect or improve public health or individual health. In fact, what digital health certificates like the EU's Covid Pass and Israel's Green Pass show is human rights and civil liberties violations, along with attacks on privacy.

9. **Although, in this chapter, I will present several, urgent and essential reasons for not allowing government to force us to comply with vaccine passports that include proved ineffectiveness of vaccines and lack of proper safety studies and controls**, there is only one reason to oppose vaccine passports. *If*

we allow government to dictate what we put on and in our bodies, we are no longer free.

In the Spring and Fall of 2021 I spent a lot of time at the Ohio State House introducing citizens bills to the Ohio State legislature that I co-wrote. These bills were sponsored by legislators and began making their way through the legislative process. They have now been combined into one bill, HB 73 - The Dave and Angie Patient and Health Provider Protection Act currently being considered by the 136th General Assembly of the Ohio State legislature.

During this same period, I was invited to give testimony to the legislature's House Health Committee (I am also a Doctor of Eastern and Oriental medicine and had a practice in New York City for 15 years) in support of HB 248 - The Vaccine Choice and Anti-Discrimination Act, a bill designed to preserve religious, medical and philosophical exemptions to Covid shots. This bill was also designed to push back against vaccine passports in the state of Ohio where I currently live.

After giving my testimony, there was time set aside for state legislators sitting on the House Health Committee to ask me questions regarding my testimony in support of the bill, and my comments supporting no vaccine passports in the state. Representative C. Allison Russo who was sitting on the health committee at the time then said to me, "Today, we have laws that you must wear a seatbelt when you drive your car. Why are mandated Covid vaccines and vaccine passports any different?" She had just compared injecting a biologic into your body that has not been safety tested with wearing a seatbelt! And I told her so in my response to her question.

Immediately after the hearing I approached Rep. Russo and offered to provide her with all the data that I and my organization had collected on the Covid shots to date, including the vaccine injury data on the shots that was approaching millions of people injured, along with Big Pharma's own admission on the Covid shot websites that the shots do not prevent infection or transmission and are "Only designed to address clinically significant symptoms of Covid-19." This was also stated on the package inserts for all of the Covid shots, until people started posting the statement in social media. Big Pharma responded by replacing the package inserts with ones that are completely blank.

When I offered to provide Rep. Russo with all the data we had, and then offered to meet with her to discuss the data further, she declined. She didn't want to see the data and didn't want to talk to me. And this is the challenge we have with our elected officials, many of whom are not properly educated or informed on the prevalent pressing issues that we face as a citizenry and, instead, are wed to their own political/social ideology and/or that of their party.

In another section of the book *Scanned*, we are told the following:

"Vaccine Passport = Digital ID – The vaccine passport is nothing more than and nothing less than a digital ID. Since at least 2016 a powerful alliance of UN agencies, global corporations, and wealthy foundations has set its sights on creating and implementing digital IDs around the world. Organizations such as ID2020, the Good Health Pass Collaborative, the Vaccine Credential Initiative, the common Pass, and GAVI are the vehicles by which they hope to achieve that goal. The COVID-19 pandemic and the subsequent roll out of novel vaccine technologies have provided the pretext. In March of 2018, almost two full years before the coronavirus pandemic, ID2020 published an article titled "Immunization: An Entry Point for Digital Identity." The article stated that, "immunization (by way of vaccination) poses a huge opportunity to scale digital identity." That opportunity could not be clearer: to use global health challenges as a pretext for implementing digital identity programs around the world, which is precisely what is happening right now." [25]

In early January of 2022 and December of 2022, Senator Ron Johnson held Congressional Roundtables in which frontline medical professionals, researchers and virologists were called to testify about their experiences in addressing COVID-19 treatments and mandates. I encourage you to view the video recordings of these sessions. Here are the links. In both cases, you will need to scroll into the recording after hitting the play button to reach the start of the roundtable discussions.

COVID-19: A Second Opinion
https://rumble.com/vt62y6-covid-19-a-second-opinion.html

Sen. Johnson Expert Panel on Federal Vaccine Mandates
https://rumble.com/vokrf7-sen.-johnson-expert-panel-on-federal-vaccine-mandates.html

To better understand U.S. Senate congressional hearings conducted by Senator Ron Johnson, view *COVID-19 Vaccines: What They Are, How They Work and Possible Causes of Injuries* here:
https://rumble.com/v1ze4d0-covid-19-vaccines-what-they-are-how-they-work-and-possible-causes-of-injuri.html

The Epoch Times interviewed Senator Ron Johnson after these roundtables took place. Below is a partial transcript of that interview.

'It's All Being Covered Up': Sen. Ron Johnson on Missing Batch of Fauci Emails, COVID Origins, and Silencing of the Vaccine-Injured

Jan Jekielek:
Senator Ron Johnson, such a pleasure to have you back on American Thought Leaders.

Senator Ron Johnson:
Thanks for having me on.

Mr. Jekielek:
I have to say that I'm going to dub you a COVID response skeptic. All the way from the beginning, you were already asking pretty big questions publicly about this whole idea of shutdowns. I want to focus in on a particular time and see if you remember in mid-March of 2020, there was this moment where the whole narrative was, "It's just another virus. Nothing to worry about." Then, it suddenly shifts to, "We have to lock down our borders," and then, pretty quickly to, "We have to lock down the country."

Senator Johnson:
Oh, I remember it. First of all, I'll take that moniker. Skeptic to me is a synonym for science. Science is about being skeptical. One of the greatest tragedies of the entire pandemic episode is we haven't even been allowed to ask the questions. I remember very early on in the pandemic watching the video coming out of China with everybody in their moonsuits, it was alarming, there's no doubt about it. We didn't know what we were dealing with. We had certainly heard of Ebola and MERS [Middle East Respiratory Syndrome].

Ebola had about a 40 percent death rate or infection fatality rate. MERS had something like a 30 percent rate. SARS was eight to 10 percent.

Were we dealing with something like that? We just didn't know, until we had the Princess Cruise. You had John Ioannidis analyzing that, and his analysis of what happened on the Princess Cruise has pretty well stood the test of time. This was a deadly disease if you were elderly, and if you had certain comorbidities. But if you were young and healthy, it was going to be a flu-like type of disease. I glommed onto that analysis. I knew that there was no way you could shut down the American economy, the way people like Anthony Fauci were talking about it, a 50-day shutdown to flatten the curve.

What exactly are you going to shut down? We're still going to need hospitals operating. We're still going to need pharmacies operating. We're still going to need grocery stores operating. We're still going to need gas stations. The economy had to continue to operate.

Somewhere in that timeframe, in a comment to a reporter somewhere, it was said, "Listen, we tragically lose 36,000 people a year on the highway, but we don't shut down our highway system. We need a transportation system. We're going to have to gut our way through this thing and follow science as best we can."

"Protect the vulnerable, but we're going to have to carry on with life." Of course, Fauci heard that, which was brought up in one of those famous press conferences. He said that analogy was beyond the pale or some such comment.

Now, I remember on one of our senate calls with Anthony Fauci about this timeframe, and you get your opportunity to ask one question. My question was directed to Anthony Fauci. I said, "Dr. Fauci, you're proposing these shutdowns." "Are you taking into account the human devastation, the human toll, the economic devastation that you're contemplating here?" He just cavalierly said, "Senator, that is somebody else's department. I don't worry about that."

If you're a doctor, you may be specialized, but you have to treat the whole patient. You have to understand what your cure is going to do to the patient. He couldn't have cared less. Very early on, nothing about our response made sense. I was an early advocate for early treatment. I heard about the possibility of the drug hydroxychloroquine. If you remember, there was a state senator in Michigan that was treated with hydroxychloroquine. I heard about Dr. Zelenko, and Didier Raoult in France. I'm reading about these things. My concern was that we wouldn't have enough of it.

I'm calling up the head of Novartis and texting him. They donated 30 million doses to the national stockpile, but it wasn't being distributed. My main concern was, again, would we have enough manufacturing capacity for a cheap generic drug like hydroxychloroquine?

I had never heard of ivermectin at that point, and at that time I hadn't heard of budesonide. I hadn't heard of all these other molecules. I had heard of vitamin D, which by the way, Anthony Fauci took and told no one. Isn't that curious? He upped his intake of vitamin D. Why wasn't he talking about that early on?

I've been vilified, and I've been ridiculed throughout this process. During Omicron was when the pandemic had really become politicized. Democrats were freaked out by it. The Republicans were walking around saying, "There's no way I am going to wear a mask." I was on a telephone town hall with a few thousand constituents, and I was telling my constituents, and a lot of them were probably Republicans, I said, "Take Omicron seriously. It's probably more contagious, probably less lethal, but it can still be a deadly disease. Take it seriously. There are things you can do. You can take vitamin D, vitamin C, and gargle. There are things you can do."

I mentioned gargling, because there was a study on the CDC's own website saying that gargling can reduce the viral load. Why not? What's the worst thing that can happen? Fresher breath. But I've got Democrat operatives in those town halls. Within 10 minutes after that town hall, we had national media calling my office, "What's this thing about Senator Johnson saying, Listerine will replace the vaccine?" Of course, I didn't say that, but that was the narrative for two weeks.

For whatever reason, there was a concerted effort to not promote or research or push any kind of early treatment, anything that might mitigate and lessen the severity of the disease. It was just, "Get tested. We'll spend tens of billions of dollars on tests." But then if you test positive, do nothing, go home afraid, isolate yourself, and hope you don't get so sick that you have to go to the hospital.

But if you do go to the hospital, then we'll slap Remdesivir in your arm, costing over 3000 bucks. You've had doctors on here, I'm sure, talking about how that can be pretty harmful to your kidneys. We'll put you on a vent, knowing that 80 to 90 percent of people that went on ventilation never got off it.

Nothing made sense to me. I'll be 68-years-old soon, and as long as I've been alive, it has been early detection that allows for early treatment, which produces better results and better healing. That's how we treat every other illness and cancer. You're trying to go for early detection. But for COVID it was early detection, and then do nothing. It was insane. With our response to COVID I would say that's probably the best word to sum it up—insane, a miserable failure.

Mr. Jekielek:
But the response went in the face of all established, suggested responses, including the CDC's own guidelines. There was a very small number of people, especially at the beginning, who were asking these sorts of questions. What was it that you knew? You said you were reading these different things, but what was it that you knew to look at, that a whole lot of people didn't?

Senator Johnson:
It was because I didn't have the level of fear others had. I certainly had a concern up front. Again, you saw the Chinese in the moonsuits. You heard from these doctors that were treating, and then young doctors just dying. I had that concern. But then, with John Ioannidis' study on the Princess Cruise ship, he said, "Okay, we'll get through this." I didn't have the level of fear that they imposed on the rest of society.

That was their main tool. The technocrats and the Faucis of the world made sure that the world was deathly afraid of this. As a result, when you're deathly afraid, you're looking for some relief from that fear.

Then, you have a guy like Fauci saying, "I've got the cure here. I've got a vaccine." What was insane about it is that we didn't pursue early treatment.

We didn't look at all the different molecules, all the different generic drugs that were on the shelf. They have been used for decades, safely. They had the kind of properties that you'd be expecting in terms of being antiviral or anticoagulant or working with respiratory illnesses. We just threw all that aside.

There was nothing in the pandemic plan that called for shutdowns. Fauci said up front, "Masks aren't going to work." They didn't. All you needed to know was, "Here is the particle size of the virus and here is the opening pores of the mask. This isn't going to work." It might be marginally effective, but it wasn't something that you would impose on everybody in your society.

The way we shut the economy down, we shut down all the little mom and pop shops, but we let the big box stores open. Bobby Kennedy writes in his, "A Letter to Liberals," that a 2021 study showed there was almost a $4 trillion transfer of wealth from the middle class to the Big Tech social media giants. Those are the people that were in charge of the narrative.

That is what has opened my eyes up. I've been referring to them as the "Covid Cartel." I'm talking about the Biden administration, the federal health agencies, Big Pharma that has captured the federal health agencies, and legacy media. The Big Tech social media giants and Big Pharma captured the media as well.

They controlled the narrative, and they controlled the narrative in a way that was highly beneficial to them.

Amazon did great during the pandemic. The social media companies did great during the pandemic. Why? Because society was shut down. You had to use social media. You had to use Big Tech.

Mr. Jekielek:
There was also a societal hysteria around this fueled by some of these different players. This is another debate that's out there. On one end of the debate there are these puppeteer overlords that are pushing their message onto the society, and society just responds. On the other side, we've simply turned into a safetyist kind of society, where the smallest threat can create a mass hysteria like this. Where do you land on this spectrum?

Senator Johnson:
Unfortunately, it's very easy to manipulate a population. We've seen this for decades. Go back to the beginning of newspapers and mass media. You tell the big lie, and as people have said, "The truth hasn't even put on its shoes, and the lie travels around the world many times." Unfortunately, it's very easy to manipulate a population, and the best way to manipulate them is with fear.

I look at the pandemic as just an extension of climate change. Again, I don't deny climate change. I'm just not an alarmist. Climate has always changed. You look at the Vostok ice core sample, we're in our fifth cycle of temperature variations of 22.7 degrees in over four hundred and some thousand years.

I know this is a diversion, but do you know how much the sea level has risen in the Bay of San Francisco since the last glaciation period 10 to 20,000 years ago? 390 feet. Again, the climate has always changed. We have to adapt. We can't hold back the tides.

And yet, there's a political movement that has seized on climate change. It used to be global cooling. I'm old enough to remember that, either a nuclear winter or a climate-induced winter, and we wouldn't be able to grow crops. Then, that changed into global warming, and then, they couldn't quite decide.

They just said, "Let's use the catchall phrase, climate change," and they used that to scare people. You have this little Scandinavian girl that says the world's going to end in 12 years. AOC has done the same thing. The world's not going to end in 12 years. We will adapt. Unfortunately, for the climate change alarmists, they weren't able to seize control to the extent they wanted to. They looked at the pandemic and said, "This is even better. We can really scare the you-know-what out of the global population, and we can gain control. We can start doing things like vaccine passports, and we can restrict travel."

People ought to be very concerned, because now what are we going through? A potential bank crisis. Be very concerned about a central bank digital currency, where they can just turn on and turn off your ability to purchase certain goods based on your social credit score. That's what happens in China. Do we want that in the U.S.? There certainly are people like the technocrats in the U.S. that would like to see that. With this banking crisis, all of a sudden we're insuring every deposit, no matter how large. Start asking some questions and be skeptical.

Mr. Jekielek:
I want to go back to this question of why you knew to look in all sorts of places? Like you said, you were reading John Ioannidis very early, but it seems like most

people weren't, even people that should be, and even people whose job it is to do so.

Senator Johnson:
First of all, I'm not a fan of the federal government. I think our founders were geniuses. They knew we were imperfect men and women. If we don't want to live in anarchy and chaos, we need some government, but it better be limited. Because they came from tyrannical regimes, they understood that as the government grows, your freedom recedes. The one essential ingredient in America is freedom. And unfortunately, I've been witnessing it over my lifetime, slowly but surely, that our fellow citizens are willingly giving their freedom away for a false sense of security.

I try to remind people, Venezuela is an oil rich nation, a successful South American nation. Those people, the Venezuelans, voted themselves into poverty. They did it to themselves. Okay, we could do the same thing here. I ran in 2010 on a platform of freedom. I've never abandoned that platform and I'm watching the potential of shutdowns to limit people's freedom. You shut down churches, but you keep liquor stores open. What is that about?

Again, every action the Faucis of the world prescribed didn't make sense to me. I remained skeptical. I was fortunate enough, because I was chairman of a committee, to hold hearings. Early in February, we had Scott Gottlieb and others talking about how we don't produce drugs in this country, not the precursor chemicals, and not the active pharmaceutical ingredients.

That's a vulnerability. We ought to address that. We still haven't. A trillion dollar-plus infrastructure bill, and we didn't address that problem. But then, I held my May hearing with John Ioannidis, because I was trying to put this into perspective. I was trying to calm things down. I remember even talking about the differences between Ebola, MERS, SARS and Covid. That's where I got introduced to Dr. Pierre Kory, who testified very late. I heard about him a couple of days before the hearing, and I tacked him on. He was one of these doctors practicing in New York, a courageous doctor with the compassion to actually treat COVID patients.

He had an affiliation with the University of Wisconsin at Madison. He came on and talked about his use of corticosteroids. Of course, he was vilified for it. That wasn't the standard of care, and Fauci hadn't blessed it. But about eight weeks later, they had the study come out of the UK on dexamethasone, a corticosteroid, and all of a sudden people were using it.

I got connected to a group of doctors, a global network of eminently qualified doctors and medical researchers who had a completely different take on Covid; the writers of the Great Barrington Declaration, and Michael Yeadon, a 30-year employee of Pfizer, who retired as a senior vice president of research with a background in toxicology. I'm talking to him. He was beside himself when he heard what his colleagues were going to do with this gene therapy. He couldn't believe it. He said, "I'm not understanding this. There's no way we're going to produce something that is going to have the body produce its own toxin," which is what the spike protein does, "and then it is encapsulated in something that is designed to permeate barriers."

Remember we were told the vaccine was going to stay in the arm. They knew it wouldn't. They had the biodistribution studies on the lipid nanoparticles from the Japanese regulators that had to FOIA (Freedom of Information Act) it. They knew it was going to biodistribute all over the body.

Now, you've got this gene therapy potentially biodistributing to the ovaries, heart, brain, and permeating the blood-brain barrier. We've got mad cow disease cases now being written about. Let's say this thing attaches to heart muscle. It does two things. It juices the mitochondria, which is the engine of the cell, so that it has the energy to produce a spike protein that's toxic to the body. Now, the body's going to attack the heart muscle. That's how you get myocarditis. Again, I'm not a doctor or a medical researcher, but this stuff can be explained in layman's terms.

What happens if that gene therapy attaches to a cancer cell? It's juicing the cancer cells mitochondria. I'm certainly hearing and reading about cancers coming out of remission and roaring back to stage four. We're hearing about all the gynecological issues that are occurring, but it's all being covered up.

I got connected to a group of doctors who were educating me, telling me of their concerns. Geert Vanden Bossche wrote his four-page letter to the WHO saying, "The last thing you want to do in the midst of a pandemic is do mass vaccination. You will drive variants." Don't we have a lot of variants? What is that caused by?

You're going to always have variants anyway; the Muller's ratchet, the natural evolution of a virus would be to become more contagious but less lethal, because the virus variant wants to survive. It doesn't survive very well if it kills its host. It wants to keep the host alive, but it wants to get a lot more hosts. These are just basic scientific principles of virology and immunology that were completely ignored. They could be very easily explained to a layman like me that could understand, along with things like natural immunity.

I had an asymptomatic case of COVID in late September, early October 2020. I was around people, and because I'm going to the White House and that type of thing, I'm always being tested. I was around people that had COVID. I got tested, tested positive, and never had a symptom. From that experience, I suppose I had less fear, plus I had natural immunity.

When I was asked, after the vaccine came out, probably around February, "Senator, are you going to get vaccinated?" My response was not to denigrate the vaccine, but first of all to be as honest as I could and say, "Listen, there aren't enough vaccines right now for the elderly who want them, so I'll hold off." What I could have said was, which would have been completely honest, "There's no way I'm going to get that vaccine." I didn't say that. I didn't discourage the use. I just didn't promote it. Because again, I'm not a doctor and I'm not a medical researcher, but I was skeptical. During that interview, I said, "Besides I've already had COVID and I've got natural immunity. It's probably going to be better than the vaccine."

I was savaged for that. I was called an anti-vaxxer, which is probably just underneath murder, rapist, racist, and pedophile—the last thing you want to be called is anti-vaxxer. That is part of our problem now in terms of getting to the truth, in terms of the pandemic and other things as well. But no, again, I was exposed. I was talking to people. I had the good fortune of being connected to these doctors and medical researchers that just had a completely different take, which is why in January of 2022, I held the event COVID-19: A Second Opinion. I thought it was about time that the public heard a different opinion on how we should be handling this pandemic, a different opinion on vaccines and vaccine injuries.

Mr. Jekielek:
Some of this information came out in your January 2022 hearing. You had another hearing in December of 2022, and it was very slow to come out. Natural immunity is finally something that's understood to be superior to vaccination, which is what you would expect, as we've already known about it. But there are still many areas, including early treatment, that are unknown or vilified in the way that you just described; as being horse dewormer or anti-vax. There are a whole bunch of slurs out there.

Senator Johnson:
It's a Nobel Prize-winning drug, and the FDA is denigrating it. Here is my history of hearings: in February with Scott Gottlieb, in May with Pierre Kory and John Ioannidis, then in November with Peter McCullough and Harvey Risch and George Fareed on early treatment. They were really focusing on hydroxychloroquine. We were all vilified as the snake-oil salesmen of the Senate by Dr. Jha, who never treated a COVID patient.

Then, in December of 2020, there was a hearing with Pierre Kory, focusing on ivermectin. By the way, Dr. Kory thought the pandemic was over. He had the studies on the use of ivermectin. He was using it, and others were using it. He said, "You don't even need the vaccine. We've got this covered." He was way too optimistic in terms of the World Health Organization and NIH actually looking at the science. I started looking at the VAERS system. Francis Collins was very cavalier in his comment to me around March or April, when there are already thousands of deaths reported on the VAERS system. He said, "Well, Senator, people die."

I got connected to the vaccine injured groups through Bri Dressen and Ken Ruettgers and his wife. I held an event in June of 2021, letting these people tell their stories. Let the vaccine injured tell their stories. We were all vilified for that. I had another one in DC in November 2021 with not only vaccine injured, but also medical experts. Then I followed up with the Second Opinion event in January 2022. The final one was in December of 2022 about vaccines; what they are, how they operate, and how they can cause injury. I've been pretty consistent on this.

I have written over 50 oversight letters, and things on lot-to-lot variations. What are they doing granting full approval for Comirnaty, but still extending the emergency use for what's available here in the U.S.? Why are you pulling the wool over the eyes of the American public? What are you trying to do here? I've asked so many relevant questions, and gotten so very few answers on this. Again, it just increases my skepticism.

Mr. Jekielek:
The information in many cases is actually out there. The studies have been done to show mechanisms of harm with the vaccines in a whole bunch of areas. With Pfizer itself we did the FOIA, and we saw they knew about 500 different types of harm. You've written 50 oversight letters. My question is about impact. Do you feel like this is having an impact? You're a very lonely voice, not alone in Congress, but a lonely voice.

Senator Johnson:

I try to tell other people on this journey with me that, "Those of us who have our eyes open and have been fighting this battle, take some comfort in the low uptake of the Covid vaccines in the very young. We are having some impact. Parents aren't subjecting their children to this. That's a good thing." I would also say the excuse for suppressing all this information, the excuse for censoring it, and the excuse for vilifying people like me and others is that, "We can't do anything that will increase vaccine hesitancy."

If you really want to get to the core issue here, that's it. They have failed miserably. By lying to the American public, by labeling truth as disinformation, and by not being transparent and honest, they've increased vaccine hesitancy. A guy like me who was never an anti-vaxxer, I've gotten them all. My kids got them all.

But now, I'm skeptical. I started reading books like Dissolving Illusions, and Turtles All the Way Down. You can see the documentary, "Vaxxed." You read a host of other books and you wonder, "Why isn't this being talked about? Why aren't questions even allowed?"

With the laws they passed in 1986 when it seemed like we were going to just completely bankrupt or eliminate all vaccine manufacturing, because of our litigious society, you probably needed some protection so that we could produce some vaccines. That was certainly the narrative back then, "You have to pass these laws to protect the vaccine manufacturers." I don't think it was contemplated that would lead to an explosion of childhood vaccines, because there's no liability on the part of the manufacturers.

When I first talked to Bobby Kennedy about this, he said, "Ron, let me give you a five-minute primer on vaccines," and then it was about 45 minutes later. But he starts out, "We're about the same age. When we were growing up, we got three vaccines. Now it's 60 or 70, and they're doing them in multiples." We're finding out with the COVID vaccine and things like antibody-dependent enhancements that things can go wrong. Now, after so many doses, your body is producing the antibodies that actually suppress your immune system. It's the same stuff that they try and juice to suppress reaction to allergies, and to alleviate allergic symptoms.

Again, I'm not a doctor and I'm not a researcher, but there's so much of this information out there that certainly concerns a guy like me. Why isn't it concerning the Anthony Faucis and the Collinses and Walenskys and the people who have replaced these folks? Why isn't it concerning our federal health agencies? The answer is pretty obvious—they are thoroughly and completely captured by big pharma.

The video, which was pretty interesting, about the serial passing for mutations, that Project Veritas undercover video, more important than the statement, was really the way he was just talking, just as a given, about the revolving door between the federal health agencies and Big Pharma. As a regulator, you're not going to really seriously regulate or question your future employer or your previous employer, who will be your future employer once again. It's a thoroughly corrupt process right now.

You can view the entire interview with Senator Ron Johnson here: https://www.theepochtimes.com/epochtv/its-all-being-covered-up-sen-ron-johnson-on-missing-batch-of-

fauci-emails-covid-origins-and-silencing-of-the-
vaccine-injured-5148765. You may need to subscribe
to The Epoch Times to access the full interview but it is
well worth it.

Biometrics and Digital IDs

Biometrics data is the most precious of all.
Biometrics systems are used to identify and
authenticate our identity by using physical and
behavioral characteristics that include personality traits,
fingerprints, face and palm prints, iris patterns, voice,
gait, breath and DNA information. These technologies
are already being used in Africa, Southeast Asia,
Pakistan, the EU and recently introduced in the U.S.
(Amazon One). The intention is for digital IDs to
include all of this data, and to connect all our
biometrics data to our money and our use of money.
This means that digital IDs will not only include a
digital health certificate and vaccine passport, but will
also be the interface to central bank digital currency
(CBDC).

Digital IDs will then be used to adopt a social
credit system and social credit score that will be linked
to our ability to access our money, based on our social
credit score that will function just like the one they
have in Communist China right now. The intention for
establishing digital IDs is to also usher in CBDCs as the
only available currency for our use, worldwide.

Once CBDCs and digital IDs become synonymous
and interoperable between all nations, the government
will have total control over our access to and use of our
money, based on their absolute control of our social
credit score.

Not up to date on the latest, ineffective Covid
shots, access to your money is turned off until you get

the jabs. Make a post on Facebook or X or anywhere else on the Internet that is critical of the government, access to your money is turned off until you remove the posts. Refuse to purchase an electronic vehicle by the imposed deadline, suddenly you can't use your money to buy gas. These are just some of many examples.

All of this is an urgent concern due to the fact that government and private corporations are merging and, in ever-increasing fashion, private corporate conglomerates are dictating public policy. In the U.S., we have a Constitution that is the highest law of the land. Since governments cannot be seen violating state constitutions and the federal constitution, the way government is now circumventing the Constitution is to get corporations to implement policies that include control over our behavior and our money. This is what ESG is all about. See Chapter 6 for more details.

All of our activities will be monitored under one digital hub, worldwide, based on digital IDs. This hub will be run by Artificial Intelligence (AI) systems that will be controlled by Big Tech. This is the immanent future of our society unless we act now to prevent digital IDs and CBDCs from being implemented (also see Chapter 5).

Digital IDs and Man-Made Pandemics

The means to force the world population to fully comply with digital IDs will likely be driven by man-made pandemics, real or imagined, in order to keep the public and lawmakers frightened. The U.S. (among other governments) has a history of using weapons of mass destruction on other nations, even when the U.S. has signed treaties agreeing not to do so. Historically, it is a fact that nations who use these warfare measures on other nations will eventually come to use them on their own citizens. Meryl Nass, MD is an Internist in Bar Harbor, Maine. Meryl Nass completed medical school at University of Mississippi School of Medicine. Following her education, Dr. Nass was board certified by the American Board of Internal Medicine. She is also a researcher who proved the world's largest anthrax epidemic was due to biological warfare. She also revealed the dangers of the anthrax vaccine.

Dr. Nass is a highly regarded champion of medical/health freedom who has exposed a lot of the fraud surrounding the COVID-19 pandemic. She is one of several doctors whose medical license has been suspended for using FDA approved repurposed drugs like Ivermectin and Hydroxychloroquine to effectively treat Covid. She is suing the State of Maine medical board to have her license reinstated. In a recent article, Dr. Meryl Nass offers us some very important information on this topic. Here is an excerpt from that article:

"The WHO's Proposed Amendments Will Increase Man-Made Pandemics"

This report is designed to help readers think about some big topics: how to really prevent pandemics and biological warfare, how to assess proposals by the WHO and its members for preventing and responding to pandemics, and whether we can rely on our health officials to navigate these areas in ways that make sense and will help their populations. We start with a history of biological arms control and rapidly move to the COVID pandemic, eventually arriving at plans to protect the future.

Weapons of Mass Destruction: Chem/Bio

Traditionally, the Weapons of Mass Destruction (WMD) have been labelled Chemical, Biological, Radiologic, and Nuclear (CBRN).

The people of the world don't want them used on us— for they are cheap ways to kill and maim large numbers of people quickly. And so international treaties were created to try to prevent their development (only in the later treaties) and use (in all the biological arms control treaties). First was the Geneva Protocol of 1925, following the use of poison gases and limited biological weapons in World War I, banning the use of biological and chemical weapons in war. The US and many nations signed it, but it took 50 years for the US to ratify it, and during those 50 years the US asserted it was not bound by the treaty.

The US used both biological and chemical weapons during those 50 years. The US almost certainly used biological weapons in the Korean War and perhaps used both in Vietnam, which experienced an odd outbreak of plague during the war. The use of napalm, white phosphorus, agent orange (with its dioxin excipient causing massive numbers of birth defects and other tragedies) and probably other chemical weapons like BZ (a hallucinogen/incapacitant) led to much pushback, especially since we had signed the Geneva Protocol and we were supposed to be a civilized nation.

In 1968 and 1969, two important books were published that had a great influence on the American psyche regarding our massive stockpiling and use of these agents. The first book, written by a young Seymour Hersh about the US chemical and biological warfare program, was titled "Chemical and Biological Warfare; America's Hidden Arsenal." In 1969 Congressman Richard D. McCarthy, a former newspaperman from

Buffalo, NY wrote the book "The Ultimate Folly: War by Pestilence, Asphyxiation and Defoliation" about the US production and use of chemical and biological weapons. Prof. Matthew Meselson's review of the book noted:

Our operation, "Flying Ranch Hand," has sprayed anti-plant chemicals over an area almost the size of the state of Massachusetts, over 10 per cent of its cropland. "Ranch Hand" no longer has much to do with the official justification of preventing ambush. Rather, it has become a kind of environmental warfare, devastating vast tracts of forest in order to facilitate our aerial reconnaissance. Our use of "super tear gas" (it is also a powerful lung irritant) has escalated from the originally announced purpose of saving lives in "riot control-like situations" to the full-scale combat use of gas artillery shells, gas rockets and gas bombs to enhance the killing power of conventional high explosive and flame weapons. Fourteen million pounds have been used thus far, enough to cover all of Vietnam with a field effective concentration. Many nations, including some of our own allies have expressed the opinion that this kind of gas warfare violates the Geneva Protocol, a view shared by McCarthy." [26]

You can read the entire article here: https://brownstone.org/articles/who-amendments-increase-man-made-pandemics/

In addition, Dr. Nass was recently interviewed on *The HighWire*. The subject of the interview is *Bio Warfare Expert Exposes W.H.O. Pandemic Treaty Threat*. You can view the full interview here: https://bhaktaschool.org/dr-meryl-nass-highwire-interview-on-who-pandemic-treaty/. In addition, there is a very important video entitled "Is the WHO's House of Cards Collapsing?" with James Corbett and Dr. Meryl

Nass. You can view that here: https://bhaktaschool.org/is-the-whos-house-of-cards-collapsing-james-corbett-dr-meryl-nass/. You are also encouraged to visit Dr. Meryl Nass's website, Door to Freedom here: https://doortofreedom.org/.

You have never pledged your body to any government or other organization or agency. However, this is what the WHO Pandemic Treaty is all about. So, it is absolutely necessary to preserve your bodily autonomy from all government and private control, whether that be by local, state, federal, private or international governments, agencies or organizations.

Also, the U.S. Sovereignty Coalition, which is comprised of elected officials in the U.S. House of Representatives, has revealed ties between the Chinese Communist Party (CCP) and the WHO. The coalition believes that the CCP is partnering with WHO leadership to formulate Pandemic treaties. This is the same CCP behind the release of COVID-19 from the Wuhan Institute of Virology. The CCP hopes to use the WHO to rollout its globalist plans for collectivism. The primary target for this plan is America and, if America falls, the world falls.

You can view press conferences held by the U.S. Sovereignty Coalition here: https://bhaktaschool.org/exit-the-who/ where they discuss the necessity for the U.S. to exit the WHO and why. I also encourage you to watch their video conference presentation entitled *Soft Coup, Hard Tyranny: Spawning Global Governance*, here: https://rumble.com/v3jo44k-webinar-soft-coup-hard-tyranny-spawning-global-governance-on-september-20.html. In addition, the U.S. Sovereignty Coalition held a conference entitled "The Fundamental Transformation of the WHO from a Health Advisor to Global Dictator." I strongly encourage you to view the recorded video of the conference here https://bhaktaschool.org/brief-on-whos-transformation-from-health-advisor-to-dictator/.

You can also use a fully automated message system to email a prewritten message to your elected officials in the U.S. Congress by going here https://stopvaxpassports.org/take-action-stop-global-tyranny/. The web page will also walk you through posting the message to your elected officials on Facebook and X, and also provides a call script and a one-click means of calling your elected officials with the same message to exit the WHO and the pandemic treaty.

What to Do About It

1. **Exit the WHO – No WHO Pandemic Treaty Without U.S. Senate Approval – No U.S. Taxpayer funding for the WHO.** According to U.S. Constitution the Federal government does not have the authority to negotiate on behalf of the states. Only the states have the constitutional authority to negotiate with the WHO.

Under Article VI, Section 2 of the U.S. Constitution any treaty entered into with foreign entities or governments by the U.S. government becomes part of the U.S. Constitution and 'the supreme law of the land.' President Biden has signed the WHO Pandemic Preparedness Treaty. This means that whatever measures the WHO decides must be used to address any future, declared pandemics, including the WHO mandating mandatory vaccination, quarantines, masks, social distancing, hospitalization and sending troops to enforce such mandates must be followed by every state and person in America, state laws to the contrary notwithstanding. *The treaty also requires that the U.S.*

pay for 20% of all medical supplies necessary to fight a pandemic anywhere in the world!

Therefore, in order to protect our health freedom and bodily autonomy, it is now necessary to support the passage of laws to prevent these things from happening, while also pressuring the President to repeal the signatory to the treaty.

There are four bills introduced into Congress for this purpose. They are:

H.R. 4665 which has been passed by the House Appropriations Committee to defund the WHO – The bill is now headed to the U.S. Senate for a vote. You can read/download the bill here: https://www.congress.gov/118/bills/hr4665/BILLS-118hr4665rh.pdf. You can watch a video clip about this bill here: https://www.youtube.com/watch?v=FNSF_NcsAl.

Email and call the elected congressional senators in your district to express your support for passage of this bill. To find the contact information for senate representatives in the U.S. Congress for your district go here: https://www.senate.gov/senators/

H.R. 79 - WHO Withdrawal Act. You can read the bill here https://www.congress.gov/bill/118th-congress/house-bill/79/text
Email and call the elected congressional officials in your district to express your support for passage of this bill. To find the contact information for House and Senate representatives in the U.S. Congress for your district go here: https://www.senate.gov/senators/

https://www.house.gov/representatives/find-your-representative

In addition, Stand for Health Freedom has established a web page with an automated email and petition campaign to congressional lawmakers and you can use their page to generate emails to elected officials in your district. You can access that page here: https://standforhealthfreedom.com/actions/exit-the-who/

There is also a second bill introduced into the U.S. Congress that, if passed, would require approval of the U.S. Senate before the WHO could carry out any of the pandemic treaty responses on U.S. soil. That bill is S.4343 - No WHO Pandemic Preparedness Treaty Without Senate Approval Act and you can read the bill here: https://www.congress.gov/bill/117th-congress/senate-bill/4343/text. Contact the elected House and Senate officials in your district and express your support for this bill via email with a followup phone call. When calling the office of your elected congressperson, if you get voice mail, leave your full name, phone number, address and a brief message of your support.

There is another bill introduced into the U.S. Congress that, if passed, would prevent U.S. taxpayer dollars from being used to fund the WHO. That is H.R.343 - No Taxpayer Funding for the World Health Organization Act. You can read that bill here: https://www.congress.gov/bill/118th-congress/house-bill/343/text

Contact your house and senate congressional representatives in your district to express your support of this bill. You can find a sample email for this

purpose on this page:
https://bhaktaschool.org/breaking-news-on-vaccine-mandates/

2. No Vaccine Passports. In order to protect our health freedom and bodily autonomy and take the important first step in resisting digital IDs, it is necessary to pass laws preventing the use of vaccine passports. You can start by supporting H.R.118 - No Vaccine Passports Act. You can read the bill here:
https://www.congress.gov/bill/118th-congress/house-bill/118/text

Contact the congressional representatives in your district to express your support for the passage of this bill.

3. Vote No on S. 884: Improving Digital Identity Act of 2023. This bill has just been introduced. The bill states, among other things, that "The lack of an easy, affordable, reliable, and secure way for organizations, businesses, and government agencies to identify whether an individual is who they claim to be online creates an attack vector that is widely exploited by adversaries in cyberspace and precludes many high-value transactions from being available online."

We already have effective ways to be identified. They are: driver's license, passport, copy of utility bills, voter registration card, social security card, other photo IDs. *There is no threat to identifying us.*

The bill goes on to state that there is a necessity for digital IDs to prevent financial fraud and identity theft. This is nonsense and an idiotic statement. Credit cards are digital IDs used in financial transactions. They are a primary source of identity theft. Financial fraud in the digital world is commonplace, as is money laundering. Furthermore, anything in digital form connected to the Internet can be hacked. Pentagon servers, NSA servers, DOD servers, U.S. Postal Service Servers and all major bank servers have been hacked repeatedly. So, to say that a digital ID will improve security is a lie because all IDs, no matter what form, use the Internet to confirm already.

The narrative around digital IDs being needed to improve security and privacy is one that is based solely on coercion. To date, there is no proof that a centralized, government-controlled, global digital ID will improve security and privacy. And the people promoting digital IDS do not provide any evidence of this. Their narrative is wholly based on spreading fear. What digital IDs will do is lock us into a digital control grid that will mark the end of our Liberty. In addition, the real reason digital IDs are being pushed is to provide the necessary tech platform for vaccine passports and CBDC.

You can read the bill here: https://www.congress.gov/bill/118th-congress/senate-bill/884/text

Contact the congressional elected officials in your district and urge them to vote NO on this bill.

4. **Pay for your purchases with cash whenever possible** and avoid using your credit cards or a check (which is also a form of digital currency that is tracked) whenever possible.

5. **Do not comply with mask mandates or vaccine mandates.** Non-compliance and civil disobedience in

this regard is essential if we are to resist the push for digital IDs.

6. Reduce your exposure on the Internet, particularly in social media. All social media platforms track your posts, your likes and other activity you engage in on social media. Increasingly, this information is being turned over to governments, in addition to corporations. This practice has increased the amount of surveillance we undergo. This increased surveillance is another reason for the push to implement digital IDs, as these IDs make it easier for government, corporations and globalists to track and compile data on our behavior. You want to communicate with friends and family? Call them. You want to shop online? If the stores you shop at are within a convenient driving distance to your home or office, shop in the store rather than on the Internet. Unless you're a celebrity promoting a fan club, avoid posting pictures of yourself, your kids and loved ones on the Internet whenever possible.

Remember, the Internet is also surveillance tool.

7. Do not give out any of your biometric information unless required to interface with your doctor or other health/medical professional who is treating you. And do not take wellness visits with your insurance company, as any information collected during such a wellness visit will be biometric data that is shared digitally. Instead, if your insurance company requires health and medical information, have your doctor provide that to your insurance company. In this way, the insurance company has to uphold both your and the doctor's privacy. The only exception is when there is an insurance claim that must be addressed, outside of payment to your doctor after a deductible. An example of this is if you are hospitalized.

8. Consider the steps in the Liberty Action Plan presented in Chapter 8.

Additional information and data relevant to this chapter can be found here: https://bhaktaschool.org/dharma-and-the-preservation-of-liberty/

Chapter 5
The Growing Attack
On Our Liberty
Central Bank Digital Currency

American Socialism is part of the plan for one world government. The destruction of our Liberty by establishing socialism in America has not been accomplished by force, but by way of economics. The basis for the challenges to all of our Constitutional, human and civil rights is how the U.S. economy and the world economy is structured and run. In the end, it all comes back to money. *To be clear, the challenge is a moral and ethical one because the challenge itself is a monetary system based on fraud.* Indeed, the love of, the infatuation with hoarding, controlling and manipulating money is the root of all evil.

For those who say that we need to fight, now more than ever, to prevent socialism from being established in America, you don't understand money and, therefore, what you have not yet realized is that the United States of America is already a socialist nation of collectivism, and has been for more than a century. If you were to understand central banking and the commercial banking system, along with how fraudulent it is, you would, at once, know that a mix of socialism and fascism has long since plagued this great nation. And, truly, we are closer to a hybrid of a socialist, fascist, communist form of governance (collectivism) than you may know.

This chapter is designed to reveal this fact to

you. *The fight is now one of destroying American socialism in order to return our union to that of a true Constitutional Republic.*

Our Constitution has been trampled on repeatedly. *This happens because the American citizenry is largely ignorant of how our economy works and why government tampering with it leads to the destruction of the only economic stabilizing force on Earth, the free market.* In addition, government repeatedly gets away with free market interference because the majority of the citizenry is ignorant of how money works and how our economy is structured. On top of that, the majority of the U.S. citizenry is ignorant of our Constitution and, for the most part, they are not actively engaged with their elected officials.

In this chapter, we will briefly examine the economic foundation for American Socialism, along with the centuries-old strategy for implementing a One World Government on the back of American Socialism. Pay particular attention to the referenced books and articles that you are strongly encouraged to read. One such reference that is a must read is *The Creature from Jekyll Island – A Second Look at the Federal Reserve* by G. Edward Griffin. Another is *The Tyranny of the Federal Reserve* by Brian O'Brien. You are also encouraged to view the documentary films, *Money For Nothing – Inside the Federal Reserve* produced by Liberty Street Films and *Inside Job* produced by Sony Pictures Classics.

As you read this chapter, keep the following in mind. **The essence of socialism is the redistribution of financial wealth.**

Also, the subject of money and how it is created is a very broad topic that cannot be fully addressed in the limited space here. So, this chapter will be a combination of mostly blunt statements designed to trigger your desire for further education. In this regard, pay attention to the referenced books/documents that you are encouraged to read and study on your own to expand your understanding of money, and to support the statements made.

What is money? Money is anything that is accepted as a medium of exchange. In his book *The Creature From Jekyll Island*, G. Edward Griffin accurately speaks about the four categories or types of money:

1. Commodity money
2. Receipt money
3. Fiat money
4. Fractional money

Commodity money began with the trading of food, livestock and tobacco. As human beings used metals to make weapons, the metals themselves became valuable. Copper, tin and bronze were traded. These became the first coins and their value was determined by weight [1]. The use of gold and silver evolved from this practice and, over time, gold and silver have become the chief form of commodity money [2]. They are also the best stabilizers of an economy - particularly gold, as gold guarantees price stability [3].

Receipt money evolved from the practice of people storing their gold and silver in vaults that goldsmiths owned and maintained. When a person stored a certain amount of gold and silver in the goldsmith's vault, that person was given a paper receipt that expressed the amount and value of the gold/silver stored in the vault. Over time, rather than going back to the vault to retrieve their gold and silver to spend, people holding these receipts began to trade them as money. Thus, receipt money was born and receipt money is the precursor to paper currency that is backed primarily by gold.

Fiat money is paper money that is not backed by precious metals such as gold or silver. In fact, fiat currency is not backed by anything other than the word and/or legal mandate of the issuer. For example, in America we have been forced to continue to use paper money as 'legal tender' that is not backed by gold as it once was. This has undermined and destabilized the U.S. economy [4,5,6].

Fractional money evolved out of the practice of lending coins [7,8]. The merchants who did so were called "scriveners." Scriveners charged interest on the coins they lent. This is how they made money. Observing this practice, goldsmiths decided to start lending out other people's money (gold and silver) that was stored in their vaults, for which they had issued a paper receipt to the depositor. Since few of the depositors wanted to withdraw their coin at the same time (only 10-15% was withdrawn at the same time), the goldsmiths became scriveners, lending depositors' money out with interest. Initially, depositors were unaware that their money was being lent out, so the interest the goldsmiths made was not shared with depositors. That changed when depositors found out and were outraged. So, goldsmiths were acting as loan brokers on behalf of depositors without their consent, lending out up to 85% of the deposits, which they did not have the right to do [9]. *Banking, as we know it today, was born.*

Now, what happens when a depositor wants to withdraw his/her money that has been lent out? And what happens when many depositors want to withdraw their deposits that are no longer there? The Great Depression of 1929 is a perfect example of what happens. On the back of poor economic news and a crashing stock market, depositors rushed to get their money out of banks. Because little of their deposits were still in their accounts, banks had to release deposits out of reserves that were quickly exhausted *because the reserves were never equal to or greater than the total deposits.* The run on the banks was so huge that banks went out of business overnight. Other banks locked their doors, refusing to allow depositors to withdraw their money – money that was no longer 'in the vault' because they had lent it out. The banks that did this did so to protect their reserves, to the detriment of depositors.

What is inflation? Inflation is a substantial rise in prices that is caused by superficially increasing the money supply. This results in the currency losing its value. In terms of purchasing power, this means that the currency buys less and less. When there is much more money circulating in a free market, manufacturers, distributors and retailers raise their prices. This is a natural, free market correction. The superficial increase in the money supply is caused by the excessive printing of money, primarily when loans are made.

Hyperinflation is money printing on steroids. Deflation is what happens when the circulating money supply is reduced and becomes more scarce. This forces manufacturers, distributors and retailers to discount their prices. This is also a natural, free market correction.

Another thing to keep in mind is this: when interest rates are high, people tend to save money, borrow less and spend less. This also means they carry less debt. When interest rates are low, people tend to save less, borrow more and spend more. This means they carry more debt. Each of these is also true on the part of borrowing, spending and saving engaged in by entire countries.

What is central banking and what is the U.S. Federal Reserve? Central banks are made up of bankers who have formed a banking cartel to protect its members from competition by way of controlling the flow of money throughout the world. Central bankers have convinced the public that this banking cartel called the Federal Reserve is an agency of the United States government. This was done on purpose.

However, the U.S. Federal Reserve is not a federal agency or branch of any government and there are no reserves. The U.S. Federal Reserve is a partnership between the American government and central bankers, and a fraudulent one at that.

In 1910, several bankers and government officials met in secret on Jekyll Island in Georgia [10]. They were:

- *Nelson W. Aldrich.* Aldrich was the Republican 'whip' in the U.S. Senate, Chairman of the National Monetary Commission and a business associate of J.P. Morgan.
- *Abraham Piatt Andrew*, Assistant Secretary of the U.S. Treasury.
- *Frank A. Vanderlip.* Vanderlip was president of the National Bank of New York, representing most of the largest banks at that time. He also represented William Rockefeller and the investment bank of Kuhn, Loeb & Company.
- *Henry P. Davison,* who was a senior partner of the J.P. Morgan Company.
- *Benjamin Strong*, the head of J.P. Morgan's Bankers Trust.
- Company. (There is some debate over whether Strong was present at this meeting. Vanderlip says he was. Other accounts are that he was not. But all agree that he knew of the plan hatched in this meeting.)
- *Paul M. Warburg.* Warburg was a partner in Kuhn, Loeb and Company. He also represented the Rothschild banking cartel in England and France.

He was the brother of Max Warburg who was head of the Warburg banking consortium in Germany and the Netherlands.

The purpose of the meeting between these six individuals at the Jekyll Island Club on Jekyll Island was to agree on the structure of a banking cartel in order to maximize profits and minimize competition between its members, and to make it extremely difficult for new competitors to enter the banking field. It was also decided that they needed the authority of government law to enforce the cartel agreement. This was to be the blueprint for what we have come to know today as the Federal Reserve.

The challenges that this group addressed were the following:

1. How to ensure that the control of the nation's finances remained in their hands and how to stop any influence from growing small banks perceived to be rivals.
2. How to expand the money supply in order to reverse private capitalization and capture the commercial loan market.
3. How to pool the limited resources of the nation's banks into a single large reserve in order to motivate all banks to follow the same loan-to-deposit ratios in order to protect banks from currency drains and bank runs. (A currency drain occurs when banks, rather than depositors, demand money.)
4. How to shift losses from bank owners to taxpayers, should there be any collapse of the banking system.
5. How to convince the Congress that their scheme was derived in order to protect the public.

Each of these challenges has been met in the establishment of the U.S. Federal Reserve.

Our entire monetary system is based on debt and this is why debt, particularly the national debt, is never going away in the current environment. Money is created out of nothing when a loan is made by a bank. That's right. The money is printed the minute a loan is made. What is known as "interest" is then charged as part of the loan repayment. Morally and ethically, it is really not interest that is being charged, as interest is something that is charged on something earned through labor that is then lent out. Bank interest is really a service fee or kickback for printing the money. **In fact, it is why the money is printed in the first place – to create income for central bankers and commercial banks.** *And they didn't earn the money, they simply printed it.*

To help you further understand this scandal let's calculate a loan. If you borrow $100,000 at 11.00% interest to be repaid over 30 years, your monthly payment will be $952.32. Your payment on interest (really a service fee/kickback) will be $242,836.42 over the term of the loan. That's almost two-and-a-half times the amount loaned to you! (If you don't own a Hewlett-Packard 12c hand-held financial calculator, you can find loan calculators online.) A percentage of that service fee or kickback is shared with commercial banks (commercial banks borrow the money from the central bank at a service fee called interest, and then lend it out at a higher rate). The rest goes to the central bankers and the politicians who keep the central banks alive by passing laws that force us to use this monetary system.

Here's the plain truth. *Under the current monetary system, there would be no money without debt.* Whatever money you have in your wallet, purse or bank account is money that you or someone else borrowed.

If no loans were made there would be no money in circulation.

Furthermore, the service fee on printing the money comes from our labor. We have to earn to repay the kickback known as 'interest.' So, in our present monetary system the total of human effort at earning money is to benefit those who create the fiat currency. So, who are we working for really?

The destruction of the gold standard in the American monetary system created the fiat money we use today. Remember that fiat currency is money that is not backed by precious metals such as gold. In early 1971 in the U.S., there was still a monetary policy that allowed people and countries to cash in their dollars for gold. In the years of the Johnson presidency, there was a run on the gold held by the U.S. Treasury that became unsustainable during the Nixon presidency. The dollar was still backed by gold but many foreign countries were trading in the dollars they held for the gold in the U.S. treasury. This caused a run on that gold that could not be sustained. There just wasn't enough gold left to make good on the dollars traded in. This is due, in part to the excessive printing of dollars for loans made to foreign countries.

In addition, because money in most countries was still tied to gold and the amount of gold on the planet is limited, this meant that the amount of world currencies in circulation was also limited. The International Monetary Fund (IMF) and the World Bank had, as one of their goals, the complete elimination of the gold standard and the gold exchange standard [11,12] worldwide so that they could establish unlimited currency circulation as part of a long term plan for one world currency. This resulted in ever increasing pressure on the U.S. government to abandon the gold standard. So, in 1971, President Nixon took the dollar off of the gold standard [13].

Up to this point, the U.S. dollar was tied to gold and all the other currencies of the world were tied to the dollar in terms of their ultimate value. In 1971 all that changed. The world's currencies remained tied to the dollar but the dollar was no longer backed by gold – meaning that the strength of the dollar was only backed by the word of the U.S. government and the Federal Reserve, and people's faith in that word. This also meant that the dollar now had to compete with the other currencies in the world, particularly the mark and the yen. All of this marked the beginning of the devaluation of the dollar worldwide.

Since 1971, due to a number of factors including a weakened U.S. economy racked with booms and busts, other countries around the world have lost faith in the dollar. *This is part of the setup for the devaluation of the dollar as a viable currency.* Because, in order to have one world currency, the U.S. cannot remain the world's currency leader. The demand for dollars by the rest of the world has to be minimized. This is being executed by the U.S. Federal Reserve through a process known as *controlled demolition* that is part of the completion of the plan for American Socialism under digital IDs and CBDCs.

Money For Nothing
The Name of the Game Is Bailout

As you read this chapter, remember: *The essence of socialism is redistribution of financial wealth.* Here's something else to remember: The Federal Reserve creates booms and busts for their own gain and that of politicians, to the detriment of all others.

Now, here is the mechanism by which America has become a socialist country, leading the way to the One World Government being planned by the wealthy elite. *The name of this game is bailout.*

Banks cannot stay in business if they continue to make bad loans without adequate reserves to cover growing defaults. And it is a fact that the central banks, including the U.S. Federal Reserve bank, have little or no reserves to back the trillions of dollars in loans they make. So, in order to continue to perpetuate their scheme to provide money for nothing in order to profit from the kickback called 'interest,' they have to have a constant, steady flow of cash to cover the losses that they consistently create. Enter the International Monetary Fund (IMF) and the World Bank.

In 1944, the scheme that established the U.S. Federal Reserve went global after a conference that was held in Bretton Woods, New Hampshire, dubbed the United Nations Monetary and Financial Conference [14]. This conference was led by John Maynard Keynes and Harry Dexter White, Fabian Socialists with ties to the Communist party [15]. It was in this conference that the IMF and the World Bank were created. Touted as arms of the United Nations, in truth, they were designed and still function as independent enterprises.

The World Bank is the lending agency to the IMF. These two enterprises were established under the guise of providing aid to feed the hungry, to bring a better life to those in underdeveloped nations and to achieve other humanitarian goals. The asset base is comprised of a pool of money collected from member nations and held in reserve to be doled out as necessary. The central banks of member nations provide a line of credit to the IMF that, when used, is lent out in the form of an SDR (special drawing right), the IMF's reserve currency [16]. However, most of the money provided by way of SDRs is lent as part of a rich nation's club to support the economic interests of those nations. Close scrutiny of the IMF shows that funds are lent to bailout bureaucrats in nations where the economies are failing, while also directed to prop up the Euro by devaluing the dollar.

Funding for these enterprises comes from member states (governments of industrialized nations) in the form of smaller amounts of cash (seed money) and promises to deliver more if the Bank gets into trouble. This functions like the FDIC of the world *but with no reserve fund.* The World Bank uses this scheme to leverage loans in the commercial loan market to borrow the larger sums needed at very low interest rates. These loans are backed by governments of industrialized nations who promise bailouts if the loans go sour, which most are destined to do. This means these governments have promised to force the taxpayers to make the payments on any default. *The truth is, under this arrangement, the American taxpayer covers the majority of the losses.*

The World Bank then takes the seed money funds and re-lends them to the underdeveloped nations at higher rates of interest, thereby making a profit. *These loans are almost never paid back.* Often, the governments of these underdeveloped nations can't even make the interest payments. The loans are then restructured and rescheduled to throw even more money at the failing loan arrangements in order to keep the kickbacks of interest payments flowing.

It is also important to note that the money going into the World Bank reduces investment in the private sector of the member nations by siphoning off the financial resources available to private industry and funds available for job creation and consumer loans. This is an inherent step for establishing world socialism. Remember: **the essence of socialism is redistribution of financial wealth.**

Then there is the matter of reserves. When a decision is made that there should be some reserves from time-to-time, those reserves are also raised by member nations taxing their citizenry, with the majority of these reserves coming from the American taxpayer.

Through the IMF, underdeveloped nations are able to exchange worthless currencies for dollars that they then use to pay their bills, one bill of which is the interest they pay on the massive loans that come from the World Bank.

It is important to note that the underdeveloped nations who get this funding (loans amounting to billions of dollars each) are typically nations over which Socialists and Communists have the greatest control. In effect, the World Bank pays the bills of these underdeveloped nations. And, usually, the one paying the bills owns the property!

So, to recap, the IMF is fashioned after and structured in the same way as the U.S. Federal Reserve. It, along with the World Bank, is the conduit for massive loans that go to underdeveloped nations where the funds are obstructed by government bureaucracies and poisoned by corruption. The governments of these underdeveloped nations squander the loans without properly investing them in any private enterprise where they have a chance of turning a profit. There is no possibility of the repayment of these loans.

Eventually, these nations are even unable to pay the interest on the loans. So, the IMF then has to fall back on its 'reserves' and assets that it does not have, or 'credits' it continues to issue, *and then to the final destination of all of these loans – the taxpayer bailout.* **Therefore, in truth, this is one big Ponzi scheme.** If any of us engages in such a scheme, we go to prison. When the government and central bankers do it it's called sound monetary policy and no one is indicted.

It can certainly be said that, without the U.S. Federal Reserve Ponzi schemes, the U.S. Federal Government would have little or no need to charge income tax on American citizens. *With respect to these*

bailouts, there is a long litany of fraud that taxpayers,
particularly U.S. taxpayers, have paid for. A short list of
examples is:

The Monetary Control Act of 1980, passed by the U.S.
Congress, authorized the United States Federal Reserve
to print money to be granted and loaned to any and all
foreign governments. Until then, the Fed could only
print money for the U.S. government and population. It
was now able to act as the central bank for the world.
This was a tremendous coup for the Fabian Socialists, a
big leap toward the completion of their plan for One
World Government under one world currency.

Panama fell into arrears on all its loans. In 1977, with a
one-vote margin in the Congress, the American
government gave away the Panama Canal to Panama so
that it could generate income to begin paying, at least,
the interest on those loans. The Canal was U.S. public
property that could have continued earning income
funneled to the American citizenry in the form of large
tax reductions and funding for U.S. infrastructure.

In 1989, the U.S. Congress passed into law the Financial
Institutions Reform and Recovery Act (FIRREA) 'to
safeguard and stabilize America's financial system.'
This paved the way for the Fed to loot Americans
through taxes and inflation, in order to bailout the
failed Savings & Loan banks to the tune of
approximately $532 billion dollars. The real cost, when
all is said and done, is closer to one trillion dollars [17].

1991 in Zimbabwe saw a bailout of 42 billion rands
($2.6 billion U.S. dollars) through the IMF/World Bank.
American taxpayers funded the majority of that [18,19].

In 1982 in Mexico, the Mexican government defaulted

on $85 billion in loans. In 1985, through the IMF/World Bank, the U.S. taxpayer shouldered about $49 billion in new loans to put towards that default. The principal on these loans has never been repaid. But the central bankers have earned their kickbacks – the 'interest' payments on the loans. Eventually, the U.S. Federal Reserve began acting directly as the central bank of Mexico. In 1995, Mexico was, again, in default of its loans. Congress ordered another $30 billion to be appropriated to Mexico that the American taxpayer paid for [20]. And that was not the end of it. Through a maze of loan swaps and agreements for Mexico to buy U.S. Treasury bonds, the American taxpayer has borne an even greater financial burden.

In 1982, Brazil announced that it was unable to make payments on its loans. More than $20 billion dollars in loans was made to Brazil to enable it to make payments on the previous loans [21]. No repayment date was ever set. This enabled the banks to continue to collect the kickback of interest on higher and higher amounts of principal. Ultimately, the U.S. taxpayer covered the defaults.

In 1982, Argentina was unable to make substantial loan payments totaling more than $2 billion dollars. Their loans were extended and the IMF infused Argentina with another $2 billion and change so that it could make the interest payments on its loans [22]. Less than a year later, Argentina announced that it could not make any more payments for another year. Payments were then stretched out with an extra $4.2 billion loaned to Argentina so that interest on the debt could keep flowing to the banks. This continued to be a reoccurring scenario through 2002. This portfolio of debt was sold to the American taxpayer, while the bankers reaped the profit of 'interest' on all of the loans.

This same scenario has played out numerous times in foreign, developing nations including Poland, Russia and China. Remember: *The foundation of socialism is redistribution of financial wealth.* In the January 1946 issue of *American Affairs*, an article written by Beardsley Ruml who was chairman of the Federal Reserve Bank of New York summed it up well. The title of his article: "Taxes For Revenue Are Obsolete." In this article, Ruml states: "The second principal purpose of federal taxes is to attain more equality of wealth and income than would result from economic forces working alone. The taxes that are effective for this purpose are the progressive individual income tax, the progressive estate tax and the gift tax. What these taxes should be depends on public policy with respect to the distribution of wealth and income." In this regard, worth studying is the Mandrake Mechanism [23]. *In a stable U.S. economy little or no tax would need to be collected if it were not for the Federal Reserve acting as the lender to the world.*

If the aim is to establish One World Government, as it certainly is, then there must also be one world currency. Establishing both is part of a plan that was created centuries ago – a plan designed to usher in such a government gradually, by economic and public health policy manipulation, rather than by brute force. The leadership for instituting this plan was taken up by a group of wealthy elites known as the Fabian Socialists [24,25]. Members of this group are also card-carrying members of the American Eugenics movement [26,27,28,29], the funding for which began back in 1906 (just a short time before the U.S. Federal Reserve was created) before the movement was formerly established in 1926. Eugenics is inherent in the plan to establish one world government. Again, because this planned world takeover is based on controlling and manipulating world economies, as part of the plan, there must be one world currency. Enter Central Bank Digital Currency (CBDC) and the Digital Wallet/Digital Vaccine Passport. I have spoken about digital IDs and digital vaccine passports in the previous chapter.

Central Bank Digital Currency and the Digital Wallet/Digital Passport

The plan to move the world onto a central bank digital currency (CBDC) is already in play. In parts of Africa and Asia people already use this digital currency in place of paper currency. The intention is to institute CBDC as part of the plan for one world currency controlled by one world government. The Covid-19 pandemic, as part of a plan that we now refer to as the Coronavirus Era, has provided a perfect environment in which to rollout a digital wallet connected to this currency. That's what vaccine passports are intended to become. In their plan, the vaccine passport is a massive step toward the worldwide digital wallet, as well as the excuse for implementing it.

CBDC works on a block chain similar to Bitcoin. It is likely that central bankers intend, at some point, to push for abolishing Bitcoin in favor of CBDC because Bitcoin is fully transparent and not controlled or manipulated by any government. Central bankers, in partnership with the government, want to control it all. The digital wallet is the final step in a planned, worldwide social credit system [30] that is being fashioned after the one being rolled out in China right now [31].

Digital ID systems connected to a digital wallet were first rolled out as early as 2005 in developing nations such as India, Mexico and Africa. Since that time they have been tested in the global south and parts of the global north in a way that can increase the effectiveness of human, civil and social rights violations. Chief among these systems is ID4D and the most established of the ID4D platforms is the *Aadhaar* system being tested in India. These systems have shown to have a *high failure rate* and robust evidence of purported benefits is *rarely provided*. The benefits are assumed, not proved. They are ill-defined and poorly documented. Furthermore, the biometric technology inherent in these digital wallets is usually downplayed to avoid public resistance to implementation.

According to the primer *Paving a Digital Road to Hell?* (pages 51-52), in 2018, former ID4D Working Group coordinator Mariana Dahan offered a report in which she stated: "But then something terrible happened, something unplanned. In a stream of high-profile security and privacy breaches...the world realized that we are on the cusp of something critical for our humanity. The risks of creation of an Orwellian system too obvious to be ignored." The Center for Human Rights & Global Justice at the NYU School of Law has published this excellent primer entitled *Paving a Digital Road to Hell?* You are strongly encouraged to read it and you can download the entire document for free here: https://chrgj.org/wp-content/uploads/2022/06/Report_Paving-a-Digital-Road-to-Hell.pdf. This brings us to March 9, 2022. "Sovereign money is at the core of a well-functioning financial system, macroeconomic stabilization policies, and economic growth. My Administration places the highest urgency on research and development efforts into the potential design and deployment options of a United States CBDC. These efforts should include assessments of possible benefits and risks for consumers, investors, and businesses; financial stability and systemic risk; payment systems; national security;

the ability to exercise human rights; financial inclusion and equity; and the actions required to launch a United States CBDC if doing so is deemed to be in the national interest." This quote is taken from Section 4 of Executive Order 14067 issued by President Biden. If you examine the order, you will see that POTUS has issued a mandate for a plan to be formulated in 180 days of the issuance of the order. This means that implementation of a United States central bank digital currency is immanent. You can read the entire executive order here:
https://www.presidency.ucsb.edu/documents/executive-order-14067-ensuring-responsible-development-digital-assets

After you read the executive order, you should also examine The Depository Trust and Clearing Corporation's *Project Lithium*, a plan to build a prototype system for exchanging central bank digital currency and tokenized assets on a distributed ledger to provide for a bank-to-bank infrastructure for clearing digital currency transactions between large commercial banks and central banks. You can read that here:
https://www.soonparted.co/p/project-lithium

Then you should study the information on *Project Hamilton*, a research and development project being run out of MIT to further develop and implement CBDC in a way that the United States becomes the world leader in the issuance, development and control of central bank digital currency. See Project Hamilton information here:
https://dci.mit.edu/project-hamilton-building-a-hypothetical-cbdc

In order to fully establish CBDC around the world, central bankers need the United States, Great Britain and Canada to fully comply, based on the current roll out in other countries. Then the rest of the world will follow. Again, vaccine passports are the tool for this mass manipulation scheme to end all paper currency and establish a worldwide social credit system.

In the U.S., a bill has been introduced in Congress to discontinue paper currency and go to a digital fiat currency. This bill is in play right now - sponsored by Senator Sherrod Brown (D) Ohio. The bill was introduced in 2020 and is stalled in the Senate. It is likely that supporters of the bill in Congress may be trying to roll this up into another bill in order to hide its pending passage from the public. You can view the bill here, along with its progress. https://www.congress.gov/bill/116th-congress/senate-bill/3571/text. You can view the patent document here that the U.S. government has contracted with, guess who? – Yes, none other than Bill Gates/Microsoft and Google to develop the digital wallet currency. https://patents.google.com/patent/US20200151682A1/en. You will notice that item #7 on page 28 of the document mentions the removal and destruction of all physical currency [32]. In the meantime, Gates is developing his own digital currency [33] and Visa has also jumped into the act [34].

Another bill, just introduced in 2022, gives Wall Street and the Central bankers the power to track every digital currency spent and control how we spend this digital currency, including locking us out of our digital wallet for any of several reasons that the government decides. It also provides for CBDC to be traded on the stock exchange. The bill is H.R. 4741 and can be read here: https://www.congress.gov/bill/117th-congress/house-bill/4741/text. Also, Gates has formed a Better Than Cash Alliance.

Connected to all this and the plan to abolish all physical currency, to be replaced with CBDC, here are some additional links to information that you should view:

https://www.gatesfoundation.org/Ideas/Media-Center/Press-Releases/2012/09/Better-Than-Cash-Alliance

https://www.betterthancash.org/

https://id2020.org/

All of this is being driven by the central banks, with the U.S. Federal Reserve cartel at the helm. **It is time to abolish the Federal Reserve.**

Why Abolish the Federal Reserve?

After almost one hundred revisions of its charter, operating under both political parties with plenty of situations that it has been called upon to address, the Federal Reserve has never achieved the objective for which it states it has been established – to stabilize the economy. Furthermore, this has never been the true objective of the U.S. Federal Reserve System.

- In the current monetary environment, the central bankers *are* the government. This is true of the Federal Reserve in the United States and most of the rest of the world. And this has been the case for almost two centuries.

- It is a cartel, a banking cabal that operates against the public interest.

- It has become the primary economic tool for establishing socialism in America and across the globe. Central bankers are globalists who want collectivism in order to establish one world government with one world currency that they control.

- It engages usury – charging 'interest' on loans that are not really loans, but rather mechanisms for robbing the public of money while, at the same time, ensuring economic collapse through booms and busts, over and over again, by manipulating economies.

- Inflation is a hidden tax that would not exist without fiat currency. And fiat currency in the U.S. is generated solely by the Federal Reserve.

- The Federal Reserve System is the means of robbing the American taxpayer to ensure that the wealthy elite continue to hoard financial wealth. In this way, it provides for the destruction of the middle class, dividing the world into the wealthy and the poor. An example is vaccines. The CDC is the largest purchaser of vaccines and Covid shots. POTUS has held press conferences recently stating, over and over again, that the Covid shots are free, but they are not. The Federal Reserve prints the money that is loaned to the Federal government to pay Big Pharma for the shots, earning their kickback in the process (interest). That interest is paid to U.S. central bankers by the U.S. taxpayer and the principal on the loan will, likely, never be repaid. Instead, if there is even a hint of default, the Federal Reserve will reschedule and restructure those loans for a steady stream of kickbacks. In the case of the Covid shots, the Federal government does not want to raise taxes. So, the kickback to the central bankers will be raised through the hidden tax of inflation. This is why, headed into the summer and fall of 2022, we saw the greatest inflation in more than 40 years.

- The Federal Reserve is a Ponzi scheme. As such, it is solely based on fraud.

- Instead of robbing U.S. taxpayers to pay interest rates to commercial banks and central bankers, the U.S. Congress has the Constitutional Authority (Article 1, Section 8, Clause 5 of our Constitution) to print money to pay for labor. The history of the greenback supports this. The Legal Tender Act of 1862 allowed the U.S. Congress to order the printing of the greenback currency. The greenback was legal tender that was not redeemable for gold [35]. This was initiated as an emergency war effort. Congress printed several issues of the greenback that allowed the North to pay for the war effort without having to borrow a lot of money from banks or increasing taxes. *The greenback was a non-debt-based currency.* The greenback became the U.S. Note and remained in circulation until 1993 when the U.S. Treasury destroyed the last of the greenbacks. When Federal Reserve Notes were introduced in 1913, the U.S. Note and the Federal Reserve Note were in circulation at the same time [36]. The U.S. Note was free of interest whereas the Federal Reserve Note was backed by debt issued by the Federal Reserve that generated interest for U.S. central bankers and commercial banks. Due to the actions of the Federal Reserve, today's monetary system has been designed specifically to place our government in perpetual debt to bankers, off the backs of U.S. taxpayers.

Why doesn't the government stop the fraud of the Federal Reserve? Because government is a partner in the fraud! Politicians receive campaign contributions as part of the huge lobbying effort to keep the Federal Reserve alive. Since the Federal Reserve is in partnership with the federal government, bailouts can be initiated at any time to make politicians look like saviors while enabling these same politicians to execute financial favors all over the world in return for the same. They don't want the gravy train to end.

Why continue to print money? Under the current system, commercial banks and central bankers make money (kickbacks on loans + exchange rates) when it's printed and/or when a ledger entry is made at the stroke of a computer key – which happens most often when banks lend money to each other and repurchase each other's loans (repurchase market, a.k.a. repo market). Money is printed and circulated in the economy when a loan is made.

The plan for digital currency is the same, except that there will be no costs for printing currency and minting coins because these will be obsolete if their plan is successful. You see, they have always created money in an electronic ledger with a keystroke on a computer. So, why should they bother to print and coin money when they can perpetuate the fraud electronically, and in a way that gives them even more socio-economic control.

Where the Federal Reserve is concerned, the American taxpayer is the sacrificial lamb in perpetuity. For a better understanding of this, you should study the Mandrake Mechanism [37]. But it doesn't have to be this way. We, the people, can change this. There is a window of time, right now, in which to do so. But that window is closing fast and we have to act NOW, with massive effort.

What to Do About It

1. **Most people are not informed about CBDCs and have no idea as to how far along these measures are toward worldwide implementation.** So, go to this web page and view the videos and all the information on this page. Share this page with as many people as you can so that they can become fully informed. https://bhaktaschool.org/central-bank-digital-currency-and-the-control-of-your-life/

2. **You can't protect something that you don't have a good understanding of.** Most people on the planet do not know how money works or how the monetary system and policy that governs their money works. I encourage you to enroll in *How to Prevent the Death of Your Money*. This is a video-on-demand course that will educate you on how your money actually works and all the things that impact your use of it and the cost for you to use it. Get enrollment and course information here: https://bhaktaschool.org/how-to-prevent-the-death-of-your-money/

3. **Support the H.R. 1122 - CBDC Anti-Surveillance State Act.** You can view the bill here: https://www.congress.gov/bill/118th-congress/house-bill/1122/text
Contact your elected congress people in your district by email and by phone and tell them to vote YES on this bill. Encourage other people you know to do the same.

4. **The state of Florida has banned the use of CBDCs in commerce and redefined CBDCs as not money.** SB 7054 was passed and signed into law in Florida in July 2023. You can view the bill here: https://www.flsenate.gov/Session/Bill/2023/7054/BillText/er/HTML

Email this link and bill information to the elected officials in your district for your state legislature and demand that they introduce a similar bill banning CBDCs in your state. Then follow up with a phone call and encourage other people you know to do the same.

5. Two bills have been introduced in the state of Ohio that, if passed, would ban the use of CBDCs in the state, as well as defining CBDCs as not money. You can view and download these bills here:

HB155 – Ohio https://search-prod.lis.state.oh.us/solarapi/v1/general_assembly_135/bills/hb155/IN/00/hb155_00_IN?format=pdf

HB 163 – Ohio https://search-prod.lis.state.oh.us/solarapi/v1/general_assembly_135/bills/hb163/IN/00/hb163_00_IN?format=pdf

Email these links and bill information to the elected officials in your district for your state legislature and demand that they introduce similar bills banning CBDCs in your state. Then follow up with a phone call. Encourage other people you know to do the same.

Additional information and data relevant to this chapter can be found here: https://bhaktaschool.org/dharma-and-the-preservation-of-liberty/

Chapter 6
The Growing Attack
On Our Liberty
Environmental Social Governance
(ESG)

I am a lover of Nature and natural beauty. I also love planting flowers and vegetables and, no matter where I have lived, I have always grown something. Even when I have lived in apartment buildings I have planted flowers and produce in pots. I also love to get my bare feet in dirt and grass, and I love getting my hands dirty in soil. My desire to protect our environment and to preserve natural beauty has grown out of my direct contact with planting things and watching them grow.

My interest for investigating climate change began when I studied the documentary *An Inconvenient Truth* in which then Vice President Al Gore goes on a rant about the imminent end of the world by global warming. It was then that I realized that any information I had gathered about global warming came from politicians, not scientists.

So, I began to research global warming in the scientific literature, and what I can tell you is that the science on global warming is far from settled. What I can also tell you (and I will provide supporting information and data in this chapter) is that the end of the world due to global warming is not coming any time soon. We have time to address the most important, current factors for which there is a lot of scientific data.

As I write these words, it is 4 degrees Fahrenheit where I live in Youngstown, Ohio and we have 2 inches of snow on the ground. And North America has seen more snow combined in the 2023-2024 winter season than it has in decades. [1] So much for global warming!

There are many climate change alarmists and climate change alarmism has become popular. Fear is unintelligent and any strategy based on fear and alarmist agendas will, ultimately, be ineffective at addressing climate change. There are also many climate change deniers. These people are only creating barriers to getting to the truth about climate change. People in both of these groups, the alarmists and the deniers, have been repeatedly caught "gaming the numbers" (an old Wall Street term) in an attempt to make the data on climate change match the ideology they are promoting.

The Truth is there is data on climate warming and cooling that has been measured going back as far as 125,000 years, with a lot more collected over the last 10,000 years. Then, if we go back 2,000 years, the data is very robust. So, there is enough data to accurately determine what we should address first, and enough data to say that we cannot blame all of global warming on greenhouse gases. And, not all of global warming is anthropogenic (caused by us humans) either. In addition, measured over a period of the previous 2,000 years, there is ample data that shows that today, in 2023, *the planet is actually cooler than in previous times during this period.*

This chapter is divided into two parts. In the first part I will address why *we are not* in a climate change emergency. In the second part I will provide compelling evidence of why we still need to act now, and in ways that will be the most effective – along with why we don't need (and you really don't want) top down measures by government that will mandate changes that are not designed to address climate change as much as they are designed to promote and enforce an ideology that expands globalist efforts at one world government while creating massive investment income in green technology startups.

It is imperative that we take addressing climate change out of the hands of politicians and hedge fund/asset managers, while demanding and supporting rigorous scientific presentation and debate on the data and the facts.

Inaccurate, Alarmist Claims Based On Malthusian Ideology

Thomas Malthus was a British economist, cleric and demographer who lived in a period from the late 1700s to early 1800s in England. Malthus is best known for his *theory* that population growth will always tend to outrun the food supply and that betterment of humankind is impossible without stern limits on reproduction. This thinking is commonly referred to as Malthusianism and is the foundation for climate change alarmism and the global push to control population growth through artificial means, the idea of which has grown out of Eugenics. Malthusianists believe and promote the notion that all of climate change and global warming is anthropogenic, primarily due to population growth.

In the early 1970s, a diplomat and chief advisor to heads of state named Henry Kissinger began a campaign to influence government policy to address both population growth and climate change. Kissinger was both a malthusianist and a eugenicist. In 1974, he produced the *National Security Study Memorandum 200,* commonly known as The Kissinger Report. The report comprises his assessment of implications of worldwide population growth for U.S. security and overseas interests. This report remained classified until July of 1989. You can download the full report here: https://bhaktaschool.org/pdfdownload.php?file=NSSM-200.pdf

     There are numbered points in the Executive Summary. I have taken some of those points and I present them here. These points have been completely debunked by time.

10. Rapid population growth creates a severe drag on rates of economic development otherwise attainable, sometimes to the point of preventing any increase in per capita incomes. In addition to the overall impact on per capita incomes, rapid population growth seriously affects a vast range of other aspects of the quality of life important to social and economic progress in the LDCs (least developed countries).

**In fact, the reverse is true. Per capita income in the U.S. was an annual $5,600 per family in 1960 and has only grown since then. Today, the U.S. per capita income average is $76,399. [2] In fact, the per capita income for the entire world has only increased since that time, with Ireland being the only country on the planet with a slight decrease around 2020. [3]

The United Nations Conference On Trade and Development also reports that, although there is more work to be done, real Gross Domestic Product (GDP) for LDCs has increased fivefold, climbing from roughly $200 billion in 1971 to $1 trillion 118 billion in 2019, due to rapid demographic growth. Real GDP per capita has expanded at a much slower pace than real GDP

(1.3% per annum), rising from roughly $600 billion to $1 trillion 82 billion over the same period. [4]

11. Adverse economic factors which generally result from rapid population growth include:

-- reduced family savings and domestic investment;
-- increased need for large amounts of foreign exchange for food imports;
-- intensification of severe unemployment and underemployment;
-- the need for large expenditures for services such as dependency support, education, and health which would be used for more productive investment;
-- the concentration of developmental resources on increasing food production to ensure survival for a larger population, rather than on improving living conditions for smaller total numbers.

**Family savings and investment from approximately 1970 to 2022, as a percentage of GDP, has steadily increased by 60%, with a slight dip for investments during the COVID-19 pandemic [5]

**Unemployment rates have bounced up and down since 1970. The global unemployment rate was higher in 1970 than it is today. In 2022, the unemployment rate decreased globally by 0.4 percentage points (-6.45 percent) over the previous year. The underemployment rate has also decreased steadily in the last decade. [6]

**Primary, worldwide crop production has increased steadily since 1970, with an additional increase of 52% from 2000 to 2022 for a total of 9.3 billion tonnes in 2022. [7]

12. While Gross National Product (GNP) increased per annum at an average rate of 5 percent in LDCs over the last decade, the population increase of 2.5 percent reduced the average annual per capita growth rate to only 2.5 percent. In many heavily populated areas this rate was 2 percent or less. In the LDCs hardest hit by the oil crisis, with an aggregate population of 800 million, GNP increases may be reduced to less than 1 percent per capita per year for the remainder of the 1970s. For the poorest half of the populations of these countries, with average incomes of less than $100, the prospect is for no growth or retrogression for this period.

**Actually, this did not take place in the 1970s, nor in the following decades through 2022 (see my comment under #11 above).

13. If significant progress can be made in slowing population growth, the positive impact on growth of GNP and per capita income will be significant. Moreover, economic and social progress will probably contribute further to the decline in fertility rates.

**This statement is moronic and not based on any statistic whatsoever. Worldwide GNP from 1962-2022 has averaged an increase of more than 6% per year. [8]

**Worldwide population growth has averaged a steady 2% per year increase from 1970 through 2023. [9]

**Fertility rates increased dramatically worldwide, beginning in the late 1970s and have slowed from the early 2000s through 2023, but are still increasing slightly every year. [10]

14. High birth rates appear to stem primarily from:

a. inadequate information about and availability of means of fertility control;

b. inadequate motivation for reduced numbers of children combined with motivation for many children resulting from still high infant and child mortality and need for support in old age; and

c. the slowness of change in family preferences in response to changes in environment.

**This is false. High birth rates are, in most countries, due to increased financial prosperity. See my comments under #11 above.

15. The universal objective of increasing the world's standard of living dictates that economic growth outpace population growth. In many high population growth areas of the world, the largest proportion of GNP is consumed, with only a small amount saved. Thus, a small proportion of GNP is available for investment - the "engine" of economic growth.

Most experts agree that, with fairly constant costs per acceptor, expenditures on effective family planning services are generally one of the most cost effective investments for an LDC country seeking to improve overall welfare and per capita economic growth. We cannot wait for overall modernization and development to produce lower fertility rates naturally since this will undoubtedly take many decades in most developing countries, during which time rapid population growth will tend to slow development and widen even more the gap between rich and poor.

**As I shared in the statistics above, population growth has not slowed development and neither has increasing fertility rates. In addition, the number of millionaires worldwide has increased dramatically, at an average rate of 3.85% each year since the 1990s, with more than 20 million millionaires today in the U.S. alone. [11]

**Although it is true that those who hold monetary wealth have been increasing their wealth, the statement that a small proportion of GNP is available for investment is not accurate. In 1979, the Dow was trading at 844. In 1989, that increased to 2,519 and as of October 2023, the Dow is trading at 33,407 - all while population has been steadily increasing. [12] So, the proportion of GNP available for investment has increased, even as the cost of living has increased.

More Alarmist Claims
Based On Malthusian Ideology

The Council of Rome, a.k.a. The Club of Rome is an organization established in 1965 that functions similarly to the WEF and the Bilderberg Group. The Club of Rome meets in private, invitation-only conferences where the wealthy elite, unelected government bureaucrats and diplomats come together to determine how they can advance their own interests through the capture of world governments. The aim is world dominance by way of socio-economic control of the world with collectivism as the means. Henry Kissinger was a member of the Club of Rome and attended and spoke at most of their conferences.

In 1991, the Club of Rome produced a report entitled *The First Global Revolution*. The report is designed to frame key areas that require attention in order to establish greater one world (global) governance. On page 115 of the report, under the subheading "The Common Enemy of Humanity Is Man," it states:

"In searching for a new enemy to unite us, we came up with the idea that pollution, the threat of global warming, water shortages, famine and the like would fit the bill....The real enemy, then is humanity itself."

From the way this is worded, their intention is very clear: Use the idea of the threat of pollution, the threat of global warming, water shortages, famine and the like to frighten the world into compliance with their formulated intentions and policies. This is not unlike the fear mongering promoted by the WEF, as evidenced in the book *COVID-19: The Great Reset* by Klaus Schwab and other rants that can be found at the WEF's web site. You can purchase *The First Global Revolution* in looseleaf form on Amazon. It is a very telling study on the push to world dominance by establishing one world government through globalism, i.e. collectivism.

What Is Environmental Social Governance (ESG)?

Environmental Social Governance is a set of global governance policies designed to implement a social credit scoring and worldwide surveillance system that is also connected to Digital IDs and Central Bank Digital Currency (CBDC). ESG is also an essential part of the plan to install a one world government run by the wealthy elite, corporate conglomerates and unelected, government bureaucrats.

At the heart of ESG is a social credit scoring system that is modeled after the current system used in China (see the opening of Chapter 4). The Chinese social credit scoring system is designed to score every person alive, based on a number of measured factors that include compliance with all government mandates.

If you are not in compliance with mandated vaccines, mandated foods, mandated vehicles that you drive, mandated political and social support for the government, mandated speech, mandated dress codes, mandated home and office environment (just to name a few), your social credit score is reduced to the point where your movements in society are severely restricted.

For example, with a low social credit score, you are unable to shop for food, unable to travel to work and unable to access your bank accounts (among other things). And, if you try to aid someone who has a low social credit score and is unable to buy food or access his/her bank account, your social credit score is lowered. Again, ESG social credit scoring is tied to Digital IDs and CBDCs. If allowed to become established globally it will make the COVID-19 pandemic mandates and lockdowns look like child's play.

The Truth About Climate Change And Global Warming

Climate researchers utilize a variety of direct and indirect measurements to investigate Earth's climate history comprehensively. Direct measurements include data from satellites in space, instruments on the International Space Station, aircraft, ships, buoys, and ground-based instruments like temperature stations. When scientists focus on climate from before the past 100-150 years, they use records from physical, chemical, and biological materials preserved within the geologic record.

The Earth holds climate clues dating back over three billion years, contained in rock layers, polar ice sheets, lakebeds, and more. Organisms (such as diatoms, forams, and coral) can serve as useful climate proxies. Other proxies include ice cores, tree rings, and sediment cores. Chemical proxy records include isotope ratios, elemental analyses, biomarkers, and biogenic silica. Collectively, these proxies significantly extend our understanding of past climates, reaching far back into Earth's history.

Greenhouse gases are partly to blame for global warming. They are gases in Earth's atmosphere that trap heat. They let sunlight pass through the atmosphere, but they prevent the heat that the sunlight brings from leaving the atmosphere. The main greenhouse gases are:

- Water vapor
- Carbon dioxide
- Methane
- Ozone
- Nitrous oxide
- Chlorofluorocarbons

Of these, carbon dioxide (CO_2), methane and nitrous oxide are at the top of the list of harmful, greenhouse gases.

Before getting into more specifics, it is important to remember that weather trends are not climate change. The two are often confused. Measuring trends in changing weather is not measuring climate change. To the detriment of climate change reporting, weather trends are often reported as climate change and have become part of the ideology of climate change alarmists.

The Intergovernmental Panel on Climate Change (IPCC) is a body established and managed by the UN.

The IPCC issues an annual report on climate change that world governments use to set policies and laws regarding climate change response. As most climate scientists will tell you in private, the IPCC has become a political organization. As such, scientists are under increasing pressure to support the IPCC narrative on climate change or they lose their research funding and are blacklisted in the scientific community.

The annual reports issued by the IPCC are known as assessment reports that are usually released in three phases: Working Group 1 (WG1) report, Working Group 2 (WG2) report, and then a final report called the Synthesis Report. IPCC is now on its sixth (AR6) assessment report since its formal inception. [13] All of the annual reports can be accessed at https://www.ipcc.ch/.

If you dig down into these reports, you will notice glaring contradictions in the reporting that include tiny type references in the back of the reports that attempt to explain away the obvious contradictions. In addition, the AR6 report contradicts the previous, AR5 report.

In several cases, the names of working scientists have been removed in report references because those scientists left the working group before completion of the reports, due to their disagreement with the narrative they were being asked to base their findings on. In addition, the IPCC reports are primarily based on predictive models that do not match what is actually taking place in the environment.

Some of you may remember that the predictive models that came out of Bill Gates's Institute For Health Metrics and Evaluation (IHME) for Covid infections, hospitalizations and deaths worldwide were proved to be completely flawed. Unfortunately, during the first year of the COVID-19 pandemic, these models were used by most world governments to establish

Covid mandates and lockdowns. This is the problem with modeling.

In addition, it's important to follow the money with respect to who is presenting the models, along with their conflicts of interest. Using the IHME as an example, Bill Gates, through organizations like GAVI, invested heavily in the Covid shots and made a return on that investment that totals over $300 million dollars. Recently, Gates was interviewed as admitting that the very jabs he helped create do not prevent infection and transmission (something most of us knew from the beginning). [14] The fact is Gates produced the flawed Covid models that put huge amounts of money in his pocket. This same scenario is playing out in the climate change arena. I will address this shortly in this chapter.

To simplify the presentation of points on climate change, I'm going to present points that are referenced from video interviews and presentations that you can find on the following web pages: https://bhaktaschool.org/the-climate-change-hoax/ https://bhaktaschool.org/the-climate-change-hoax-2/

Climate Intelligence (CLINTEL – clintel.org, https://clintel.org/videos/) is an independent foundation that operates in the fields of climate change and climate policy. CLINTEL was founded in 2019 by emeritus professor of geophysics Guus Berkhout and science journalist Marcel Crok. CLINTEL's main objective is to generate knowledge and understanding of the causes and effects of climate change as well as the effects of climate policy. CLINTEL has provided a World Climate Declaration entitled *There Is No Climate Emergency* that has now been signed by 1,824 climate scientists from all over the world. That's more scientists than the IPCC has in all of its working groups combined.

The Center for Environmental Research and Earth Sciences (CERES) is a multi-disciplinary and independent research group. The aim of CERES is to address important issues in the fields of environmental and earth sciences. The group strives to foster original and timely scientific understanding, in addition to re-examining old analyses with fresh insights.

The above climate change organizations and scientists presented in videos are listed at the top of the first web page. There is also a link to a very important interview of Steven E. Koonin by Joe Rogan that I encourage you to view. In addition, Steven E. Koonin's book, *Unsettled: What Climate Science Tells Us, What It Doesn't, and Why It Matters* is worth taking the time to read.

In addition, I will reference a very important book produced by the scientists at clintel.org entitled *The Frozen Climate Views of the IPCC – An Analysis of AR6*. This book is a bit technical but if you understand graphed statistics and are comfortable reading more technical data, this book is essential for understanding the truth about climate change. It can be purchased at clintel.org.

Also, I will present points supported by three, recent peer-reviewed studies. They are *The Detection and Attribution of Northern Hemisphere Land Surface Warming (1850–2018) in Terms of Human and Natural Factors: Challenges of Inadequate Data* which you can read/download here: https://www.mdpi.com/2225-1154/11/9/179, *Challenges in the Detection and Attribution of Northern Hemisphere Surface Temperature Trends Since 1850* which you can read/download here: https://iopscience.iop.org/article/10.1088/1674-4527/acf18e, and *Evidence of Urban Blending in Homogenized Temperature Records in Japan and in the United States: Implications for the Reliability of Global*

Land Surface Air Temperature Data which you can read/download here: https://journals.ametsoc.org/view/journals/apme/62/8/J AMC-D-22-0122.1.xml

A Brief Examination of Critical Data

1. Climate is chaotic by nature and moves up and down in cycles, constantly, and over long periods of time, from a decade to 1,000 years or more.

2. Measurements taken for global surface temperatures between the late 1300s through 2021 indicate that our planet has been warming and cooling in consistent cycles, mostly below 1.0 degrees centigrade. There was a spike in the mid 1700s, up to 2.5 degrees centigrade. Then the planet cooled considerably, and then began warming and cooling again in cycles between 0.5 degrees centigrade and 1.8 degrees centigrade, with a cooling period from the early 1900s through the early 2000s, with measurements below 0.5 degrees centigrade in the early 2000s. [15] Since about 2016, our planet has begun to heat up again.

3. In the three, peer-reviewed studies mentioned above, as well as in the videos mentioned, data is presented that shows how the reporting of actual climate change numbers is skewed through "urban blending." Large cities produce what is known as the urban heat island effect. Due to dense populations, large cities generate a greater land warming effect in the areas where they are located. *This is not a global effect. It is a localized effect.* It can be said that this localized warming effect is, mostly, anthropogenic and many climate scientists believe that this urban heat

island effect probably comprises 40-50% of the total reported impact on climate warming.

Urban blending occurs when the data for the localized urban heat island effect is mixed into the data for all the other areas of the planet, thereby skewing the warming numbers higher. This data has to be separated out of the total data for climate change and considered separately in developing a response that is targeted at large cities.

4. Total Solar Irradiance (TSI) is now believed to be the probable cause of up to 50% of the rest of global warming climate change. It is a known and measured fact that solar output from radiating sunlight increases and decreases over long periods of time in cycles. Measured solar output is on the rise again over the last 100 years.

5. Moon output also increases the overall temperature on earth because, at times, it reflects more sunlight that hits the earth than at other times. This causes both warming and cooling.

6. 125,000 years ago during the last interglacial period there was little ice on the Earth and the land temperature was 2 degrees warmer than today. Sea levels were about 25 feet higher than they are today. This is due to changes in Earth's orbit and how that impacts the amount of sunlight falling on the Earth. These periods last thousands of years, occurring between ice ages or glacial epochs.

7. The U.S. emits only 13% of global greenhouse gases and U.S. Economic impact of global warming is minimal between now and 2100. Countries like India, China and

parts of Asia are the ones emitting the majority of greenhouse gases.

8. Warming around the globe is not happening at the same rate, and there are parts of the globe that are cooling. For example, arctic areas are warming faster as the southern hemisphere is cooling mildly.

9. Hurricanes do not kill more people because they are growing in intensity due to global warming. They kill more people because there are more cities that are a lot more populated than in past centuries.

10. Are storms getting more intense? No. They go up and down over long periods of time, up to 100 years or more. This is true even when there has been much more anthropogenic influence on climate change in recent decades. This means greenhouse gases are not the primary cause of climate change.

11. Sea level rise is not accelerating. Tide has gone up less than a foot per century and we have adjusted to this slight increase. The politicians complaining about rapidly rising ocean levels due to climate change all have houses on the beach. If they believed what they are hyping, they would have moved by now.

12. There are natural variations in ocean current that occur over 80-100 years at a time.

13. Glacial melting is not a recent phenomenon. Glaciers started melting 20,000 years ago, so this is not due to a global warming catastrophe.

14. There are cycles of ocean currents and winds in the Northern Hemisphere that cause ice to melt and freeze

over extended periods of time. This is what causes glacial melting and freezing.

15. Climate changes occur over long periods of time - from 100 years to 10,000 years.

16. Natural variabilities are a greater influence on climate change than anthropogenic influence. We are not headed for climate catastrophe. Mainstream media, the UN and politicians have inflated the challenge by wrongly placing 100% of the blame on anthropogenic causes.

17. The IPCC and most climatologists have completely ignored the fact that cloud cover acts as a natural thermometer to warm and cool the Earth and stabilize the Earth's temperature. The understanding of how clouds control land and atmospheric warming and cooling is a huge missing link in the understanding of natural climate change.

Nobel laureate John Clauser was recently interviewed by The Epoch Times about this phenomenon and why spending billions of dollars on CO_2 and methane removal is a waste of time and money. You can watch a video of the interview or read a transcript of the full interview here: https://www.theepochtimes.com/epochtv/nobel-laureate-john-clauser-there-is-no-climate-emergency-climate-models-miss-one-key-variable-5486017

18. Direct air capture technologies are being designed to capture CO_2 from the atmosphere. However, the best way to capture CO_2 is to plant trees, stop deforestation and increase organic regenerative farming.

19. Organic farming using organic super fertilizers like biochar to repair dead soil is a primary means of capturing CO_2 from the atmosphere and converting it to carbon. The earth has gotten 40% greener since 1980. Plants need carbon and carbon makes plants, trees and grass grow.

20. There is enough certainty about some of the data, particularly that industrial/factory farming with synthetic fertilizers is a major anthropogenic cause of the release of carbon dioxide and nitrous oxide into the environment. So, this is where we should start to address the challenge of global warming.

21. The current, proposed ESG changes by the government are not scalable by 2030 or 2050 or even 2075. These changes have to be made at a slow, steady pace that is based on actual data, is effective, and also accepted by the public.

22. The science on climate change is not settled and there is no broad consensus on all of the causes. However, even given this fact, there is enough verifiable data that is worth acting on. This will be addressed further in this chapter.

The Real Costs of The ESG Rollout

The ESG rollout in the U.S. and other parts of the world is focused, as a first step, on replacing gas-powered vehicles with Electric Vehicles (EVs). So, for the purpose of this section, I will focus on the real costs of the ESG mandates for the rollout of EVs and the outlawing of gas-powered vehicles.

The process for manufacturing the high-voltage batteries necessary to power EVs is an environmental nightmare.

1. Most of the high-voltage batteries used to power EVs are made in India and China. These batteries are a combination of lithium, cobalt, and nickel. Other countries, including the U.S. are now looking at mining these minerals for EV battery production. India is running out of lithium reserves and is now relying on China for these batteries. It is uncertain how much lithium, cobalt and nickel reserves exist in the U.S. and other countries. What is certain is that it is a finite number, after which there will be no more of these materials left to make the batteries. [16,17,18]

2. Mining these materials, however, has a very high environmental cost, a factor that inevitably makes the EV manufacturing process more energy intensive than that of a gas-powered vehicle. The harm to the environment in making these batteries is far worse than digging for oil and fracking for natural gas. The toxic fumes released during the mining necessary for EV batteries are very damaging to the environment. The process for EV battery mining is uses up a great deal of water that remains contaminated when the mining process is complete.

In 2016, hundreds of protestors threw dead fish plucked from the waters of the Liqui River onto the streets of Tagong, Tibet, publicly denouncing the Ganzizhou Ronga Lithium mine's unethical practice of polluting the local ecosystem through toxic chemical leaks. Similarly, the production of lithium was halted in China's Yichun city after an investigation into the water quality of the Jin river, the main source of residential water, revealed the presence of toxic pollutants. [19,20,21]

3. The additional environmental cost of transporting these batteries results in a higher carbon footprint than gas-powered vehicles. A 2021 study comparing EV and gas-powered car emissions found that 46% of EV carbon emissions come from the production process while for a gas-powered vehicle, they only account for 26%. Almost 4 tonnes of CO_2 are released during the production process of a single electric car and, in order to break even, the vehicle must be used for at least 8 years to offset the initial emissions by 0.5 tonnes of prevented emissions annually. Furthermore, producing one tonne of lithium (enough for 100 car batteries) requires approximately 2 million tonnes of water, which makes battery production an extremely water-intensive practice. [22,23,24]

4. In light of this, the South American Lithium triangle consisting of Chile, Argentina, and Bolivia, experienced heavy water depletion due to intensive lithium extraction in the area. In Chile alone, 65% of the region's water was used for lithium extraction. The U.S. State of Nevada recently saw protests on account of the Lithium Americas Project due to the prophesied use of enormous quantities of groundwater. Nickel and cobalt have similar reputations. Satellite analysis in Cuba has shown a devoid of life in over 570 hectares of land and contamination of over 10 kilometres of coastline where nickel and cobalt mines are present. [25,26,27]

5. The Philippines had to shut down 23 mines, many producing nickel and cobalt, because of the environmental degradation that it caused. Stories like these are a testament to the hazards of metal extraction, but they are not exclusive to EV

manufacturing – all portable electronic devices contribute to this. Recycling and reusing batteries can provide some relief to the mining process but the technology surrounding it is still inefficient. Currently, the Japanese car manufacturer, Nissan reuses the batteries from its EVs to power the automated guided vehicles in factories. [28,29] Then there is the health problem. Smoke from lithium-ion batteries is toxic. When these batteries burn to provide electricity for the EV, hydrogen fluoride and carbon monoxide are released into the air, which can have acute and chronic health effects on a person's respiratory system. [30]

6. Volkswagen and Renault have set up recycling plants for batteries. Despite this, only 5% of the world's total batteries are currently recycled. This is mainly because of the cost and the rather long process required to recycle batteries. Batteries ending up in landfills add to the environmental footprint. [31,32,33]

7. While manufacturing has the biggest footprint, powering batteries also contributes to environmental degradation, especially in developing economies like India. This is because the source of electricity used to power them determines how eco-friendly an EV really is. Personal electrical vehicles require more lithium per rider than electric buses.

According to the Ministry of Power, as of 2021, India sourced 61% of its power from thermal sources including fossil fuels like coal, which accounts for 60% of the country's total emissions. Added to this, is the environmental cost of transporting coal to India. India is currently the world's second largest exporter of coal to meet the demand and enhance the quality of coal.

The use of coal leads to health hazards due to noxious fumes, higher CO_2 emissions, loss of forests and water pollution through mining wastes. Coal also kills aquatic life forms. This is further exacerbated by the underutilization of power capacity (wherein the ability to produce power is higher than what is produced due to archaic power plants and obsolete technology), resulting in wastage that adds to the environmental impact. [34,35,36,37]

8. To ensure emission-free mobility, renewable sources of power are required to power batteries. At present, however, only 21% of installed capacity is accounted for by renewable sources in India. China is even worse.

In addition to the referenced articles in this section, for more information about the environmental impact of lithium batteries, you can also read the Institute for Energy Research's article here: https://www.instituteforenergyresearch.org/renewable/the-environmental-impact-of-lithium-batteries/

9. All of the above will amount to ever-increasing retail costs for the EV batteries that go into EVs, thereby increasing the cost of EVs over time. Then there are the other two questions that must be answered now, before nations start making policies and passing laws that force us to buy/drive EVs. Is EV battery mining sustainable long-term? What will be the total impact on the global environment due to EV battery mining and how will that impact be addressed where toxic pollution of the environment is concerned, as more and more EVs come to market?

10. According to data from Cox Automotive, parent of Kelley Blue Book, the average transaction price for electric cars was $53,469 in July 2023, vs. gas-powered

vehicles at $48,334. The cost for EVs starts at around
$25,000 and can go as high as $125,000 or more. EVs
are more expensive than gas-powered vehicles *and they
cost twice as much to insure.* [38] Personally, I wouldn't
mind paying more if I were convinced that EVs are
better for the environment. I'm not and I will explain
why here.

11. The value of a new car decreases dramatically over
a short period of time. Carfax data show that cars
typically lose more than 10% of their value in the first
month after you drive off the lot, and it keeps dropping
from there. According to industry experts, the value of
a new vehicle drops by about 20% in the first year of
ownership. Over the next four years, you can expect
your car to lose roughly 15% of its value each year –
meaning the average vehicle will be worth just 40% of
its purchase price after five years: A 5-year-old vehicle
that sold for $40,000 when new will be worth $16,000.
A 5-year-old car that sold for $30,000 will be worth
$12,000. [39] The relevance of this point will become
clear further down this list.

12. Although world governments claim that their
power grids will be ready to handle the increased
output necessary to meet the demand of EV charging
under 2030 implementation policies, the difference
between these policies and engineering reality is huge.
In places like California and the Netherlands where
they are passing laws to abolish gas-powered vehicles
by 2035, they have already had issues with their grids
going down due to increased EV charging demand. In
the U.S. and elsewhere, nations are starting to realize
that, in order to meet any increase in EV charging
demand, they will have to bolster or rebuild their power
grids. It is clear that, globally, nations are not ready to
meet an increasing demand for EV power by 2030, even

though they say they will be ready. [40,41] As of the publication of this book, 2030 is only six years away.

13. The other issue is charging stations. Currently, in states like California and New Jersey that are adopting very aggressive policies and laws to retire gas-powered cars in favor of EVs, there are big issues with charging stations. From broken connectors to dead chargers to sticking cables to broken credit card machines for making payment, the number of charging stations, along with their reliability, is not keeping pace with EV sales. For example, in states like California and New Jersey, there are more than 50 EVs for each available public charging station. [42,43,44,45]

This means long wait times to get into a charging station to charge the EV. There are over 400,000 Tesla EVs on the road in the U.S. Over the last two holiday seasons, Tesla's Supercharger stations were overcrowded and many Tesla owners faced an hours-long wait to recharge their electric vehicles. That does not include the actual recharging time.

14. There are fire and safety risks associated with all EV charging stations. Land and building owners have to be cognizant of the risks to installing EV charging stations in their parking lots, garages and other locations. First, there is a significant risk of smoke and fire that accompanies them. So, when installing these EV charging stations in parking garages and other locations, fire protection of the area must be taken into consideration, as well as the placement of these charging stations themselves, to ensure that if an incident does occur, the fire can be contained quickly without spreading and causing further damage.

Another important element to consider is whether the current electrical system of your building can manage the power of the charging stations. Some questions to answer when deciding this would be to determine when your buildings electrical system was last updated and whether the building currently meets fire and electrical codes. It is also important to note that electrical fires are not always visible immediately and often burn in unseen areas for a while, so it is equally as important that certified electrical workmanship and solid infrastructure are in place to support the installation of EV chargers. [46]

Home charging stations can be purchased, but the same challenge exists of whether the home's electric system can safely meet the electric output required to operate the home EV charging station.

15. On top of the challenge to find and get into an EV charging station is the time it takes to fully charge an EV. There are three charging levels: slow, fast and rapid. The charging level you are able to use depends on the EV you buy. Charging on level 1 (slow) takes 8-30 hours, depending on the wattage of the main battery. Fast charging (level 2) takes between 3-12 hours, again depending on the wattage of the main battery. Level 3 (fast) takes 32 minutes to 2 hours. [47]

16. What happens when the EV battery dies? There are two batteries in EVs. The first is a standard, 12-volt car battery that can be charged when it is low, jump started with cables or replaced inexpensively, as necessary. The second battery is the main, high-voltage battery that powers the driving of the vehicle. There are warning gauges on the console that tell you when the main battery is getting low. You cannot jump start the main battery.

If that battery goes down, you need roadside assistance to come charge the battery enough (per the times indicated in number 15 above) to get you to the nearest charging station or home. Also, towing an EV due to a dead main battery is not always an option, as many EVs have regenerative braking mechanisms (to reduce the amount of drain on the battery needed to brake the vehicle) that won't allow for towing. [48]

17. All batteries eventually die. So, what happens when the main, high-voltage battery on an EV has to be replaced? EVs sold in the U.S. come with at least an 8-year/100,000-mile battery warranty. That's 8 years or 100,000 miles, whichever comes first. [49] Some EV manufacturers provide a 10-year/150,000 mile warranty. To replace the main battery on a Tesla EV can run you more than $20,000. *The labor charge to replace the battery is additional.* To replace the main battery on a Toyota Prius will run $1,500-$4,000 depending on the model and whether you buy a new or used battery. *That's also before labor costs.* But there is something else you need to consider and that is the depreciation in value of your vehicle.

So, let's run some numbers. As I shared in number 11 above, the value of a new car decreases dramatically over a short period of time. Carfax data show that cars typically lose more than 10% of their value *in the first month* after you drive off the lot, and it keeps dropping from there. According to industry experts, the value of a new vehicle drops by about 20% in the first year of ownership. Over the next four years, you can expect your car to lose roughly 15% of its value each year – meaning the average vehicle will be worth just 40% of its purchase price after five years: A 5-year-old vehicle that sold for $40,000 when new will be worth $16,000. A 5-year-old car that sold for $30,000 will be worth

$12,000.

For the sake of example, let's say you purchase a $40,000 Tesla EV with a warranty on the main battery of 8/100,000. Always remember that, by stating a warranty, the manufacturer is telling you how long they expect your car to run under standard driving circumstances. Now, per the depreciation stated above, in 5 years, your Tesla EV will be worth about $16,000. You decide to drive the EV past the warranty period and, in the ninth year, the main battery on your Tesla dies. You get a quote for $20,000, not including labor costs, to replace that battery. But, at this point, the EV is only worth $16,000. The cost for replacing the battery is more than the car is worth. So, now, unless you want to pay more for less, you will likely have to purchase a new EV.

18. The true cost to power EVs, based on the cost to recharge, is the equivalent of $17.33 per gallon of gas. This is a lot higher than the $1.21 per gallon industry estimates. As long as this remains the case, it is unlikely that President Biden's goal of 100 percent EVs by 2040 will ever become a reality as EVs will remain more expensive than gas vehicles. And with various subsidies, regulatory credits, and charging costs of an average model year 2021 EV, add $53,267 to the vehicle's price over a decade. [50,51]

19. The other very important concern about EVs is that they are connected to the Internet via the charging stations. There is a push to make EVs part of the control grid that includes Digital IDs and CBDCs. This would place all EVs under the same global surveillance system and allow government to make EVs part of a social credit scoring system. Have a low social credit score? Now, you can't charge your EV until you improve

your social credit score as dictated by the government. The technology to make this happen is already in place.

With respect to EVs, there is much more to be considered and addressed before the public should accept any mandates or laws requiring the use of EVs over gas-powered vehicles.

More Real Costs of The ESG Rollout

In addition to mandates for EVs, in the U.S., President Biden has issued Executive Orders to ban all gas-burning stoves and air conditioners that are placed in windows, by 2030. In addition, if you have central air conditioning, due to additional mandates designed to abolish Freon A/C altogether, the cost of Freon coolant refills for central A/C has gone from $600 per pound to $1,800 per pound.

According to Consumer Watchdog, the Biden Administration climate regulations add $9,100 per year in total expenses for a typical American household. [52]

Then there is a national security issue that is raising more and more concerns. Many of the green tech companies are Chinese and operate out of China. These companies are backed by the CCP and the CCP does an excellent job at mining data over the Internet that it then uses to further its strategy of world dominance, targeting the U.S. in particular.

From computer chips to steel to batteries to the computers in everything from our cell phones to our home and office computers, to the computers that operate EVs and EV charging stations, China has cornered the market on the manufacturing of these. There is a growing and valid concern that the CCP will use the data it collects from its green technology to undermine the security of the U.S. and other nations, particularly where intelligence is concerned. [53]

Solar and Wind Power

Solar panels and wind turbines are clean sources of energy that, while operating them, has little or no impact on the environment. However, *the manufacture of these devices* requires the use of processes and equipment *that rely heavily on fossil fuels to operate.* So, greenhouse gases are released into the environment during the manufacturing process and this has yet to be addressed by the industry or government. In addition, when solar panels die they are thrown in landfills and the toxic chemicals in the panels leech out into the ground and, eventually, contaminate the ground water.

Solar panels become toxic waste. They are made with a host of toxic chemicals like cadmium and lead that are both carcinogenic. [54,55,56,57] Currently, there are no effective recycling policies in place for solar panels.

Wind farms produce less energy than hoped for and comprise a small percentage of the overall power required for consumption. Wind farms also affect local weather, raising temperatures by as much as 2.7 degrees. In addition, they require large tracts of land, as the turbines have to be positioned a good distance from each other. Then there is the hazard of death to birds and bats. And, if the wind farms are located in the ocean, the ecosystem in the water is gradually destroyed as fish are killed off. This has become a big complaint of the fishing industry that is resulting in lawsuits around the world. People living near wind farms have consistently complained of noise and vibrations that rock the foundation of their homes. In addition, *the manufacturing process for wind turbines is usually run on fossil fuels* that cause greenhouse gases to be emitted. [58,59,60]

Every new technology has its "growing pains" that need to be worked through. In addition, most new technologies (as well as some old ones) have an impact on polluting and degrading the environment. So, the question becomes which of the technologies harm the environment the least while preserving our Liberty, rather than destroying it. This requires that the public be fully informed and not coerced or forced.

Again, climate change cannot be 100% blamed on anthropogenic causes (caused by us humans). There are too many facts and too much data that show that climate change is also cyclical (warmer, then colder, then warmer again) when measured over long periods of time, and that climate change is also due to natural causes like increased solar output.

Once you embrace this fact, it becomes necessary to examine the natural causes of climate change, not just the anthropogenic causes. And once you do that, it becomes necessary to embrace the likelihood that climate change is subject to both anthropogenic causes and natural causes. Once you understand this, the examination has to turn to the degree to which climate change is caused by each, and how.

Where To Begin To Address Global Warming

One of the greatest challenges to climate change and the protection of Mother Earth is the fact that the majority of the masses on the planet do not have a relationship with our Earth. I know of no person who plants something who does not take steps to protect the environment. So, it is essential that we begin educating people in how to grow plants, flowers and produce in home gardens, pots and planters. This education should also become a standard part of the K-12 school curriculum, globally.

Industrial/Factory Farming

According to many studies and thousands of climate scientists, industrial and factory farming (non-organic farming) accounts for 90% of the release of greenhouse gases like carbon into the atmosphere. Other scientists say that figure is more like 50%. So, for the sake of argument, let's average those two out. That comes to 70%. This means that more than half of all greenhouse gas emissions are due to industrial and factory farming. So, this is where we should start to address the challenge of global warming.

The information and data presented in this section is referenced from several sources, including two very important documentary films that offer many additional references. These two are: *The Need to Grow* that you can view as video-on-demand here: https://vimeo.com/ondemand/theneedtogrow/ and here: https://grow.foodrevolution.org/screening/. You can also purchase the DVD here: https://www.earthconsciouslife.org/shop-tntg. Then there is the documentary *The Seeds of Vandana Shiva* that you can view here, free: https://bhaktaschool.org/the-seeds-of-vandana-shiva/.

If your plan is for one year, plant rice.
If your plan is for 10 years plant trees.
If your plan is for 100 years, educate children.
~ Confucius

Some important points to be informed about are:

1. You can't feed the world from dead soil. Industrial agriculture/factory farming is the most destructive activity on the planet because it kills healthy soil through the tilling process, and by the use of toxic chemicals and synthetic, toxic fertilizers that deplete the soil of all nutrients while releasing carbon dioxide into the atmosphere.

2. Tilling soil involves turning soil carbon into atmospheric carbon dioxide. As soil dies, this carbon dioxide from tilled soil is released into the environment and atmosphere, causing the planet to heat up.

3. We have an estimated 60 years of farmable soil left on the planet and the Earth has lost a third of its farmable soil in the last 40 years. It is estimated that today, 70% of the planet's soil has already been destroyed.

4. In the United States we are losing soil at 10 times the rate it takes to regenerate it. Industrial farming costs the environment $3 trillion a year in what is required to address the harm to the environment.

5. Plants and produce that are grown in healthy soil absorb CO_2 from the atmosphere and convert that to carbon. Because this is the case, it is possible, through organic farming, to remove that 70% of greenhouse gases from the atmosphere that is caused by non-organic farming. The excess carbon not taken up by the organic crops stays in the soil and helps keep the soil healthy.

6. Permaculture uses a natural, organic process that takes atmospheric carbon and stores it in the soil. This is an incredibly useful tool for removing CO_2 from the atmosphere to reduce global warming and not enough

people know about it. And governments are not engaged in fostering permaculture in farming and homesteading. To learn more about permaculture visit The Permaculture Academy at http://www.permacultureacademy.com/

7. The reason governments are not engaged in permaculture initiatives is that, as an example, in the U.S., industrial and factory farming companies have successfully engaged in regulatory capture of the FDA, the EPA and the U.S. Department of Agriculture. These same companies have also captured mainstream media. All of this must stop. Pay attention to the plan offered in Chapter 8.

8. One of the challenges is that industrial farming relies on short-term boosts in production yields. Even smaller farmers have adopted this approach by insisting on using synthetic fertilizers that kill the soil in the long term. The focus on short-term increased crop yields through industrial/factory farming comes at a major cost to soil longevity through the use of these synthetic fertilizers and other chemicals that eliminate the biodiversity of the soil.

9. Globally, 44 billion pounds of chemical fertilizers are used each year. Up to 50% of nitrogen fertilizers are washed away by rain and groundwater. This pollutes the ocean. This also creates ocean dead zones.

10. In the U.S., more than one-third of all fossil fuels, more than 50% of water, and 80% of our farmland is used in animal factory farming.

11. The glyphosate chemicals that are used in industrial farming create toxins that also run off into our water supply, including rivers, streams and

eventually the ocean. This happens by way of the ground water being poisoned.

12. 32 million tons of food are thrown out every year in the U.S. 97% of food waste ends up in landfills. When you have millions of tons of organic matter and garbage that is going into landfills and rotting away, that garbage itself emits CO2, methane and nitrous oxide into the environment. So think about all of these landfills that are open, and stuff is rotting in open air. That is contributing to global warming.

13. Industrial/factory farming destroys the amount of available seed varieties.

Organic Farming

Organic farming is regenerative. When permaculture is applied to organic farming this is the primary means of drawing CO2 from the atmosphere and turning it into carbon that is stored in the soil, while causing robust, healthy crop yields. Long-term organic farming has been shown to provide greater crop yields than industrial farming. The reason for this is that, as industrial farming produces high, short-term yields using toxic chemicals, the soil dies. Once that happens, the yields decrease dramatically and then the soil stops producing crops.

Organic farming is regenerative farming. As organic crops are grown, the soil gets healthier, producing increased yield over the long term. During World War II, 20% of home and community gardens produced 40% of organically grown food in communities in the U.S. As homesteading increased, this percentage grew.

A Rodale Institute study (done over a period of 30 years) showed that organic farming matches or surpasses conventional farming without destroying the soil and while emitting 35% less greenhouse gases and utilizing 45% less energy. With permaculture and other forms of regenerative farming, the percentage of greenhouse gas emissions is reduced to zero.

No-till farming, cover crops and composting, all forms of regenerative farming, help retain water in the soil; these are techniques that protect the soil year-round. They increase carbon, which is an essential nutrient in the soil and these approaches make the soil carbon-rich. Humic substances are a critical component of decomposing organic matter. This is how composting helps to create permaculture that enriches the soil.

A tablespoon of healthy soil contains 6 billion microorganisms. Every 1% of organic matter that is added to the soil causes the soil to retain 25,000 gallons of water per acre. This reduces the risk of drought and flood. Composting also turns food waste into new soil.

Urban Agriculture
and Global Warming

There is a globalist plan that has been formulated to create smart cities that are tied to Digital IDs, CBDCs and ESG. The plan focuses on huge, forced reductions in the manufacture and availability of all things consumed by the public living in urban areas. You can download and read The Future of Urban Consumption In a 1.5°C World – C40 Cities Headline Report here: https://bhaktaschool.org/pdfdownload.php?file=Arup-C40-The-Future-of-Urban-Consumption-in-a-1-5C-

World.pdf. This report is mostly about top-down measures dictated by city government mandate that does not include informing or educating the public. It also does not include known, viable alternatives to reducing CO_2 and nitrous oxide emissions in urban environments.

It is possible to grow 100% organic, nutrient dense foods in urban environments by creating community gardens that can even be established in vacant lots and other spaces where there is not soil. In this way, urban agriculture can also remove CO_2 and nitrous oxide from the urban environment in much the same way as described earlier in this section.

Erik Cutter is one of the subjects of the documentary *The Need to Grow* that I mentioned at the beginning of this section. He is a former oncologist who left his practice to create urban agriculture systems that create zero waste and outperform industrial agriculture without the use of toxic chemicals. His is a 2-part system. Using hydroponic vertical towers he has grown 40 plants of produce for every 2 square feet of space. This system uses 90% less water and 50% less fertilizer than industrial/factory farming. To give you an example of the extraordinary yields of this system, Erik grows 10,000 heads of lettuce on 1/10th of an acre of space.

The second part of Cutter's urban agriculture system is what he calls the Organic Soxx system for growing produce anywhere without having to dig down into dirt. This system uses long socks as planters that grow crops using 70% less water. It causes crops to grow 2-1/2 times faster, using 50% less fertilizer. With Organic Soxx gardens produce can be grown anywhere, even in concrete spaces. Imagine the impact on reducing global warming generated by cities if there were these urban agriculture systems all over every city – generating healthy, nutrient dense organic foods at the same time.

Most of our produce, including organic produce that we buy in stores, travels an average of 15,000-20,000 miles from the farm to the store. That is an average of one week to 10 days from the time it is harvested to the time it gets to the store. And then it sits on the shelf until it is purchased. Through Erik Cutter's Urban Farming System, it's farm-to-table in one hour or less.

Bringing Dead Soil Back to Life

Michael Smith is the inventor of the Green Power House. Before dedicating his life to regenerative farming and soil repair, he worked for Walt Disney, NASA and the FBI creating artificial intelligence systems that were used in everything from digital remastering technology to video games and movie animation to simulation systems and 3D printing.

The Green Power House is a house that embodies a system for making biochar, an organic substance that regenerates and repairs dead soil. Biochar is also used to generate electricity that is used in homes. The electricity is a byproduct of the manufacture of Biochar.

Imagine a physical structure that houses a system that generates this magical, organic regenerative substance from a combination of organic matter that converts algae – while completely closing the loop so that there is absolutely no waste matter created in the manufacturing process that then has to be discarded – and no combustion that is then released into the atmosphere. And, at the same time, the manufacturing process itself generates zero greenhouse gases while providing all the electricity needed to power the entire plant. That's the Green Power House.

This genius of an invention creates biochar that is a substance that upregulates plant growth by stimulating roots. Biochar also completely repairs dead soil. Utilizing this closed-loop system that begins with power being generated by the main product, Biochar, *the Green Power House generates more electricity than 3 acres of solar panels, as a byproduct of running the Green Power House.* Again, biochar is created without any combustion, and that is important because this is part of the closed-loop system where there is no waste going into the environment.

Biochar is the infrastructure for soil regeneration. When dead soil is treated with biochar that locks stable carbon into the soil that will remain in the soil for more than 1,000 years. One Green Power House stabilizes over 1 ton of carbon every day by trapping it deep down into the soil. It takes roughly 50,000 trees to do the very same thing that the Biochar does. The reason why this is such an important point is because trees store carbon in the roots, so this is another recommended method for reducing climate change: to plant a lot of trees. The problem is that takes time, and trees take awhile to grow.

The Green Power House converts algae that, when combined with Biochar, creates a natural fertilizer that regenerates the soil even if the soil is dead. Through this process, it takes 4 or 5 days to accomplish what other forms of organic regenerative farming take at least a month to accomplish.

The methane that is produced by the Green Power House is used to power the machinery that creates the Biochar so that it doesn't escape into the atmosphere. Methane is used as fuel, to power the breakdown of the wood matter into Biochar and it is used as fuel to power the mechanism that reduces the wood to Biochar. The methane never escapes into the atmosphere. It is part of the closed-loop power system.

Once this combination of Biochar and algae is used to regenerate the soil, it allows the soil to absorb CO_2 and nitrous oxide from the environment. CO_2 and nitrous oxide are the two major components of greenhouse gases. With Biochar, something that could take Nature decades to accomplish can be done in a matter of days. We need this system replicated everywhere on the planet. The reason you don't hear about The Green Power House and the reason governments everywhere are not financing the building of these units all over the planet is due to regulatory capture.

Billions of dollars each year are made on the sale of synthetic fertilizer alone. Then there are more billions made on the sale of the glyphosate feed that is used in the factory farming of animals. Big Agra doesn't care about killing soil, animals or humans. Nor do they care about the toxic pesticides like glyphosate that they make even more billions on that are known to cause cancers of all kinds in animals and humans.

Even after successfully being sued in numerous court cases over their products causing cancer and numerous deaths, they continue to make and sell their toxic products. This is so because they have a huge, legal war chest set aside for litigation that does not even begin to impact their bottom line. That's how much money they make – and enough money to bribe government officials through campaign financing and lobbying.

The other challenge is that many elected government officials are not properly educated in the available, non-toxic methods that are also much more effective in agriculture. We, the people, have to educate them. Pay close attention to the plan discussed in Chapter 8.

Plant A Lot of Trees

In addition to the use of Biochar, trees are a very good means to reduce global warming. Trees soak up carbon and trap the carbon in the roots. The carbon does not escape into the atmosphere. By planting a lot trees, particularly in and around urban areas and big cities, we can reduce carbon emissions to a great degree. [61,62,63,64,65,66,67] Deforestation is a challenge that must be addressed. For every tree that is cut down, two should be planted. Rather than having government pressure to establish the current ESG policies as law, we the people can pressure our lawmakers to pass laws that protect forests and trees in urban areas against deforestation through carefully executed plans to plant trees.

To Sum It All Up

The Malthusian notion that global warming is an immanent threat to life on Earth due to overpopulation is false and has been debunked over and over again. The notion that humans are the cause of climate change (anthropogenic causes) is not entirely true. At least 70% of global warming is a direct result of industrial/factory farming that causes carbon to escape into the atmosphere as carbon dioxide and nitrous oxide, while killing the soil.

Carbon dioxide emissions from gas-powered vehicles and methane from cow farts and gas stoves may represent no more than 15% of the total cause of global warming. In fact, the processes used to manufacture EV batteries, any lithium-ion batteries, solar panels, wind farms and digital, smart cities – each claimed to be saviors to reduce global warming – all rely on fossil fuel power to be manufactured. When taken in total, this represents an even greater percentage of greenhouse gas emissions than those from gas-powered vehicles, methane from cow farts and methane emissions from gas stoves. Furthermore, nobody is talking about the large amounts of methane emissions created by the processing of wastewater connected to sewage.

Bill Gates, a notorious whack job who has paid people to promote him as a genius, is now promoting and financing companies that make food out of bugs. Gates wants us to eat bugs in order to reduce the world's dependency on meat, particularly red meat and pork. The idea is that, if people everywhere eat bugs, there will be less need for cows and pigs, thereby reducing methane emissions (and also putting small farmers out of business). Less farmers on the planet, particularly smaller farming operations, will place the control of the world's food supply in the hands of genetic engineering companies who want to replace healthy, nutrient dense organic foods with their GMO products.

It is my feeling, based on observation and research, that any top down measures by government, in collaboration with corporate conglomerates to force people to stop eating meat is anti-Liberty, anti-Freedom and focused on the elimination of choice and our God-given rights. Let the people decide how they want to eat and what to eat.

Furthermore, there is no one set of ways to address climate change threats and we live on an exceedingly abundant planet that is not now and has never been threatened by population growth (more about this in the next chapter). What we need now is to advocate for open scientific debate on climate, in conferences that are open to the public, that are independent of government and corporate financing.

The United Nations Development Program (UNDP) has become a political organization engaged in socialist aims, based on big government that is globalized. UNDP has formalized a plan known as Agenda21 for achieving this aim. To better understand this, I strongly encourage you to download and read *A Guide to Understanding the Hoax of the Century. Thirteen ways of looking at disinformation.* You can download this eBook here by placing this link in your web browser. https://bhaktaschool.org/pdfdownload.php?file=A Guide to Understanding the Hoax of the Century-Tablet Magazine.pdf

Any government that is a signatory to UNDP's Agenda21, is focused on passing laws to force us to drive electric vehicles, to outlaw our gas stoves and force small farmers out of business. *That's because ESG is not intended to save the planet from global warming and climate change.* ESG is a political movement to ensure that government and the wealthy elite get more and more socio-economic control of the masses everywhere. In this regard, they are using China and the CCP as the model for this and are openly praising China's form of governance.

It is essential that the public become fully educated and informed on climate change and global warming in a way that is not subject to the political narratives of the day. It is also essential that we demand that government be transparent in providing information about climate change, without any attempts to coerce or force us into top-down measures of any kind.

What to Do About It

1. **It is imperative that you get involved in advocating for your freedom, human rights and civil liberties** by

262 DHARMA AND THE PRESERVATION OF LIBERTY

contacting your elected officials to let them know how you feel and what you want.

In matters like those discussed in this chapter, it is best that you take a group of like-minded people and meet with the elected officials in your district face-to-face. Often, they will meet with you in your district, or you can schedule a meeting and travel to their office. Start with your state representatives, as there is a lot the states can do to pass laws that prevent any ESG encroachment by the Federal government. If you don't live in the U.S., start with the elected officials in your province or parliament. For more about how to go about this, see Chapter 8.

2. **If you live in America, you can follow the documentation, data and activities of the U.S. Sovereignty Coalition**, a group of U.S. congressional elected officials who have formed this coalition to push back on globalist measures, of which ESG is a part. You can view their website here: https://sovereigntycoalition.org/.

3. **Watch the video** *Soft Coup, Hard Tyranny: Spawning Global Governance* for more insights and action items. https://rumble.com/v3jo44k-webinar-soft-coup-hard-tyranny-spawning-global-governance-on-september-20.html

4. **Use this link to sign an email petition that will automatically send notice to the elected officials in the U.S. Congress in your district**, as well as the White House to stop the global tyranny associated with ESG and other measures. https://stopvaxpassports.org/take-action-stop-global-tyranny/

After submitting the notice, it is best to then follow up with those elected officials by way of a phone call and email to emphasize the message in the notice.

MUST WATCH: Climate the Movie: The Cold Truth
https://bhaktaschool.org/climate-change-and-the-cold-truth/

Additional information and data relevant to this chapter can be found here: https://bhaktaschool.org/dharma-and-the-preservation-of-liberty/

Chapter 7
The Growing Attack
On Our Liberty
Censorship of Free Speech

"If freedom of speech is taken away, then dumb and silent we may be led, like sheep to the slaughter."
~ *George Washington*

I may not agree with what you say and I may find what you say to be vulgar, abusive, stupid or dangerous. But I will always advocate in defense of your right to say it. Also, as much as I dislike it, hate speech is free speech. If you don't like what you are viewing, hearing or reading and something being said upsets you, you can walk away, you can turn the page, put the book down, stop the video, click out of the web page or change the channel. You have the freedom to do that. You also have the freedom to voice your concerns or upset directly to the person or organization speaking. You also have the right to voice your own opinion about something that someone else has said, including decrying what someone else has said. You can also file a harassment lawsuit against anyone who you feel is using hate speech to harass you (in a free society, that's what the courts are for).

We all have these freedoms. The reason we have them is that, in most free countries, there are constitutions and/or other laws that protect our free speech. In fact, free speech is the cornerstone of any free society where Liberty and the function of a free democratic society are protected.

Allowing government, corporations and other institutions (including, in some cases, social media platforms) to begin regulating hate speech is a recipe for tyranny. Who gets to decide what hate speech is? If governments get to decide then any form of speech the government doesn't like will be deemed "hate speech," including any form of speech in dissent of how the government operates. Once we allow this to happen we will have the kind of tyranny that is prevalent in China where any form of speech that the government feels is unacceptable is punishable by a reduced social credit score, fines, imprisonment and even death. In another example, recently, the EU passed a law that allows the EU government to censor anyone for what it deems hate speech and misinformation. I strongly encourage you to view the David Thunder interview by The Epoch Times in which he reviews the written law to uncover how vague their definition of hate speech and misinformation is. You can view the video here: https://www.theepochtimes.com/epochtv/is-eu-censorship-coming-to-america-heres-what-you-need-to-know-david-thunder-5535769

In the United States, the First Amendment to the U.S. Constitution, which is the highest law of the land in America, guarantees the American citizenry the right to free speech. This is also the case in other countries across the globe like the UK (UK Human Rights Act of 1998) where free speech is mostly protected. However, with the growth of collectivism/globalism across the world, the protection of free speech is being eroded rapidly. The ultimate aim of this calculated erosion of free speech is to convince you that you cannot be trusted with your own mind. This is the premise on which the collectivists/globalists are acting.

In this regard the attacks on free speech in America over the last four decades, and especially as a result of the COVID-19 pandemic, have led myself and others whom I associate with to begin calling this country the United States of China. In fact, with respect to the destruction of free speech, America is looking more and more like China every day. And so are many other parts of the world with regard to freedom of speech.

Permanently Banned

As I have stated earlier in this book, I hold degrees in Eastern and Oriental Medicine and had a practice in New York City for fifteen years. In that time I helped people completely heal from cancer, heart disease, diabetes, lung infections, kidney failure and liver disease. I did so using natural, alternative therapies that included little or no pharmaceutical medications of any kind. I was well trained in many natural healing modalities that included cellular nutrition, acupuncture, herbal medicine and lifestyle medicine.

85% of my clients were completely cured of their illnesses. I tracked clients' progress over a minimum period of 5-7 years to ascertain if there were any relapses of illness. In addition, I have logged over 20,000 hours of additional study in biology, microbiology and cellular biology. I have interfaced with more than 175 medical doctors, researchers, epidemiologists and virologists, some of whom I have developed personal friendships with.

In March of 2020, in response to the declared COVID-19 pandemic, my staff and I wrote and published a book, *The Coronavirus Era; What You Need to Know and How to Prepare for What Is Coming Next.* This book was revised and republished in late 2021. This book was a result of our ongoing contact and discussion with frontline doctors who were treating patients infected with SARS-CoV-2, and our contact with researchers and statisticians who were blowing the whistle on inflated Covid hospitalizations and death counts.

At that time, our school had accounts on Vimeo, Youtube, X (formerly Twitter) and Facebook. After publication of this book we started to make posts and videos of our published findings in these accounts. Within a month of doing so, all of these accounts were shut down. We have since been permanently banned from each.

In every case, we were told that our posting information about inexpensive, effective therapies, like Ivermectin and Hydroxychloroquine for treating Covid constituted misinformation. We were accused of misleading the public and, potentially, causing harm to people, even though all of the information in our presentations was backed by early peer-reviewed studies on Covid treatment, along with video interviews and written statements from medical professionals who were successfully treating patients with these repurposed drugs.

Since the early 1990s, there has been a rise in what can only be referred to as the censorship industrial complex. This expansion of censorship began after the passage in the U.S. of the National Childhood Vaccine Injury Act of 1986. This law releases vaccine manufacturers from any and all liability for damage done by their vaccine products (see Barbara Loe Fisher, Chapter 2).

As the parents of vaccine injured children and the doctors who treat them began to speak out publicly about vaccine injury and the inadequacy of the Vaccine Adverse Events Reporting System (VAERS) and vaccine court, the censorship industrial complex went into

268 DHARMA AND THE PRESERVATION OF LIBERTY

overdrive to censor parents and to vilify medical professionals, researchers and anyone else speaking out about vaccine injury. Doctors who spoke out publicly had their medical licenses revoked permanently. Parents who questioned doctor's recommendations that their child get the vaccines on the CDC vaccination schedule were told to leave their offices.

This can fully be understood in a report, *Blacklisting and Censorship Violates Freedom of Thought, Speech and Conscience* presented by Barbara Loe Fisher who runs the National Vaccine Information Center. You can view a video about this important report here: https://rumble.com/v3rwot4-blacklisting-and-censorship-violates-freedom-of-thought-speech-and-conscien.html. And you can read the entire report here: https://www.nvic.org/newsletter/nov-2023/censorship-violates-freedom

During and after the Covid pandemic, censorship by world governments has increased exponentially.

Covid Censorship

A month after we were banned for publishing our Corona Virus Era book, we found out that Representative Adam Schiff who, at that time, was the chairman of the U.S. House Intelligence Committee, had sent letters to all of the Big Tech companies urging them to halt the spread of misinformation and disinformation during the pandemic by actively censoring free speech on their platforms. [1,2]

Less than a year prior, Adam Schiff sent a letter to Google and Facebook expressing his concern over declining vaccination rates in America, and urging them to take action to address any anti-vaccine information posted on their platforms. [3]

Of course, these two incidences are connected. And it makes one wonder how much Adam Schiff knew about the looming pandemic back in February of 2019 when the above-stated letter was sent, and when a pandemic had not yet been declared. The other point is that Adam Schiff made this a covert intelligence matter. In a related incident, information about the potential risks of the Covid shots that was based on people being injured by them, along with information about the effectiveness of Ivermectin in treating Covid was combined into a book by Dr. Joseph Mercola. Due to high sales of the book, it topped Amazon's search results for COVID-19.

Rep. Adam Schiff and Senator Elizabeth Warren sent letters to Amazon complaining about the book and vilifying both Amazon and Dr. Mercola for the book's high sales and its presenting Ivermectin as a treatment for Covid. [4] They called the book a hoax and demanded to know what Amazon's misinformation policies were and to what degree Amazon was taking steps to silence people like Dr. Mercola. They also claimed that, because the book promoted Ivermectin for treatment of Covid, that its recommendations were killing people, even though they could not present a single shred of evidence that Ivermectin used to treat Covid killed anyone. This was just another call to censorship.

In fact, over the three years of the COVID-19 pandemic Ivermectin has been shown over and over again to be both an effective prophylaxis for COVID-19 infection and a cure for it. Please refer to Chapters 2 and 3 for the information presented on this fact.

Free Speech Is Now Hate Speech

Whenever a government gets involved in controlling the speech of others anywhere, whether it be on or offline, tyranny and rule by dictatorship is at hand. The above-stated steps taken by Rep. Adam Schiff and the Democratic Party led to the formation of government censorship by proxy in the formation of two organizations that are actively engaged in censoring free speech. The first is the Center for Countering Digital Hate (CCDH), based in the UK, and the second is CISA, the Cybersecurity and Infrastructure Security Agency that is part of the Department of Homeland Security in the U.S.

CCDH was behind the campaign against what it called the Disinformation Dozen. CCDH, and later, President Biden, created a huge, worldwide media campaign stating that 12 people were responsible for most of the misinformation and disinformation being generated about COVID-19 alternative treatments to the Covid shots and vaccine injury from the Covid shots. President Biden even held a press conference in which he stated that these 12 people were responsible for killing people. [5]

Murder requires an investigation into deaths and who committed the crimes. Then people have to be indicted and court has to be convened. Guilt is usually determined based on trials and the outcomes of those trials. Even then, the courts don't always get it right. So, to make such a statement, particularly coming out of the mouth of the President of the United States, is not only foolish but dangerous to the public welfare. The fact is, Biden made this claim based on information he was fed by CCDH.

Here is the list of the disinformation dozen.
1. Dr. Joseph Mercola, https://www.mercola.com/
2. Robert F. Kennedy Jr.
https://childrenshealthdefense.org/
https://therealrfkjrmovie.com/trailer1/

3. Ty & Charlene Bollinger, https://thetruthaboutcancer.com/
4. Dr. Sherri Tenpenny, https://drtenpenny.com/
5. Rizza Islam, http://intellectualones.org/
6. Dr. Rashid Buttar, https://www.centersforadvancedmedicine.com/
7. Erin Elizabeth, https://healthnutnews.com/
8. Sayer Ji, https://greenmedinfo.com/
9. Dr. Kelly Brogan, https://www.kellybroganmd.com/
10. Dr. Christiane Northrup, https://www.drnorthrup.com/
11. Dr. Ben Tapper, https://rumble.com/vxptru-must-watch-the-time-is-now-2021-documentary.html
12. Kevin Jenkins, https://childrenshealthdefense.org/authors/kevin-jenkins/

I've given you web links to their information to encourage you to visit their web sites, review their information and presentations and decide for yourself if they are murderers. The truth is these twelve were singled out, not just because of how outspoken they are, but because they have large followings online and their publications and products sellout. CCDH has repeatedly violated UK rules of law and is now refusing to cooperate with a U.S. Congressional inquiry. [6]

It's important to understand government censorship by proxy. In the U.S., we have a Constitution that protects our right to free speech under the First Amendment. Because this is the case, government in America cannot violate free speech. However, businesses can. With rulings that started in 2010, the U.S. Supreme Court decided that corporations are people with the right to free speech and certain religious rights, as well. This is why Big Tech platforms like Facebook, Google, X, Vimeo and Instagram can legally edit or delete your posts, based on their user policy. This includes banning you for statements that you make that they decide violate their user policy, which they can update at any time. This is why U.S. Congress members Adam Schiff and Elizabeth Warren sent letters to these platforms urging them to crack down on our free speech. Government can't violate our free speech but corporations can.

Censorship By Proxy

Although this has always been the case, the act of government colluding with corporations and, in this case, Big Tech, to censor speech online has grown dramatically since the start of the COVID-19 pandemic. And, it is against the law in the U.S., as delineated in the First Amendment of the U.S. Constitution. In the U.S., this has become mass censorship of everyone who does not speak in alignment with the official government narrative. Enter CISA. The Cybersecurity and Infrastructure Security Agency that functions as a branch of the Department of Homeland Security is an intelligence agency that was established to monitor online speech that might indicate the formation of terrorist plots against the U.S. government.

During the COVID-19 pandemic, President Biden opened a discussion with Democrats in Congress over the fact that Covid shot uptake has flatlined, as more and more people are deciding against taking the shots and the boosters. This has resulted in a proposal to use CISA to monitor our text messages, and to use 'fact-checkers' to dispel vaccine misinformation about the Covid shots. [7] America is getting more and more like China.

In addition, Biden has ordered the FBI to classify Donald Trump and his Make American Great Again (MAGA) supporters as domestic terrorists. [8,9] I am not a Trump supporter but I am against these kinds of censorship efforts. In this case, clearly Biden is using the FBI to smear his political opponent and to silence his opponent's supporters. To classify a portion of the voting public as terrorists for the purpose of denying their free speech and support of a political opponent is disgusting behavior for a President of the U.S. and any department he oversees. We, the people, have to put a stop to it.

In documents released by the House Select Subcommittee on the Weaponization of the Federal Government, it is shown that Facebook was pressured by President Biden to restrict online searches of certain media outlets deemed undesirable, and to deplatform users deemed undesirable by his administration. The statement he made to Facebook was "Kick people off." [10] In a court case brought against Big Tech in this regard, a Federal judge has ruled that President Biden likely violated the First Amendment during the COVID-19 pandemic. Google, Meta and X are all named in the lawsuit. [11,12,13] Biden got a temporary stay against the judge's order to halt this government censorship in order to prepare a defense. This case is going to the U.S. Supreme Court.

In addition, Biden told his administration to push Attorney General Merrick Garland to issue a controversial memo to "intimidate parents" against speaking out against leftist policies in schools and at school board meetings. You can view the article that broke this news here: https://www.theepochtimes.com/us/biden-admin-put-pressure-on-garland-to-intimidate-parents-conservative-legal-group-5554592

But it doesn't stop there. Even though Facebook is named in the above-mentioned court order and ensuing case, Meta, the parent company of Facebook has hired a former CIA agent to head up its election

274 DHARMA AND THE PRESERVATION OF LIBERTY

censorship division ahead of the upcoming 2024 elections. Meta's election censorship division is designed to do just what its title says: Censor posts to allow Meta to control the election narrative and Facebook/Instagram searches for election information. [14]

The House Select Subcommittee on the Weaponization of the Federal Government

The House Select Subcommittee On the Weaponization of the Federal Government is engaged in ongoing hearings on the behavior of the U.S. Federal Government that violates the U.S. Constitution and our human rights and civil liberties. A portion of these hearings have been dedicated to examining the censorship engaged in by the U.S. Federal Government in violation of the First Amendment. Robert F. Kennedy, Jr. was one of several people invited to give testimony to the subcommittee and testified in a session that was broadcast live on the internet. You can watch the video of the hearing that contains Robert F. Kennedy, Jr.'s testimony here: https://www.youtube.com/watch?v=WRPezfR_jIY. The hearing footage begins at about 18 minutes into the video recording. I watched the hearing live.

If you don't know, Robert F. Kennedy, Jr. is one of the most censored people in America, primarily due to his activities as an attorney who has litigated many court cases against corporate environmental polluters, as well as, Big Pharma (for vaccines that have not been properly safety tested and have injured millions of people). Big Pharma has consistently targeted him as a quack in mainstream media and online, simply because he has used compelling evidence to repeatedly blow the whistle on them.

In his testimony before the committee he spoke a great deal about government censorship of all his activities and provided the subcommittee with compelling examples. In turn, the Republican subcommittee members asked him questions while the Democratic subcommittee members made statements attempting to embarrass him and frame him as an idiot, and to frame the subcommittee as a sham.

Censor the Censorship Hearing

In an attempt to get him disinvited from these hearings, Rep. Stacey Plaskett accused Robert F. Kennedy, Jr. of being a racist. This accusation was also made in a letter to Rep. Jim Jordan who chairs the House Select Subcommittee On the Weaponization of the Federal Government. I strongly encourage you to view this 9-minute clip on Bobby Kennedy's response where he talks about the necessity to stop trying to tear each other down and, instead, to be willing to engage in healthy, open debate with people who we don't agree with. You can view it here: https://www.youtube.com/watch?v=GEAm21alji0

The purpose of the letter I mentioned above was to convince the chair, Rep. Jim Jordan, to disinvite Robert F. Kennedy, Jr. from the hearings. It was sent by the Executive Director of the Congressional Integrity Project. Here is the letter in its entirety.

July 16, 2023

The Honorable Jim Jordan
Chairman, House Select Subcommittee on the
Weaponization of the Federal Government

2138 Rayburn House Office Building
Washington, DC 20515

Dear Chairman Jordan:

I'm writing to formally call on you to disinvite Robert F. Kennedy, Jr. from next week's so-called weaponization of the federal government hearing. Not only is he a known conspiracy theorist whose anti-vaccine views have put lives in jeopardy, a Russian propagandist who has sided with Putin over Ukraine, and a total whack job whose views and conspiracy theories would be completely ignored but for his last name, but we now have video evidence of his horrific anti-Semitic and xenophobic views which are simply beyond the pale.

We know because we track and respond to your work that nearly every investigation you've embarked upon to hurt President Biden, help Donald Trump and play the victim on some fanciful "weaponization" of the government against conservatives has blown up in your face. You've proved nothing against President Biden. You've proved nothing on the nonsense conspiracy theory of weaponization of social media or the government against conservatives. Your so-called whistleblowers have been exposed as crazy conspiracy theorists, disgruntled employees or former employees, and January 6th insurrection sympathizers.

And now you're desperate. Your MAGA cult leader Donald Trump expects you to deliver and you and your friend James Comer have failed spectacularly every step of the way. And now you think having Robert F. Kennedy, Jr. testify in support of your debunked theories will somehow own President Biden and the Democrats – but in reality all you're doing is proving to all the world what a desperate man you are.

But maybe we shouldn't be surprised that you invited him to testify. This is all part of the same anti-Semitic pattern from you and your fellow House Republicans. Should you require more examples of the damning evidence showing that providing Robert F. Kennedy, Jr. with a platform at a Congressional hearing is dangerous, inappropriate, and insulting, we stand ready to assist you.

Sincerely,
Kyle Herrig,
Executive Director
Congressional Integrity Project
80 M Street SE
Washington, DC 20003

What!? Well, clearly the guy didn't write the letter to get his aim considered by the chairman. And this is the problem with how lobbyists in Washington think and act. Again, I encourage you to view the video of the hearing with Robert F. Kennedy, Jr. so you can decide for yourself if Robert F. Kennedy, Jr. is a whack job.

Big Pharma's Control of Mainstream Media

Big Pharma spends billions of dollars each year on TV, radio, newspaper and online advertising for its products. If you don't believe this, start counting the number of ads for Pharma medications that you see while watching TV, while playing free music on the internet, while flipping through legacy media newspapers or watching free Internet programming for which you are paying the vendor not to be shown ads on channels like YouTube. In fact, there are more Pharma ads for medications than there are car ads.

However, what you may not know is that when a company like a broadcast network, for example, agrees to take money from Big Pharma in return for advertising, the company has to sign a contract that guarantees to Big Pharma that the company will not run ads that Pharma deems as competing with ads about its products. The company accepting Big Pharma ads also has to agree that it will not air any programs, statements or other broadcasts that Pharma deems as damaging to its products and reputation. Otherwise, Pharma pulls its advertising and, in some cases, will bring a lawsuit against that company for violation of contract. In essence, Big Pharma has captured mainstream media.

This amounts to mainstream media censorship and false reporting, at the behest of Big Pharma. For example, this is why, during the COVID-19 pandemic, mainstream media did not report on the effective, inexpensive treatments for Covid like Ivermectin and Hydroxychloroquine. It's why there was no mainstream media coverage of the vaccine injuries being caused by the Covid shots and it's why, other than the Tucker Carlson show on Fox, there were no mainstream media interviews of people questioning the official government narrative on the pandemic and the origins of the pandemic. In fact, Tucker Carlson resigned from Fox News due to the pressure he was under to stop running the new reports he presented on his show. The truth is, Big Pharma has been working to censor mainstream media for many decades, and has also gotten support from the U.S. Federal government to do so.

Commercial Banks Jump On the Censorship Bandwagon

Banks in the United States and the UK are closing people's bank accounts and even debanking the accounts of their family members and associates. These accounts are being closed due to the political and social views of the account holders, not due to financial issues with their accounts. Debanking increased during the COVID-19 pandemic and continues to increase as some banks adopt ESG scoring methods (see next chapter). In the U.S., Dr. Joseph Mercola, one of the listed disinformation dozen, had all of his Chase accounts suddenly closed without warning. Chase bank also closed the accounts of all his family members, his employees and some of his associates. Dr. Mercola believes that this happened due to his outspoken stance against Covid shots. [15]

In the UK, former member of the United Kingdom Independence Party, Nigel Farage, was debanked for his political views. And he's not the only one. [16] Censorship, either directly or by proxy has become popular and we are likely to see more of it, particularly with the growing implementation of the ESG/DEI scam that is now being perpetuated by the wealthy elite, in partnership with Big business and governments around the world.

China's Censorship Machine Is Spreading

In China all media is censored by the Chinese Communist Party (CCP). This includes all internet access and all internet content. In a recent development, as of August of 2023, the European Union

(EU) passed the Digital Services Act, or DSA. This law obliges "Very Large Online Platforms" or VLOPs, to speedily remove illegal content, hate speech and so-called disinformation from their platforms. If not, they risk fines of up to 6% of their annual global revenue.

The EU has, to date, compiled a list of 19 VLOPs and VLOSEs (Very Large Online Search Engines), most of them from the US, that will have to begin complying with the DSA in 50 days' time. [17] This is dictatorship. And, under this law, who gets to decide what is hate speech and disinformation? The government, of course. How many other governments around the world will attempt to enact such a law and what will the people do to prevent that from happening?

On September 19, 2023, the U.K. passed a new law to "regulate" (read, censor) online content. The so-called Online Safety Bill has been described as "one of the most far-reaching attempts by Western democracy to regulate online speech." The bill has been in the works for the last five years, again proving that online censorship is not something that sprang up in response to Covid. In addition to stricter regulations on pornography and content that promotes suicide and self-harm, "vaccine misinformation" and any other material that may be "harmful to health" is also barred under the bill.

On September 29, 2023, the Canadian Radio-television and Telecommunications Commission (CRTC) also announced all "online streaming services that offer podcasts" must now register and conform to regulatory controls. This full article, along with a video about online censorship, has been posted here: https://tnc.news/2023/10/02/crtc-will-require-podcasts-to-register/.

The reality is that censorship has always been a goal of intelligence agencies around the world, with the most egregious being the U.S. and British intelligence agencies. In fact, from the start, the internet has had a dual purpose, the second of which is to surveil the citizenry in order to execute measures to brainwash the masses and censor anything and everything that goes against how the closed ruling class wants us to think and act.

The people behind the growing censorship on the internet and the plans for using AI to scrub the internet as a brainwashing tool under their control, truly believe that free speech must be destroyed and Liberty severely restricted in order to protect democracy. This, they feel, justifies their breaking the law and undermining constitutional law, human rights and civil liberties. This is Orwell's Ministry of Truth on steroids and their tactics have been weaponized under the management of agencies like the DOD, CIA and NSA. There is only one reason for this behavior, and that is to protect the ruling class from ever being usurped. This is a 100-year plan to be implemented in 15-year segments, based on Agenda21 (Agenda for the 21st Century).

To better understand this, I strongly encourage you to download and read *A Guide to Understanding the Hoax of the Century. Thirteen ways of looking at disinformation,* written by former U.S. Army Intelligence Officer Jacob Siegel. This is a must read to better understand how the U.S. intelligence community in particular uses the internet to surveil and influence thinking, brainwash people, influence election outcomes and censor Americans and other people all over the globe. You can download this eBook here by placing this link in your web browser. https://bhaktaschool.org/pdfdownload.php?file=A Guide to Understanding the Hoax of the Century-Tablet Magazine.pdf

What to Do About It

1. **CCDH is a foreign organization and, as such, its activities in America must be outlawed. In addition, a permanent congressional committee must be established to monitor CISA activities, along with the activities of any like agencies within the Federal Government.** This oversight must take place on a constant basis so that Congress can pass laws to reign in all of their censorship activities as they are being monitored. Pay attention to Chapter 8 for how you can pressure your elected officials to get this done.

2. **In order to protect our free speech, the "deep state," also known as the administrative state within the U.S. Federal Government must be downsized and severely limited in its activities.** This is one of the primary objectives of the Convention of States movement, to call a Convention of States under Article V of the U.S. Constitution. I urge you to find out more about COS and to get involved in supporting the establishment of a Convention of States. Go to https://conventionofstates.com.

3. **Mainstream media is ripe with censorship and sensationalist newscasting that is designed for the purposes of entertainment.** As a result, most of the world's real journalists have left mainstream media for alternative and community media outlets. It is essential that you get your news from sources that are not engaged in censorship, and that report on all sides of a story or debate in an unbiased fashion. In this regard, there are a number of alternative media sources that are worth considering. Here is a partial list.

NTD News
https://www.ntd.com/

The High Wire
thehighwire.com/

The Epoch Times
https://www.theepochtimes.com/

The Solari Report
https://home.solari.com/

The Corbett Report
https://www.corbettreport.com/

Children's Health Defense
https://childrenshealthdefense.org/

In addition, Youtube, Vimeo and Twitter (now X) are all engaged in censorship, often in cooperation with governments, Big Pharma and Big Agra. Here are some platforms where you can find uncensored video presentations that are relevant to the topics discussed in this book, as well as other matters of interest.

https://rumble.com/
https://odysee.com/
https://www.bitchute.com/
https://twitter.com/wideawake_media

4. You are going to have to decide whether or not you want your government taking control of your mind and that of your family and children. If you have children, you are also going to have to decide whether or not you want to co-parent with your government in how your children are raised and what information your children have access to, online and off. If you live in a democratically functioning society with a constitution or other laws that protect free speech, pressure your elected officials at the local, state and federal levels to enact laws that prevent censorship by proxy engaged in by the government. Pay close attention to Chapter 8 for more on how to go about this.

5. **Stop supporting Big Tech platforms that are engaged in censorship by not using those platforms.** These Big Tech platforms farm all of your personal data and sell that data to corporate conglomerates. These corporations examine the data to determine how they can get into your head to brainwash you into buying their products and supporting their ideology. In addition, Big Tech platforms and, in particular, social media are engaged in their own brand of brainwashing. For examples of how this happens we turn to the excellent documentary, *The Social Dilemma*, produced by Netflix and directed by Jeff Orlowski and written by Orlowski, Davis Coombe, and Vickie Curtis [18]

6. **Rather than relying on making posts online to share information on platforms that may censor that information, gather in person to do so.** Community centers are great for this. Find one in your area or start one on your own and invite as many people as possible. You can draft a proposal for issues that you want community meetings to address and discuss that proposal with other people in your community who you will rely on to run the community center with you. Then you can start getting the word out in your community about the center and its purpose. Or, if you attend a church or other spiritual center, these are places where you can gather to have discussions on issues impacting your lives and you community.

One of the greatest challenges in our modern-day society with all of its technology is that, outside of the family unit, people seldom gather in a community setting to discuss and debate issues and to come up with ideas on how to best serve the community while protecting the Liberty of each person. Gathering is an important aspect of sharing our humanity.

7. **Don't accept any piece of news without vetting it yourself.** Abandon any narrative that is based in fearmongering and operates on spreading fear and alarmist views and behavior. Fear is unintelligent and is used to divide and conquer us. So, discard such narratives and reports outright, along with those alarmists who are engaged in them. Always perform your own due diligence on narratives and reports that may impact your daily existence, your God-given rights and your Liberty. You can start with the many references in this book. Also, pay attention to Chapter 8 regarding steps you can take to overcome any fear of interacting with and managing your elected officials.

8. **Download and read** *A Guide to Understanding the Hoax of the Century. Thirteen ways of looking at disinformation,* written by former U.S. Army Intelligence Officer Jacob Siegel. This is a must read to better understand how the U.S. intelligence community uses the internet to surveil and influence thinking, brainwash people, influence election outcomes and censor Americans and other people all over the globe. You can download this eBook here: https://bhaktaschool.org/pdfdownload.php?file=A Guide to Understanding the Hoax of the Century-Tablet Magazine.pdf

Additional information and data relevant to this chapter can be found here: https://bhaktaschool.org/dharma-and-the-preservation-of-liberty/

Chapter 8
Our Duty to Preserve Life, Liberty and the Pursuit of Happiness by Reforming Government

This is not the government's world. This world has been entrusted to us – the people. This is God's world, imbued with God's nature. *Therefore, in the end, righteousness will prevail here.* Dharma is executed in recognition and glorification of this fact. And it's not up to government. It's up to us. We are responsible and whatever government we get is a reflection of us, we the people.

Many spiritual traditions speak of Dharma. Dharma is the act of loving the Truth more than mundane life itself. Many of those who have gone before us lived by this principle. And many of those who did so gave their lives so that we can have Liberty under God.

Our Liberty has been gradually eroded over the past century. This has been done, primarily with our help. For example, the majority of citizens in America do not know what their rights are. They have not read and studied the United States Constitution or their state's Constitution. If you don't know what your rights are, in many cases, they are already gone.

Earlier in this book I put a spotlight on the fact that America has become a socialist country and is now turning into what some call a hybrid of socialism, fascism and communism. Socialism in America has most certainly been established economically. This has been easy for the wealthy elite to accomplish, due to the fact that the majority of American citizens don't know much about money, where it comes from and where it goes, let alone how (see Chapter 5).

It is a matter of great misfortune for the American people that the Constitution, along with money and economics, is not taught in grade school. Unless you go to college to get a degree in economics or constitutional law, you may go through your entire life without knowing much about these. The wealthy elite and government have used this fact to gradually and systematically destroy our rights and control our livelihoods. With Covid-19, the rest of the plan, that includes controlling our bodies, is now in play (see Chapter 2).

What Are You Prepared to Do?

Our Liberty is rotting away at the hands of megalomaniacs like Bill Gates and Anthony Fauci, and sycophants like President Joe Biden and others in our state and federal legislatures who are career politicians rather than public servants and states people. The Federal government in America is far too large and presidents are acting like kings rather than servants of our Liberty. This is the oath all elected U.S. Presidents take when being sworn into office. It is the same oath that President Biden took: "I do solemnly swear that I will faithfully execute the Office of President of the United States, and will to the best of my ability, preserve, protect and defend the Constitution of the United States."

Addressing the public recently, POTUS Biden displayed his mental incompetence and lack of knowledge of the foundational principles of the U.S. Constitution that he took an oath to uphold when he mocked the Declaration of Independence on which our great nation is founded. [1] He said; "We hold these truths to be self-evident. All men and women created by co you know you know the thing." Then, at a meeting in the Oval office [2,3], he stated: "The Constitution is always evolving slightly in terms of additional rights or curtailing rights." The fact is The United States Constitution is not a living, breathing document. It was conceived out of the experience of more than 700 years of tyranny under British rule, and the only way it can be changed is by constitutional amendment. Therefore, it is not an ever-evolving document. Our Constitution has always been and still is the highest law in the land. And Joe Biden is not the only President of the U.S. to violate it. In fact, the three Presidents before Biden did the same and there have been others before them.

On April 15, 2022, Biden signed an Executive Order to block property rights and use 'with Respect to Specified Harmful Foreign Activities of the Government of the Russian Federation.' [4,5] This Executive Order is not about Russia. It is actually designed to allow the Biden administration the ability to violate the property rights of American citizens and organizations. The order allows for arbitrarily linking those persons to real, imagined, or vaguely defined activities of the Russian government.

In fact, there is an unprecedented attack on our Constitution by President Biden who has consistently violated his oath of office. Surprisingly, although there has been a response from some mainstream media outlets, as yet, not a single state or federal legislator has called Biden out on his bashing of our Constitution.

Of course, the Covid-19 plandemic and the attempted plandemic that followed around monkey pox (for which there were mock events similar to Event 201 held in March of 2021 [6,7,8,9]) are clear examples of how government and the wealthy elite are scheming to destroy our Constitution using plandemics to enforce compliance. *It is a fact that, if we allow government to break the law and violate our Constitution in states of emergency, they will create states of emergency in order to break the law.*

Every time we comply with an unconstitutional mandate, executive order or law, we are setting the stage for a future where our children will not have the option of non-compliance. If we refuse to comply, a golden age awaits us, if we are willing to take full responsibility for our governance. Therefore, we must refuse to comply with any mandate, order or law that is unconstitutional.

The Constitution of The United States of America

"Any society that will give up a little liberty to gain a little security will deserve neither and lose both."
~ *Benjamin Franklin*

Today, our constitutional rights are under willful attack by a federal government that we have allowed to get far too big, and a President who we allow to act as a king, rather than a servant of the people. One example of many under Covid, related to coercing people to take Covid shots that do not prevent infection or transmission, and that have been proved to be gene therapy that alters DNA, is the blatant violation of our constitutional right to free speech by President Biden.

Biden has colluded with the CDC in a coordinated effort to get Big Tech to censor American citizens while only publishing the propaganda issued by the Federal government [10]. This censorship has included censoring the growing number of injuries and

290 DHARMA AND THE PRESERVATION OF LIBERTY

deaths from the Covid shots and other shots on the childhood and adult vaccine schedules.

Emails between the CDC and Big Tech firms support this fact. You can read the email trail between the CDC and Big Tech to further understand this betrayal of our free speech [11,12]. You can also download a complete copy of these emails here: https://bhaktaschool.org/pdfdownload.php?file=CDC-Emails-to-Big-Tech.pdf. The Biden Administration is currently being sued over these blatant violations of our free speech [13].

Again, government is always a reflection of the people who are governed. Therefore, we always get the government we deserve, based on that reflection. In the United States of America, the majority of the citizenry don't even know what kind of government we have. They are entrenched in the notion that the Federal government is the governing body of the American people and has the final say on how we are ruled.

The importance of understanding the difference between being ruled and being served will become blatantly clear shortly. The fact is, based on the U.S. Constitution, the States are above the Federal government and hold the majority of authority with respect to governance. The powers delegated to the Federal government are few and defined. *And delegated does not mean surrendered.* Today, the U.S. Federal government is far too large and has become the very thing that the framers of our Constitution intended to prevent by its adoption. They knew from experience that too much centralized authority always leads to the corruption of greed. Tyranny follows.

The United States of America (where I currently live) is a Constitutional Republic. Although it may function on democratic principles, America *is not* a democracy. Based on the highest law in the land, our

Constitution, government has been established for one reason only: to protect and serve our God-given, unalienable rights. Specifically, our Constitution has been established *to protect the minority from the will of the majority.*

Such a government under the Constitution of these United Sates is established by the people for this purpose. This is why we are not a democracy because, in democracies, the will of the majority becomes the law for the minority, as well. In such a scenario, Liberty cannot be upheld and protected. Liberty is defined by the framers of our Constitution as the intersection of freedom and morality. Freedom cannot embody immorality for, without morality, there is tyranny.

The U.S. Constitution provides for the protection of Liberty based on the proclamation that *our rights come from God, not from government.* Did you get this? I'll say it again. The U.S. Constitution provides for the protection of Liberty based on the proclamation that the rights of the people come from God, not from government. Indeed, the framers of our Constitution were God-centered people.

So, the first essential step is for the American citizenry to study, understand and know the Constitution of these United States. As part of reading and knowing the Constitution, it is very useful to also read the Federalist and Anti-Federalist papers which elucidate the clear intention of the framers of the Constitution in its creation, chapter and verse. You can purchase both a copy of the U.S. Constitution and the Federalist and Anti-Federalist papers online for about $12-$15 total.

Because the Constitution is not a teaching document, it is essential that you read the Federalist and Anti-Federalist papers to understand the "Why" of the edicts of the Constitution. I also recommend, if you are a citizen of the U. S., that you visit libertyfirstsociety.com. You can subscribe to get access to very valuable lessons on our Constitution with excellent commentary by KrisAnne Hall.

Government Has To Be Managed By The Citizenry

If you were the owner of a business, in order to ensure that your business runs successfully, you would have to properly manage your employees. It is the same with government. So, the second essential step is for the citizenry to properly manage its property, because the U.S. government, on the local, State and Federal levels, is the property of the people – Us. We own the government and its' only purpose is to protect our Liberty.

The wealthy elite and the government bureaucrats who they bribe want to establish one world government under their control. To accomplish this, they are attempting to get the citizenry and legislators to ignore the U.S. Constitution through planned panic. So, don't embrace or engage in planned panic.

Also understand that there is a difference between politics and citizen responsibility. Citizen responsibility for monitoring, managing and changing our government is an absolute necessity if we are to destroy the tyranny that is becoming entrenched in the United States of America.

As an introduction to the next section, remember that there are 50 independent sovereign states in the Union of the United States and, according to our Constitution, the President is not a king and has less authority than the Governor of a state. Now, on to the answer to all of the challenges presented in the previous chapters that we now need to address.

The Liberty Action Council Plan

Fear does not stop death. It stops Life. And worrying does not take away tomorrow's troubles. It robs you of today's peace.

As defined by the framers of the U.S. Constitution, Liberty is the intersection of freedom and morality. This is an essential definition because Liberty is not Liberty if you engage your Liberty by trampling on the Liberty of another. It's time for a revolution to re-establish Liberty in America. This is a Spiritual Revolution. There is now an individual and a collective responsibility of the citizenry to end the corruption of greed that has infected the U.S. government and impacted the lives of people everywhere in America and beyond. And the only real solution is to reform government. This reform must be led by the people, and the time is Now.

Let Justice Be Done
Though the Heavens Fall

Liberty is not free. *It must be protected by keeping our foot firmly on the neck of government.* We are told that Benjamin Franklin was walking out of Independence Hall after the Constitutional Convention in 1787, when someone shouted out, "Doctor, what have we got? A republic or a monarchy?" To which Franklin apparently responded, with an ominous rejoinder: "A republic, if you can keep it." This conversation is reported to have taken place between Benjamin Franklin and Elizabeth Willing Powel, considered one of the well-connected social figures of Colonial and early Republic Philadelphia. She played a vital role in American history as a close friend of both

George and Martha Washington. She was a prominent society figure and the wife of Philadelphia Mayor Samuel Powel.

Like Franklin, Powel was known for her wit and knowledge. She often hosted convention delegates and their wives in her home. She spent most of Washington's presidency in the temporary capital of Philadelphia. There was more to the conversation than the now famous reply "A Republic, if you can keep it." The conversation is reported to have continued in the following way. Referring to George Washington, Franklin said, "The first man put at the helm will be a good one. Nobody knows what sort may come afterwards." Franklin continued, "The executive will be always increasing here, as elsewhere, till it ends in a monarchy."

And there is an extended version of "A Republic, if you can keep it." In an 1803 account [14], Powel immediately shoots back, "And why not keep it?" Franklin responds, "Because the people, on tasting the dish, are always disposed to eat more of it than does them good." Here, Benjamin Franklin was referring to the complacency that often comes with perceived prosperity. With respect to the human condition, Franklin likely understood that a free and democratic Republic can be no different than a monarchy or dictatorship in which the masses are fed comforts that cause them to ignore governance, by way of turning their backs on their responsibility to be fully engaged in shaping their own governance. Comfort is often blind.

A New Normal

There is one statement being made by government and mainstream media that rings true. There's no going back to what we know as "normal."

However, this statement is made with a different intention in mind than that of the plandemic planners. The "normal" has been one in which the masses, particularly here in America, have traded truth for convenience. We have submitted to fear, believing that it is better to do so than risk inconvenience, confrontation and sacrifice.

We have been willing to close our eyes and turn our backs on centuries of corporate greed, government's continuous violation of our constitutional rights and civil liberties, public/private partnerships that place profits before people and "democratic elections" that have become public auctions as a spectator sport. The present Covid-19 era is just another addition in a very long trend of corporations and the wealthy elite attempting to own our government through regulatory capture. Our Federal government is too big, and that is part of our downfall.

Socialism and Fascism are on the rise, and have been for a long time. The declaration of a worldwide pandemic has presented an ideal opportunity for those who want total socio-economic control of the masses. Nowhere is this more evident than in these United States of America where public health officials tell us that the price of freedom is now vaccination. And those who dare to question the necessity, safety and effectiveness of Covid shots have been censored and vilified. Defending our freedom of speech publicly is being treated like a criminal offense – all for a virus that has an infection and mortality rate of 1-2 percent! That's less than some flu seasons. Why would we want to go back to more of the culture and environment that has fostered all this?

Without an engaged citizenry all we will have left is tyranny. Right now, we live in a time when we can stop talking about being spiritual, honorable, moral or ethical and, instead, become more so by embracing love, courage and compassion to become fearless, as fearlessness is one of the greatest spiritual principles we can embrace, no matter what the circumstance. Right now, we can invoke a huge rebirth, a paradigm shift to embrace Grace, Beauty, Intelligence and Blessings by choosing to heal, nurture and sustain our bodies holistically in alignment with Nature's bounty.

We can decrease our reliance on synthetic and often risky medical interventions that do have their place, but only when inexpensive, effective alternative holistic therapies that get to the root cause of our lack of well-being have been exhausted. And we have a privilege, right now, of serving humankind by educating them in the same.

You can only solve a problem with an awareness in Consciousness that is higher than the one that created the problem. Therefore, fear can never be a means of solving anything. Right now, we can serve Humanity by educating people in how, historically, the corruption of greed, when allowed to flourish unchecked, has always ruined Humanity, and how, historically, love, courage and compassion have always won out in the end – these being the key factors in bettering Humanity in every way - so that we can become a society that values and embraces Liberty, first based on reverence for our God-given rights.

Right now, we have the amazing privilege of actually establishing a government that is for the people, by the people. And all we have to do is to get involved and become more fully engaged. Becoming fully engaged in our governance represents an even greater potential than the "new normal." It is the very real possibility of a new birth. So, why should we pine for going back to normal when we can have something so much greater for all?

It is in the spirit of the above, that this plan for Liberty Action Councils is offered to secure our Republic in governance for the people by the people.

Courage is Love in Action

"We hold these truths to be self-evident, that all men are created equal, that they are endowed by their Creator with certain unalienable Rights, that among these are Life, Liberty and the pursuit of Happiness – That to secure these rights, Governments are instituted among Men, deriving their just powers from the consent of the governed, – That whenever any Form of Government becomes destructive of these ends, it is the Right of the People to alter or to abolish it, and to institute new Government, laying its foundation on such principles and organizing its powers in such form, as to them shall seem most likely to affect their Safety and Happiness.

Prudence, indeed, will dictate that Governments long established should not be changed for light and transient causes; and accordingly all experience hath shewn, that mankind are more disposed to suffer, while evils are sufferable, than to right themselves by abolishing the forms to which they are accustomed. But when a long train of abuses and usurpations, pursuing invariably the same Object evinces a design to reduce them under absolute Despotism, it is their right, it is their duty, to throw off such Government, and to provide new Guards for their future security."
~ Excerpt from The Declaration of Independence – IN CONGRESS, July 4, 1776 – On Which the Constitution of Our Great Nation Was Founded.

Legal Decisions and Briefs
That We Should Remember

"A law repugnant to the Constitution is void. An act of Congress repugnant to the Constitution cannot become a law. The Constitution supersedes all other laws and the individual's rights shall be liberally enforced in favor of him, the clearly intended and expressly designated beneficiary."
~ Marbury v. Madison, 5 U.S. 137 (1803)

"An unconstitutional act is not law. It confers no rights; it imposes no duties; affords no protection; it creates no office. It is, in legal contemplation, as inoperative as though it had never been passed."
~ Norton v. Shelby County, 118 U.S. 425 (1886)

"The general misconception is that any statute passed by legislators bearing the appearance of law constitutes the law of the land. The U.S. Constitution is the supreme law of the land, and any statute, to be valid, must be in agreement. It is impossible for both the Constitution and a law violating it to be valid; one must prevail. This is succinctly stated as follows:

The general rule is that an unconstitutional statute, though having the form and name of law, is in reality no law, but is wholly void, and ineffective for any purpose; since unconstitutionality dates from the time of its enactment, and not merely from the date of the decision so branding it. An unconstitutional law, in legal contemplation, is as inoperative as if it had never been passed. Such a statute leaves the question that it purports to settle just as it would be had the statute not been enacted.

Since an unconstitutional law is void, the general principals follow that it imposes no duties, confers no rights, creates no office, bestows no power or authority on anyone, affords no protection, and justifies no acts performed under it...A void act cannot be legally consistent with a valid one. An unconstitutional law cannot operate to supersede any existing valid law. Indeed, insofar as a statute runs counter to the fundamental law of the land, it is superseded thereby. No one is bound to obey an unconstitutional law and no courts are bound to enforce it."
~ 16 American Jurisprudence 2d, Sec. 177

"No one is bound to obey an unconstitutional law, and no courts are bound to enforce it. The general rule is that an unconstitutional statute, whether federal or state, though having the form and name of law, is in reality no law, but is wholly void and ineffective for any purpose, since unconstitutionality dates from the time of its enactment, and not merely from the date of the decision so branding it. AN UNCONSTITUTIONAL LAW, in legal contemplation, IS AS INOPERATIVE AS IF IT HAD NEVER BEEN PASSED."
~ 16 American Jurisprudence 2d, Sec. 256

Conflict is always an invitation to useful change. Therefore, this is a great and glorious time, a perfect time to enact this change, community-by-community, state-by-state. In this regard, to secure the above in alignment with our Constitution and the conscience of the individual, we will need many more of the citizenry to become *fully engaged* in their governance, something that we do not now have.

Human Contact and Solidarity

By convincing the healthy that they are sick when they don't have any symptoms, and then by discriminating against them (vaccine passports) to create a second-class citizenry - and by grossly inflating SARS-COV2 infection and death counts based on computer model projections, even when accurate, real-time numbers are available - and by using a virus that is no more dangerous than that occurring in an extended flu season (99% recovery rate among those with healthy immune systems) – thereby breaking the economy that the middle class relies on - and by having established a state of emergency that, for almost three years, had no clear designated end, our current government is attempting to obliterate solidarity by making us frightened of each other! What better way to punish dissent under the guise of protecting us!

Fascism

Under a fascist society, there is no need for enforcing the mandates of tyranny. Through engineered consent, and by shifting the culture of societies to a culture based on the corruption of greed that provides those commanding huge amounts of financial wealth the ability to bribe people for total socio-economic control, the masses will police each other. Fascism is a fear-based culture, by design. It has its roots in socialism/globalism that is engineered by the wealthy elite, government bureaucrats and the military for this purpose.

Why Do We Need
Liberty Action Councils?

Central banks now own the governments of the world. The implementation of the current plan for globalization, based on a social credit system, can no longer be stopped by just getting out of the banking system. The only option left is to take back our government. We need Liberty Action Councils *to develop direct and sustained contact with legislators and other elected officials.* We need Liberty Action Councils in order to engage, as necessary, peaceful non-compliance and civil disobedience when our Liberty is threatened and our Constitutional rights and civil liberties are being violated. In the U.S., this threat to our Liberty represents a clear and present danger in our times, due to the fact that the Federal government continually acts on manufactured authority not delegated to it by the States and not elucidated in our nation's Constitution.

Currently, the checks and balances provided by the U.S. Constitutional Republic, under the Constitution that is the highest law of governance in America, have been practically destroyed due to the negligence of the public in allowing government to repeatedly violate these checks and balances. Some of this statement also applies to the current state of affairs under Covid with respect to State Constitutions.

This is not a matter of a "system" being broken. Systems are made up of the people who design and run them. So, terms like "it's the system" are used to distract us from demanding transparency and accountability on the part of those individuals who are complicit in placing profits and personal gain above the people. Will we be ruled or will we insist on actual governance for the people that is by the people?

302 DHARMA AND THE PRESERVATION OF LIBERTY

Because there is a difference in these two. And any system established by the people that is not working in the best interest of the people can and must be changed by the people – Us.

The Overrated Reliance
On the Executive Branch

"Governor, to see that laws are executed; may require written information. §6 He may require information, in writing, from the officers in the executive department, upon any subject relating to the duties of their respective offices; and shall see that the laws are faithfully executed." ~ Ohio State Constitution

As just one example, under Covid emergency mandates in Ohio State (where I currently live), the powers vested in the state legislature have been abdicated to the Executive Branch of the Governor and state and local health departments, in violation of our state's Constitution. See Article II, Section 1, paragraph D, which states that only the state legislature can declare a state of emergency that can only be implemented by a two-thirds vote of the legislature. During the 2020 declared state of emergency, we heard testimony in the Ohio statehouse on the part of elected officials that, under Covid, "there should only be one general making decisions." Replace the word "general" with "king" or "dictator." This is precisely what the Ohio State Constitution is designed to prevent.

There are only five pages in the Ohio State Constitution dedicated to delineating the powers of the Executive Branch in Ohio. In delineating the powers of the three branches, the predominant number of pages in our state's Constitution are dedicated to the powers of the legislature. That's because only the legislative body has the power to make law and declare rulings and mandates under such law. Most of the Ohio citizenry are not even aware of this, as evidenced by the number of citizens, local elected officials, law enforcement and business owners who, under Covid, had wrongly stated that the Governor's mandates are law.

The power of the Executive Branch in Ohio is very limited, as is the case with America's Federal Executive branch. However, in Ohio, there are a good number of sections of the revised code (state laws) that are in direct opposition to the state's Constitution. This is likely the case with other states also. Therefore, it is of the utmost urgency to ensure that any laws on the books (for example, the Ohio Revised Code) be revised or repealed by the state legislature to bring the code into alignment with the Ohio State Constitution.

In addition, every elected official in any state in America takes an oath upon taking office, to uphold that state's Constitution. This means they have sworn to protect our God-given unalienable rights. And they have to be held to their oath by us. Ask yourself if current affairs in your state are in alignment with the separation of powers and checks and balances under your state's Constitution.

In the U.S. it is a fact that the public allows for non-delegated authority to the Executive branch on both the state and federal levels, a branch that has the least delegated powers under the Constitution. This has paved the way for Presidents, Governors and departments of the Executive Branch (the Administrative State) to successfully supersede the separation of powers designed to protect our Constitutional rights and civil liberties, and to prevent big government from running amok.

They have done so by pandering to corporate special interest in which they take bribes in return for mandating legislation and issuing executive orders that actually protect corporate economic interests and provide for our tax dollars to be spent to support corporate and private economic interests. The events that have transpired under Covid-19 show this to be the case.

As an example, although well meaning, most officials in the Executive Branch are not educated on the science of viruses/virology and toxicology and alternative, inexpensive, non-toxic therapies for treatment. Instead, they rely heavily on government bureaucrats to provide them with data from computer projection models, rather than data from professionals on the ground who are successfully treating patients and clients. These bureaucrats have kept their positions for decades by serving the special interest of big business and, in this example, Big Pharma.

In this way, corporate special interest and that of the wealthy elite often hold the Executive Branch hostage (and, at times the legislature also). We the people no longer have the greatest voice in our government. And the wealthy elite in both political parties often work together for personal gain and advancement of their ideologies. So, this is not about democrats, republicans or independents. It's about protecting our God-given, unalienable rights by upholding and enforcing the Constitution.

The Legislative Branch

"§1 The legislative power of the state shall be vested in a General Assembly consisting of a Senate and House of Representatives but the people reserve to themselves the power to propose to the General Assembly laws and amendments to the constitution, and to adopt or reject the same at the polls on a referendum vote as hereinafter provided. They also reserve the power to adopt or reject any law, section of any law or any item in any law appropriating money passed by the General Assembly, except as herein after provided; and independent of the General Assembly to propose amendments to the Constitution and to adopt or reject the same at the polls. The limitations expressed in the Constitution, on the power of the General Assembly to enact laws, shall be deemed limitations on the power of the people to enact laws." ~ Ohio State, 1851, am. 1912, 1918, 1953

The longest section delineating the three branches of our state government is this section - and for a reason: The legislative branch holds the most power of governance of the three. Review your state's Constitution, for it is likely comparable.

The Judicial Branch

"§1 The judicial power of the state is vested in a supreme court, courts of appeals, courts of common pleas and divisions thereof, and such other courts inferior to the Supreme Court as may from time to time be established by law." ~ Ohio state, 1851, am. 1883, 1912, 1968, 1973

We the people must ensure that the current practice in the way the judicial branch functions never outweighs the powers afforded to it under the Constitution. Review your state's Constitution, for it is likely comparable.

Special Interest Lobby

The challenge we have in our communities is fighting the corruption of greed that has infected our government. Ours is a capitalist society. Big business operates with the understanding that corporations provide economies on which communities and states thrive through the development and sale of their products and services, in which people are also provided jobs.

Of course, the hubris of upper management and owners of these conglomerates is such that they forget that it is their often-underpaid employees who make their companies successful. In addition, corporate greed has fueled the notion that government is in debt to private industry for creating economies. It's not enough that these conglomerates make, as their reward, vast sums of money. They believe they are the saviors of the people rather than the servants of the people and, in this regard, they feel they have the right to own government. Again, this, of course, is due to the corruption of greed and our own complacency in reining it in.

The fact is, corporations do not make economies, consumers do. Therefore, we have the power of the purse that should be exercised to protect our will and our rights.

Campaign Finance

Our elected officials have major constituents, and then there are the rest of us. Due to the outrageous cost of campaigning for office in most scenarios, people running for office get most of their campaign financing from corporations and international conglomerates. This means that those companies are the major constituents of that person, should he/she get elected to office. This has created a highly charged political environment where elected officials are forced to choose between us, their minor constituents who actually voted for them, and their major constituents who financed their election campaigns. If a decision has to be made between the two, the elected official will always represent the interests of his/her major constituents first.

This is why we have such a great disparity between serving the will of the people and serving the corruption of greed. This has been worsened by the successful lobby of the U.S. Supreme Court by big business that resulted in the high court deciding that corporations are people. Due to this, politicians now have a legal right to represent and support the interests of their corporate donors, ahead of serving the will of the majority of the people who elected them.

If, for example, a bill is considered that serves the will of the people and the interests of major donors at the same time, they call that a people's bill and proclaim that they are serving the will of the people. But when bills do not serve both, the bill will always be fashioned in a way that serves the interests of the elected official's major constituents, even to the detriment of the majority of people who voted for them.

So, if you don't know the corporations that your candidate or elected officials take money from, then you don't know your candidate/elected official. This is why we must demand campaign finance reform, while coalescing to form citizen Superpacs that raise money to finance election campaigns for candidates that the citizenry has groomed, outside of personal and corporate conflicts of interest.

Party Loyalty

One of the greatest challenges to our present system of governance is reliance on and loyalty to political parties. In the U.S., the framers of our Constitution warned that any two-party system of government will destroy governance for the people, by the people – through a culture of one party consistently attempting to gain power over the other. And this is exactly what has happened in our present times.

Elected officials are required by party leadership to uphold the ideology and initiatives of the party. This loyalty to party places elected officials at odds with the moral and ethical duty to serve the people. So, they serve their party first. There are many examples of important bills brought by citizens to state legislatures and the U.S. Congress that gained considerable support, only to be abandoned because party leadership ordered elected officials to table their support of those bills. This is a common occurrence in our government that must stop. It will only stop if we demand statesmanship and a multiple party system of governance. Otherwise, one party will always seek to override and control the other, and we see this in the redistricting practices that occur in each state, along with consistent election fraud on the part of both parties.

Lobbyists

The following is an example that should be heeded. Although it references the U.S. Congress, we have similar issues here in the state of Ohio and you may have the same issues in your state.

1. For every member of the U.S. Congress, there are, at least, 4 special interest lobbyists representing corporations.
2. These lobbyists call on our government representatives on a constant basis.
3. Corporations are still the primary source of the introduction of bills into the U.S. Congress.
4. In order to get these special interest bills passed, conglomerates finance election and re-election campaigns, offer valuable perks to legislators and donate and/or offer grants to fund causes connected to legislators.
5. We, the people, introduce few bills to the legislature. In fact, it's unheard of that bills to be considered are presented for consideration of sponsorship by communities of citizens, even though that is our right.
6. In a growing number of cases (not all), conflicts of interest often prevent legislators from initiating bills on behalf of their constituents, even when their constituents press for the bills to be enacted. This is largely due to the rise of the career politician (who places keeping his/her seat as a higher priority to serving the people) and the decline of the statesperson.
7. Our government does not hear from us. Because this is the case, our legislators assume that we are in agreement with whatever they say and do.

The above list is just a sampling of what needs to be addressed, and this is why we now need to plan and execute Liberty Action Councils in as many counties as possible across America.

Previous chapters in this book have elucidated how collectivism, a.k.a. socialism, a.k.a. globalism has been established in America for more than a century. The strategy that made America a socialist country is based on the Marxist-Leninist model, taken in the context of the evolving plan for One World

Government. This strategy is backed by the wealthy elite who have adopted particularly the primary principle of Leninism: tell them what they want to hear until you have power over them, and then betray them.

Lenin proposed three great lessons of power. Since power means a lot of things to different people, Lenin's choice of the word "power" is replaced here with the word "authority."

1. It makes no difference what you think if others hold the authority over you.
2. Authority does not seek those who are virtuous. It belongs to those who reach for it.
3. Once authority is acquired it must be used to defend itself against those who would take it from those who possess it.

Those who have not claimed authority with respect to Liberty, cannot defend Liberty. Therefore, we the people, based on our Constitution, have to now take back the centers of authority, one by one, exactly as we lost them. The goal must be to reclaim our Liberty under the authority of the highest law in the land, the United States Constitution.

We Don't Want That Here

Before I present the means for us to keep our foot on the neck of government, throughout this book I have indicated developments in countries across the globe that have put in place the mechanisms (through laws and mandates) to destroy Liberty and increase big government control over that nation's citizens. When you hear or read of such laws being enacted in other countries, you should immediately gather that information, along with a copy of the actual edict or law and contact your elected officials to tell them "we don't want this here." When the enemy is headed towards you, you sound the alarm when they are still off in the distance. Not when they are on your doorstep, because then it is too late.

The Plan

If pirates capture your ship, it will do you no good to ask or beg them to give it back and you won't get it back by doing nothing. You won't get it back by jumping ship into the shark-infested waters below, nor by finding a place on the ship to hide. A signed petition to the pirates objecting to their behavior won't work. Threatening legal action if the pirates get caught will be useless. If pirates capture your ship, the only way to get it back is to recapture the ship.

This is a good analogy for the challenges we currently face with respect to our governance. The difference is that, right now, we can engage in massive action that is both forceful and peaceful. The majority never decides anything on its own. Those in a position of authority are those who influence and lead the majority. Therefore, we must have leadership in authority that will uphold Liberty out of reverence for our God-given, unalienable rights.

Any reference here to collectivism is also a reference to fascism, socialism and communism. Collectivism and Liberty are enemies. Only one will survive.

Vision: A proposed minimum of 10 citizens per Liberty Action Council (can start with less – perhaps 5), with one Liberty Action Council per county or province.

I. Education and Outreach – the Citizenry

"If you don't know what your rights are, how do you know they are not already gone? You cannot exercise a right you do not know you have. If you are not exercising your rights, they are already gone."
~ *Krisanne Hall, Constitutional Attorney, Liberty First University*

In the United States, the citizenry is ignorant of the Constitution on which our Republic is founded. Most have not read it, nor have they read their state constitution and bill of rights that is based on the U.S. Constitution. Therefore, they have no idea of the highest of societal laws that govern them. So, how can they even begin to protect such rights?

Therefore, a principle duty of any Liberty Action Council is to begin classes, webinars, gatherings and other groups to teach people the Constitution and its efficacy for securing our constitutional rights and civil liberties.

This simple training can be led by constitutional attorneys, community leaders educated in the constitution and constitutional sheriffs of the CSPOA (Constitutional Sheriffs and Peace Officers Association) or similar organizations. These trainings can also include group viewings of constitutional lessons readily available through platforms like Liberty First University.

II. Education and Outreach – Elected Officials

Elected officials (who often need training in becoming public servants), many of whom are elected legislators, are, in some cases, also ignorant of the Constitution on which our Republic is founded. Many of them have not read it, nor have they read their state constitution and bill of rights that is based on the U.S. Constitution. Therefore, they also have no idea of the highest of societal laws on which we are to be governed. In addition, here in Ohio we have met with several state legislators who have told us that the Constitution is no longer relevant.

Given this fact, a principle duty of any Liberty Action Council is to also begin educating state legislators and local law enforcement in the Constitution on which they have taken a sworn oath to uphold.

This can be accomplished over breakfast and lunch sit-downs or Zoom meetings with these officials, in which they are graciously weaned on to direct knowledge of our highest, societal law.

This simple training can also be led by constitutional attorneys, community leaders educated in the constitution and constitutional sheriffs of the CSPOA (Constitutional Sheriffs and Peace Officers Association) or similar organizations.

In addition, it will be a priority of Liberty Action Councils to get legislators to enact laws that require that government officials and law enforcement officers take a written, graded test on their knowledge of the Constitution, because no elected or appointed official can be expected to uphold and protect laws and rights for which they have no detailed knowledge. And government officials who fail such a test should be required to take it over and over again, until their grade is satisfactory. The results of such tests should become a matter of public record.

III. Holistic Health and Health Freedom Education and Outreach – the Citizenry

Unfortunately, today too many people take better care of their cars and cell phones than they do their bodies.

The majority of U.S. citizens are still unaware of the many effective, alternatives to toxic medical interventions like most of the current vaccines, and the many pharmaceutical medications that have become commonplace.

Reaching for these toxic interventions should be the last resort when all other viable, alternative therapies have been exhausted. Instead, many people in America and across the globe are stuck in the mentality of a magic pill for everything that ails them.

The importance of medical interventions when absolutely necessary is understood and there should be no opposition to such interventions. However, rather than applying effective methods for getting to the root cause of the health condition or disease, too many people are happy to simply focus on treating symptoms. In fact, in America, we have a sick care system, not a health care system. Ours is a system dominated by a medical field that has been focused on symptom relief only, rather than getting to the root cause for permanent healing of the condition. This is so because there are no massive profits in cures, only in continued disease for which the symptoms alone are treated.

This has increased reliance on toxic medical interventions that have made us a society of drug users and drug dealers. A society that promotes prevention as the first line of defense against illness is a society that will not become reliant on pharmaceutical medications. This, then, will destroy the economies built around our sick care system that have been placed as the highest priority to maintain, ahead of prevention and cure.

Therefore, one of the duties of Liberty Action Councils is to offer, share, promote and support programs that educate people in how to care for their health, holistically, and as a matter of prevention, by way of lifestyle changes that are known to effectively address getting to the root cause of illness and lack of well-being.

There are growing numbers of doctors, scientific researchers and holistic health, healing and well-being practitioners with very strong track records of successfully helping people to reverse and heal chronic health conditions and diseases through lifestyle changes. This approach includes holistic, cellular nutrition through eating real, highly nutritious food, restful sleep, proper exercise, intermittent water fasting, meditation and yoga, herbal therapies and other methods that amount to healing and prevention of disease.

It is the duty of any Liberty Action Council to foster education in these alternatives so that the citizenry is fully informed about all of the viable choices they have for true health care, based on prevention and getting to the root cause of the ailment.

Health Freedom

"Unless we put medical freedom into the Constitution, the time will come when medicine will organize into an undercover dictatorship to restrict the art of healing to one class of men and deny equal privileges to others; the Constitution of the Republic should make a Special

privilege for medical freedoms as well as religious freedoms."
~ *Dr. Benjamin Rush, signatory to the Declaration of Independence*

Along with education in holistic health, there is the necessity to educate the public in what health/medical fully informed consent is, along with the fact that it includes the right to refuse without discrimination or other reprisal. This form of education must include getting people to understand that trust has to be earned – whether that be trust in a doctor, medical professional, health/healing practitioner, or other therapist or researcher.

When it comes to health care, too often, people give their trust blindly without insisting on a complete understanding of the science (or lack thereof) on which the recommended approach/therapy is based. Doctors and health/healing/well-being professionals are your paid consultants. They work for you and are fully accountable to you, and not the other way around.

For example, patients/clients have to be educated in how to vet the underlying science of any diagnosis and prognosis, before accepting and trusting it just because the doctor says so.

In this regard, fully-informed consent and the right to refuse can only be supported when people have all the facts and have considered all sides of the science before exercising their right to accept or refuse any proposed health/medical intervention of any kind.

Right now, in the state of Ohio, state Attorney General Yost has approved a medical right to refuse amendment initiative to the Ohio state constitution (www.MedicalRight2Refuse.com). The amendment initiative is being spearheaded by Ohio Advocates for Medical Freedom. This kind of amendment should be initiated in every state in the union.

It's not their body, it's your body and, in the end, you are the one responsible for keeping it well, not your doctor or other health/well-being professional, and certainly not the government.

IV. Holistic Health and Health Freedom Education and Outreach – Elected Officials

As stated above for the citizenry, too many elected officials are also ignorant of the many, effective and non-toxic holistic therapies for treating chronic health conditions and diseases. Many of them only know what Big Pharma tells them. This can be easily understood by observing how our government has stood by and allowed chemical companies to poison our food and water supply with GMOs and other genetically engineered poisons.

In this regard, many elected officials overlook or are not aware of the science that supports the alternative approaches to health, healing and prevention. Even now, some are calling for all such therapies to be outlawed, and some of that is due to pressure from Big Pharma to eliminate what they feel is the competition. Big Pharma can only thrive if people remain sick or are convinced that they are sick when they are not.

Therefore, another primary duty of Liberty Action Councils will be to begin an extended education campaign targeted to elected officials, designed to give them a direct experience of how these holistic lifestyle approaches can improve their health and well-being permanently.

V. Education In How to Raise Candidates for Public Office

In America, in most cases, we vote for the candidates that are presented to us. Our 2-party structure provides us with few alternatives for candidates and has created a polarizing environment that makes it almost impossible for bipartisan cooperation in protecting/upholding the Constitution and serving Liberty by first protecting our God-given unalienable rights.

Most citizens have never met their candidate in person or had a face-to-face discussion with the candidate about serving and protecting their Liberty. Instead, too many people vote based on viewing video clips of campaign stops, campaign ads in popular media (media sound bites), flawed, televised debates in which the debate questions submitted are controlled by the presiding media outlet running the debate, and/or peer pressure/discussions with family members and loved ones who have also had little or no contact with candidates. In addition to this flaw, people also vote for personalities, rather than investigating background and skill-level.

This has fostered an environment where elections have become nothing more than public auctions. We, the citizenry, have allowed this to happen because, too often, we are not engaged in raising candidates who actually represent us. This has led, in most cases, to voters feeling like they have to vote for the lesser of two evils, a tragedy at best.

Therefore, Liberty Action Councils must be actively engaged in choosing and grooming people for office who will actually represent us and serve our needs, while protecting our constitutional rights and civil liberties.

So, community-by-community, we need to foster relationships based on human contact that can be nurtured in the context of raising states people for public office. It is foolish for us to simply wait to be told who the candidates are.

In this regard, there are advocacy training portals already in place that liberty action councils can utilize to become educated in how to raise candidates. Once the council has done so, it can go about presenting candidates to the public who have been raised from inside the community, and then begin to raise campaign financing.

Part of this approach will include populating legislatures with citizens who are not interested in becoming career politicians but, rather, want to serve for a finite period of time in which to foster creative innovations to practical, representative government for and by the people.

Campaign Finance

The citizenry is victim to a system run by people who will only allow those with monetary wealth to run for office. The outrageous cost connected to running campaigns, which includes hefty media buys, is executed to keep those not part of the wealthy elite from running for office.

The premise on which this is founded is that the monetarily wealthy are smarter and more fit to run government than the rest of us unintelligent rabble. However, financial wealth does not automatically equate to intelligence, particularly when many wealthy people have gotten materially wealthy by way of the corruption of greed and the unethical and criminal acts that greed renders.

This keeps good, morally and spiritually ethical people out of the election process. And this must change. The financially rich have robbed our Republic and made our government subsidiaries of their businesses!

The Need for A Citizen's Superpac

The way to change this is for citizens across this land to band together to form Superpacs that are not associated with any political party, to raise money to run candidates for office who want to uphold the Constitution and protect our God-given, unalienable rights – candidates who will place this above party and above individual ideology.

This can be done by communities of citizens coming together with financial and campaign experts, to begin forming Superpacs to run candidates who will endeavor to reform government and enliven plans for reshaping elections around town hall meetings that are not reliant upon media ad buys and media-controlled debates.

VI. The Reading and Vetting of Bills Being Introduced to the Legislature

One of the primary duties of any Liberty Action Council will be to assemble groups of citizens in the community to read and vet every single bill being proposed to the state and federal legislatures, before those bills get out of committee and are presented for a vote.

Legislators are, at times, in the habit of reading 2-page summaries of bills, rather than reading the entire bill. Therefore, they are voting on bills that they have not fully read.

So, we, the citizenry, better know and thoroughly understand what's in these bills before they are voted on so that communities can make their support or lack of it known to their public servants. Bills must be considered based on the will of the people, not the special interest and conflict of interest of a select few.

Once the Liberty Action Council understands what's in these bills, the council can act accordingly in apprising the citizenry and arranging meetings with legislators to discuss support or opposition to the bill and what actions should be taken to represent the people.

It's easier than you might think to track all federal and state bills in the U.S. Start at billtrack50.com. It is free for citizens to search bills and the website will search simultaneously in multiple states, as well.

VII. The Writing and Introduction of Bills by the Citizenry for Consideration and Sponsorship

If corporations, either directly or indirectly, are allowed to introduce the majority of bills to the legislature, why can't the citizenry do the same!? Of course we can. In fact, if we are going to complain about bills that are being passed into law, it is our duty to provide an alternative.

One of the best ways to engage a citizenry is to get the citizenry educated in the bill writing process, along with how to effectively have them introduced to the legislature – just like corporate and private special interest do now.

In the state of Ohio, citizens have introduced several bills to the state legislature that are gaining momentum and support. This is happening in other states also. Tracking the data over a period of more than twenty years, it takes an average of three years for most bills introduced by citizens to get passed.

Therefore, it will be a duty of Liberty Action Councils to engage local citizens in education and engagement for introducing bills written by the people, for the people.

VIII. Foster Monthly Meetings Between the Citizenry and Elected Officials

If we feel that we don't have transparency and accountability in government, it's because we don't demand it. Simply complaining about a problem is not useful. Engaging the problem is more useful.

Right now, our government is like a big ghost operating in the shadows. Who are they? What do they do with their time when they are "on the clock"? Who runs what and when? The citizenry doesn't know. And yet, our tax dollars pay their salaries and they are said to represent us.

In business, there are management levels designed to monitor what is required of the employees, along with the quality of their work. With respect to governance, that management level belongs to the citizenry.

Our elected officials don't hear from us. So, they naturally assume that we agree with what they do and say. Communities don't have a strong voice in their government because they don't insist on direct, human contact with their elected officials.

It will be the duty of Liberty Action Councils to arrange monthly meetings (and more frequently as needed) with elected officials, either in-district or at statehouses and the nation's capitol. Such meetings must be engaged with regularity to foster relationships with elected officials based on direct contact, so that communities are heard and the message is sent, "You will be seeing and hearing from us all the time." Only then will we even begin to have governance that is for the people, by the people.

IX. The Monitoring of Our Schools and Community Home Schooling

For all you parents out there, when was the last time you sat in on any of your children's classes to observe for yourself what your sons/daughters are actually being taught in school? The fact is, most parents don't know, first-hand, what their children are being taught in school. They only know what the child decides to tell them, or what the teacher tells them.

In fact, the parent has the responsibility for teaching the child whatever is necessary for the child to meet the challenges of life, including helping the child to develop critical, independent thinking. Schools are actually supposed to be adjuncts that exist to serve the parent's intention for the child's education, until the child is mature enough to make decisions about further education for his/herself. This is not the case in much of our school system today.

Therefore, it will be the duty of Liberty Action Councils to establish forums that represent the will of parents in the community in how the school system must operate. This will include populating school boards with citizens who are not interested in becoming career politicians but, rather, want to serve for a finite period of time in which to foster creative innovations to schooling.

In addition, it will be a duty of Liberty Action Councils to foster alternative schooling by also developing a selection of citizen teachers who are themselves parents, to establish a cooperative community home schooling network.

This can be done to offer parents a choice in the education of their children through developing relationships with other parents who are teachers, while relieving them of the burden of having to home school alone, when faced with the challenges of reporting to work for a living.

Home schooling can present less of a challenge when, instead of parents or a single parent having to face the burden of schooling children on their own while also working a job or running a business, several competent teachers in the community can take up the charge of educating that community's children. In this way, home schooling Co-ops and charter schools can be established within communities. In fact, this is the way in which schools like the Rudolf Steiner School first got started. Workers at the Waldorf-Astoria cigarette factory needed help in home schooling their children due to their workload, and the factory owner asked Steiner to create a co-educational school for the workers' children.

X. Community Internet and ISP

The Constitutional right to free speech is a central pillar of any Republic functioning democratically. Without it, we have tyranny.

The level of censorship of our free speech on the Internet has reached epic proportions under Covid that is reflective of dictatorships.

For example, doctors successfully treating SARS-COV2 infected patients on the front lines with off-patent, effective, inexpensive and non-toxic therapies have been repeatedly censored on the Internet and had their licenses threatened or revoked. Why? Because Big Pharma and Big Government cannot force a vaccine on us if the public knows there are more effective, non-toxic and inexpensive alternatives available. So, they censor that information.

In addition, world-renowned scientific researchers, virologists and epidemiologists are also being censored for questioning the lack of science, proper research and testing behind totalitarian Covid mandates and shots. In addition, attorneys and activist groups are being heavily censored, particularly when making announcements about bills being presented to the state legislature to protect the right to health freedom through fully informed consent.

Corporate economic interests have fueled the corruption of greed in mind control schemes to tell us when to think, how to think and what to think. This is intentional. The wealthy elite want total socio-economic control of the masses. They believe they are the masters of our Universe and that we exist as commodities to consume their products, and to be traded to serve their ideology. To further understand this, you can visit the World Economic Forum's web site and also read the writings of Klaus Schwab and Yuval Noah Harari, the chief architect there. These people are not hiding their plans for how we live and breathe and have openly and publicly indicated that they want to change what it means to be human – as in Transhumanism.

To better understand their plan to control every aspect of our lives, you should also read *Covid-19: The Great Reset* by Klaus Schwab.

The Internet Today

Contrary to popular opinion, the Internet is not a public trust. It is a private going business concern. The Internet is run by corporations of wealthy elite and, in order to achieve socio-economic dominance, they have to control free speech. Therefore, in order to protect our free speech, communities either need to have a direct stake in running the Internet or severely limit interacting with it.

Dependent upon how a state allocates broadband distribution, it is possible for anyone to start an Internet service provider company. This means it is possible for communities to own their own ISPs for the purpose of providing their own low-cost, freedom of speech Internet.

IT professionals living in communities can be engaged to build web browsers like duckduckgo that provide for uncensored search that is not monitored and manipulated in any way by corporate interests, thus ensuring that the Internet remains open and transparent.

Costs for community ISP startups are being researched right now.

And, A Not So Novel Idea

And here's an idea. Close your cell phone facetime apps, get off Facebook and Instagram and Twitter and, instead, call those you want to speak with and arrange to gather and visit with each other more regularly. In a world more and more dominated by Big Tech, this is even more essential.

XI. The Monitoring and Prevention of Corporate Campaigns to Privatize Public Resources

The era of GMO foods has evidenced the fact that corporations have made repeated attempts to privatize our food supply. One only needs to read the transcripts of the court cases brought against Monsanto to understand this. And now Bill Gates, through his foundations, is buying up large amounts of farmland to produce his own version of GMO crops and food that delivers self-spreading vaccines.

Under Covid, some government officials have floated the notion that organic whole foods will be infected with SARS-COV2, as further justification for genetically-engineered foods that are grown/manufactured with carcinogenic herbicides and pesticides like glyphosate. Such a declaration can lead to the same indemnification against all lawsuits for farming that vaccine manufacturers now enjoy, thanks to our Congress and Supreme Court.

If these companies are granted the power to control our food supply under the PREP Act and state emergency acts under Covid, eventually they will own the food supply. This will be their pushback on huge losses on their GMO product due to increased public awareness and successful litigation against them.

As another of many examples, corporate pressure on government to privatize our water supply has reached a critical mass, with some elected officials in the U.S. now considering the introduction of bills to enact laws for same. They have tried this in other countries and you may be interested in viewing the documentary report of Bechtel's attempt to own the water supply in Bolivia.

After the Bolivian government, in return for a significant bribe, transferred ownership of the country's water supply to Bechtel, Bechtel successfully lobbied the Bolivian government to outlaw the collection of rainwater by farmers who could not afford to purchase water from Bechtel and were, instead, collecting rainwater for their crops. You can view the story in a posted documentary "The Corporation" here: [https://watchdocumentaries.com/the-corporation/ (starting at approximately 1:40:00 – 1:45:00)]

Another case is that of the 750 million genetically-modified mosquitoes that were unleashed in the Florida Keys by Bio Tech companies who had obtained the backing of state and local authorities to do so, ostensibly to prevent mosquitoes from multiplying, out of fear that the mosquitoes might be carriers of Coronaviruses and other new diseases. [15] This was done despite heavy protests from local communities and scientists who never got an answer to the question of long-term ramifications of such a project and questions about any scientific data to prove that this move will not turn the community into Jurassic Park.

Conglomerates are always looking to increase their market share by lobbying governments to back their proposals. The problem is there is often little incentive to enact the proper testing and safety measures to ensure no harm to the public. Instead, we have become the guinea pigs for testing their products.

For these reasons (and more), it will be a duty of Liberty Action Councils to engage in community resource management, in order to monitor corporate special interest and lobbying campaigns designed to privatize our natural resources that belong to all, so that these attempts can be preempted.

XII. The Power of the Purse. End Mindless Consumerism.

As citizens and consumers, we have the power of the purse that should be exercised in situations where businesses are clearly censoring our free speech and violating our constitutional rights and civil liberties. There is no reason to continue to give such businesses our money, or use their Internet platforms that are designed to violate our privacy by selling data about our online behavior as commodities to big business, government and the intelligence community. We can stop frequenting their businesses and Internet platforms by organizing boycotts and taking our money elsewhere.

In addition, it is high time for us to stop engaging in mindless consumerism. In doing so, we are destroying our environment and, by looking the other way and trading in truth for convenience, we are making the perpetrators of collectivism stronger and stronger.

Therefore, an aim of Liberty Action Councils is to encourage the development of a new, community-based culture in which small business networks, community gardens and farms and resource management teams can be created that are environmentally friendly. Such networks can be established as alternative places of employment for our youth and can be structured so that we do not continually send our money into the hands of those who want to manipulate our thinking and control our very bodies for their own profits.

XIII. National Virtual Call Center

National virtual call centers can be established and used by Liberty Action Councils in multiple campaigns to contact and engage the public by phone in educational initiatives designed to inform and encourage – with a call to action for further engagement. With the ever-increasing censorship of free speech that is taking place online, we need an alternative to communicate effectively with the public, and in a way that cannot be censored.

XIV. Demand Monetary Reform and Abolish the U.S. Federal Reserve System

In Chapter 5 you learned how the U.S. Monetary system is a debt-based system of usury perpetrated on the American people to enrich the wealthy elite by keeping all others impoverished in debt. By way of kickbacks on loans, this small group of wealthy elite perpetuate fraud for massive amounts of passive income that they do not ethically and morally earn. Therefore, the first step in monetary reform must be to make fractional reserve banking (discussed in Chapter 5) illegal while, at the same time, abolishing the Federal Reserve. Then the planned move to central bank digital fiat currency and the digital wallet must be outlawed by way of a Constitutional amendment.

The next step is to repeal the legal tender laws so that people can choose to reject Federal Reserve Notes if they want to. Next, recover all Federal Reserve Notes and use them to pay off the national debt and destroy all remaining Federal Reserve Notes after doing so. Then, simultaneously, bring back the U.S. Note, a debt-free currency that is based on the printing of money to pay wages, and tie the U.S. Note to precious metals such as gold and silver. Concurrent with these steps, the U.S. Congress should take over the management of our monetary system, as specified in the Constitution, in order to remove private bankers from the equation.

There are additional, viable solutions that must be put in place but this would be the beginning of a just monetary system on which a very stable U.S. economy could be built, based on free market forces that are not tampered with. Then, the shadow banking system must be made illegal. The shadow banking system is the broad collection of financial institutions managing private equity and offering the same services as commercial banks do, but in an unregulated environment in which there are trillions of trades, most of which are fraudulent. It was the reliance on and subsequent collapse of this system that brought on the global financial crisis of 2008.

XV. End Big Federal Government

The United States Federal government is far too large. As a result, it is constantly engaged in overreach and, in more than a century, has expanded its collectivist/socialist agenda by establishing agencies by powers that have not been delegated to it by the states. We must now decide whether or not to keep these agencies or to insist on their abolishment. And, if we the people decide to keep these agencies, we must push for changes in the law and/or constitutional amendments to insist that the people running these agencies are elected officials with a long, verifiable history of expertise in their qualifying field, and not appointed bureaucrats.

Some examples of these agencies are:

CDC
Established in 1946 as the Communicable Disease Center (CDC), the CDC opened its doors and occupied one floor of a small building in Atlanta. Its primary mission was simply to prevent malaria from spreading across the nation. As the organization took root deep in the South, once known as the heart of the malaria zone, CDC Founder Dr. Joseph Mountin continued to advocate for public health issues and to push for the CDC to extend its responsibilities to other communicable diseases.

DHHS
The idea behind the U.S. Department of Health and Human Services (DHHS) dates back to 1798, with a program created for the relief of sick and disabled merchant seamen. As a result, this established a national network of hospitals specifically for their care and was the forerunner of today's U.S. Public Health Service (HHS Office & Digital Communications Division, 2017).

This federal agency acts as a parent agency to over one hundred additional agencies. Some of the most well-known include the Centers for Disease Control and

Prevention (CDC), Food and Drug Administration (FDA), Indian Health Service (IHS), National Institutes of Health (NIH), and the Office of Inspector General (OIG) just to name a few. The DHHS put into place the Global Health Strategy in January 2012, stating that Americans health is linked with the rest of the world.

NIH
Begun as a one-room Laboratory of Hygiene in 1887, the National Institutes of Health (NIH) today is one of the world's foremost medical research centers. An agency of the Department of Health and Human Services, the NIH is the Federal focal point for health research.

NIAID
The National Institute of Allergy and Infectious Diseases (NIAID) traces its origins to a small laboratory established in 1887 at the Marine Hospital on Staten Island, New York.

In the 1880s, boatloads of immigrants were heading towards America, some of them unknowingly bringing with them cholera and other infectious diseases. No one knew what caused most of these diseases, and physicians relied on clinical signs alone to determine whether someone might be carrying an infectious agent.

FDA
The U.S. Food and Drug Administration (FDA) got its start with the passage of the country's first major food and drug safety bill, the 1906 Pure Food and Drug Act. That law's origins stem from a decades-long fight for the government to regulate food.

As the Industrial Revolution swept America, the production of food and medicine became a large-scale enterprise. Inventions like canning allowed foods to last long enough to be shipped around the country and sit on store shelves for extended periods. Meanwhile, "patent medicines" started being sold in catalogs for a variety of ailments. This industrialization put a new veil between consumer and product. Besides artful labels and hyped slogans, there was no way of knowing what a product really contained. Manufacturers began to exploit this ambiguity. Using spices or additives, canners could mask the taste of expired meat and other substandard ingredients. Many patent medicines ended up relying on large quantities of morphine or cocaine to give users a high instead of actually healing them.

FBI
On July 26, 1908, the Federal Bureau of Investigation (FBI) was born when U.S. Attorney General Charles Bonaparte ordered a group of newly hired federal investigators to report to Chief Examiner Stanley W. Finch of the Department of Justice. One year later, the Office of the Chief Examiner was renamed the Bureau of Investigation, and in 1935 it became the Federal Bureau of Investigation.

Seeking to form an independent and more efficient investigative arm, in 1908 the Department of Justice hired 10 former Secret Service employees to join an expanded Office of the Chief Examiner. The date when these agents reported to duty—July 26, 1908—is celebrated as the genesis of the FBI. By March 1909, the force included 34 agents, and Attorney General George Wickersham, Bonaparte's successor, renamed it the Bureau of Investigation.

CIA

The CIA, or Central Intelligence Agency, is the U.S. government agency tasked primarily with gathering intelligence and international security information from foreign countries. The controversial spy agency's history dates back to World War II, and it played a key role in U.S. efforts to combat the Axis powers during that conflict, and in the Cold War that followed. Though shrouded in secrecy, some CIA activities—such as covert military and cybersecurity operations—have drawn public scrutiny and criticism. In the 20th century the CIA has been exposed for turning its covert operations on the American people, launching many campaigns that include MK Ultra [16] and the flooding of crack cocaine into poor neighborhoods in south central Los Angeles by "Freeway" Rick Ross, as part of the CIA-Contra crack cocaine controversy [17,18].

Each of these agencies is financed by our tax dollars and the hidden tax of inflation. Therefore, these agencies belong to us, the people, and we must decide if they are useful and how, or push for abolishing them.

There is a growing movement across America to establish a Convention of States under Article V of the U.S. Constitution in order to make amendments to the U.S. Constitution to downsize and rein in our big Federal government. 19 states have passed resolutions to have a Convention of States. 34 are needed in order to hold the convention.

Among other things, such a convention will allow the states to amend the U.S. Constitution in order to downsize the administrative state within the U.S. Federal government. For example, this means that agencies within the Federal government that eat up our tax dollars and are engaged in overreach, outright attacks on our Liberty and civil rights, violations of the Constitution or gross inadequacy in their function, or are no longer necessary and will be downsized or eliminated. You can learn more about the Convention of States here: https://conventionofstates.com/.

IMAGINE THIS

This plan has fifteen provisions. That may seem daunting. However, any newly established Liberty Action Council can start by focusing on just one or two to begin.

If one Liberty Action Council can be established in every county of every state in America, we will far outnumber the total number of corporate and private special interest lobbyists in Congress and the state houses combined!

What about your county?

The Importance of Reducing Your Internet Footprint

Contrary to what many people think, the Internet is a private going business concern, not a public trust. And the web browser you use is privately owned. The owners of the various platforms you engage with on the Internet have the legal right to set and change the terms of your use. This is how platforms like Facebook and YouTube get away with censoring free speech.

In addition, the Internet has consistently been used as a tool to invade our privacy to make us commodities. Our private data is sold to corporate conglomerates and governments who use that data to sell us stuff and to influence our thinking and behavior to wed us to their products, services and socio-political agendas for our entire lives. This includes raising the next generation on their brainwashing. An example is the fact that Apple and Google Apps, in addition to how they target adults, are now targeting children, sending that data to advertisers without parental consent. [19]

The fact is, we have become addicted to Internet and cell phone usage. Before its availability to the public, we picked up the phone and called each other (on land lines), we visited with each other in our homes, churches and other places of social gathering, business meetings took place in our offices and personal contact, on the whole, was far greater. There are certainly some great benefits to Internet use, as well. However, as living under Covid has made it blatantly clear, the Internet can be used to undermine our Liberty and subvert our rights in ways previously unimaginable. The growing censorship on the Internet on the part of Big Tech is a testament to this fact.

Some say that life as we know it cannot exist without the Internet. But, if you are old enough to remember when the Internet was first announced to the public then ask yourself: What did I do before there was an Internet?

The rapid push on behalf of Big Tech and the wealthy elite to institute a global network based on Internet and cell phone technology to establish socio-economic control of the world is based on Internet and cell phone usage. This is the plan that the wealthy elite have been scheming to implement, connected to the Internet of Things (IoT), which can now be understood as the means to rule all of life based on AI algorithms.

So, you are strongly encouraged to reduce your Internet footprint right now. Their plan to rule our lives cannot be implemented if Internet usage and cell phone usage drops dramatically. Here are some steps you can take, right now, while there is still a small window of time in which to resist and disable this plan.

Credit Card Usage

Cash protects your privacy. Only use your credit cards when absolutely necessary. All credit card expenditures are tracked and those expenditures are used to develop a profile on you and your shopping/spending behaviors. That data is not only mined by the card provider but it is sold to all interested third parties (whether you've opted out or not), and those third parties then use that data in the same way. It's a cycle that keeps repeating itself as part of a standard business practice in which you are viewed as a mere dollar sign.

Considering the above, now just imagine a world in which there is no cash and all we have to transact purchases are credit cards that can be turned off and on at the will of the government.

Spend Cash Every Day

How has it come to this, you might ask? Because many people, perhaps the majority of people who have credit cards, use them instead of cash to make most, if not all of their purchases. Especially in the context of the long-planned move to a digital wallet/digital passport system, this is a very bad habit.

Use your cash to break out of the digital concentration camp. Spend cash for your purchases every day. Keep cash on hand, even if it means you have to buy a safe to lock your cash up. Don't use credit cards when they are not absolutely necessary.

Electronic Deposit of Your Paycheck

Many people opt-in to have their paychecks deposited directly into their bank accounts through a program known as direct deposit. Then they use their credit cards for the majority of their purchases and send a check to the credit card company to pay off those purchases. Worse yet, people also use a debit card tied to their checking account, so the money goes directly from their checking account to the seller. In either scenario, this means that you never see your cash.

In the present environment, this practice only emboldens the planned move to a digital wallet, digital fiat currency system – which, by its very nature will be a social credit system (see Chapters 4 and 5). So, if you are one of those people who has opted-in to direct deposit, along with spending cash every day you are strongly advised to opt-out of direct deposit. Instead, get your paycheck in hand, convert it to cash and spend cash.

Stop Using Big Commercial Banks

Get out of the big commercial banks and bank at the smaller community banks and credit unions. It is much easier to get to know bank personnel at these banks. These staff are usually much more personable and more willing to tend to your financial needs, regardless of the size of your account. Many of these smaller banks know that their existence is doomed, should there be a move to digital currency that will be controlled by central bankers. So, they are happy when you spend your cash (see Chapter 5).

Social Media

Most social media utilizes AI and other Big Tech tools to mine data that is then used to brainwash the public. This is particularly true of those under 18 years of age. The current plan to institute a central bank digital currency (CBDC) based on a social credit system will rely heavily on the brainwashing power of social media to coerce the general public into embracing CBDC, particularly the younger generation.

As an example, in 2020 social media platforms like Facebook and Instagram began floating disinformation that included a narrative that people can contract Covid from the SARS-COV2 virus being transmitted from paper money. This narrative was then adopted by the Department of Defense and the U.S. Congress was pressured into considering a "lockdown on cash" during the pandemic. The justification for the request was based on the fact that paper money circulates through many hands.

To date, there is absolutely no evidence at all that the virus can be transmitted in this fashion. However, this narrative led to a number of retail stores announcing that they would no longer be accepting cash. And other retail stores like Giant Eagle supermarkets where I live do not allow the cashiers to handle cash. The cashiers are baggers and payment is made into slots that collect the money and make change mechanically.

With your use of social media, you are the product being sold. In addition, on most social media platforms, you are censored from speaking out on matters of public health, Covid and the faults and frauds of our government. Moral of the story – get off social media. When you want to share thoughts and experiences, pick up the phone and call. Or send an email (preferably on your own server – more about this later). Better yet, gather in person.

For an even better understanding of the ins and outs of social media brainwashing and data mining, you are strongly encouraged to view *The Social Dilemma*, a documentary produced by Netflix featuring the testimony of tech whistleblowers who worked for the top social media companies. The full documentary can be viewed here:
http://www.documentaryarea.tv/player.php?title=The%20Social%20Dilemma

Shopping Online

Shopping online is a great convenience. And, often, items can be found cheaper online. However, online shopping is one of the primary means by which our privacy is breached and our data mined and sold. Also, when you do shop online, always use the guest checkout, if that option is provided. Creating accounts online to shop greatly increases your Internet footprint and makes it easier for Big Tech to mine your data. In this way, you have less and less privacy when you spend your money.

Certainly there are items online that are difficult to find locally or regionally. But, for items that can be found locally/regionally, you are strongly encouraged to support your local and regional businesses, many of which are small businesses that are the backbone of our economy. Get to know your small business owners. They don't mine your data and are not engaged in plans to control your thinking and behavior.

Online Bill Pay

Particularly if you are with a large commercial bank, this is another area in which your data can be mined and used against you. This is because most bills paid online are processed electronically. This can expose you to the same kinds of data mining that occur with your credit card usage. So, in order to further reduce your Internet footprint, you can pay your bills with a check through snail mail instead.

Your Web Browser

Your web browser is one of the data mining capitals of the world. Cookies are mechanisms by which a web browser mines your data for the owner of the browser and the owner of a web site to exploit and sell. Cookies enable your web browser to store data about your browsing habits that include all web sites that you have visited, whether or not you made a purchase at a web site, all of your social media engagement and much more. This data is then used to control what you see when you are on the Web, including which online ads are presented to you as you visit web sites and social media platforms that engage advertising.

In addition to providing web site owners with web traffic data on visits to their web sites, cookies enable web developers, online businesses, banks and other going concerns to develop a very sophisticated profile on you and your Internet usage. This profile is used in many ways, mostly to commoditize your online behavior. This is also the case with search engines, each of which uses cookies to determine what you will see in your Internet searches.

So, if you don't want Big Tech mining data on you, always delete all cookies after using your web browser. This will mean that, for example, if you return to web sites that require you enter a user ID, you will have to reenter that ID each time you go back to the web site – a small price to pay for much greater protection of your data.

Cell Phone Usage

In the period from 2012 to 2013, Edward Snowden secretly downloaded files and documents showing that the U.S. National Security Agency (NSA), as well as intelligence agencies of other countries, have been monitoring (among other things) the cell phone calls of their citizens. Whether the actual number is 20,000 or more than 50,000 documents in Snowden's possession, along with millions of secret files, is not actually known for sure. But Snowden absconded with a lot of mined data, much of which we are told comes from the monitoring of our cell phone calls. Snowden continues to stand by his assessment of what's in those documents. He has been declared an enemy of the United States. This means that if he were to ever set foot on U.S. soil again, he would be arrested and executed for treason.

With this in mind, Snowden has publicly stated that he would return to the U.S. and undergo a trial, if that trial were broadcast to the American people (like the O.J. Simpson court hearings) and face the possibility of death if there were a ruling against him – so certain is he that the evidence that would come out in such a trial would clearly back his claim regarding the United States and intelligence agencies of other countries monitoring cell phone calls of the citizenry.

NSA-gate (as it is now referred to) became a controversial topic, both in the media and in our nation's capitol. However, especially given the horrific push by America and other world governments to rob us of our rights under the guise of a pandemic, wouldn't it be essential for us to know what's in those documents that Snowden downloaded from the NSA servers? Maybe we'll never know. However, in the present environment of track and trace, of greed and the great reset, caution would be prudent.

How would you respond if there were evidence that our government is monitoring our cell phone calls and monthly usage? So, you are strongly encouraged to reduce your cell phone usage. Email instead of texting. Better yet call instead of emailing or texting. Get a landline phone and use that to make your phone calls. That will be much better for your health, as well, because with the expansion of 5G cell phone networks and 6G on the way, our bodies are being exposed to more and more toxic radiation than at any other time in human history.

One thing you can do to protect yourself is to limit your cell phone usage to when you are traveling and may need access to a phone when you are not at home or in your office. Other than that, turn your cell phone off. And, if you don't want your cell phone to be tracked at all, you'll need to remove the battery when you are not using it, as all cell phones can be tracked even when the phone is turned off, unless the battery has been removed.

Gathering In Person

The importance getting offline and gathering in person cannot be emphasized enough. Our digital culture is now serving to isolate us from each other. This trend will not end well, as it enhances and emboldens existing plans to divide and conquer. This is part of the corruption of greed that has as its foundation the desire for full socio-economic control of the masses. This plan now includes the desire to own our bodies for the sake of full compliance with their plan to rule the world through One World Government.

Protest Big Tech

Big Tech is at the heart of the plan for this one world government. Therefore, it is imperative that we not support those who are cutting our throats. It really does matter who owns the tech platform, who finances it and whether or not they are engaged in the censorship of our free speech, the destruction of our human rights, the destruction of our constitutional and civil rights and crimes against humanity. The best protest is to stop using such platforms – to stop supporting them in any way.

Chapter 9
Population Growth, Abundance and Prosperity

Governments and the wealthy elite want you to believe that population growth must be regulated and, when necessary, controlled and reduced by government, if our planet is to survive. These notions come out of a focus on scarcity and lack that is promoted in doomsday, apocalyptic scenarios that have become a hallmark of big government, the UN and globalist organizations like the WEF and Club of Rome. In fact, apocalyptic thinking has become popular among the masses.

The truth is that, as population has grown on the planet, all nations and societies have become more prosperous, and the materials and natural resources required to sustain nations and the planet have become more abundant than ever before while, at the same time, costing less.

In this chapter there are three books that I reference that I strongly encourage you to read. They are *The Ultimate Resource 2* by Julian Simon, *SuperAbundance* by Marian L. Tupy and Gale L. Pooley, and *The Surprising Story of How We Learned to Prosper Using Fewer Resources – and What Happens Next* by Andrew McAfee. These three books have many other references in them that are wholly relevant to the presentation in this chapter.

The "Fixed Pie" Fallacy

In Chapter 6, I shared information about Thomas Malthus and Malthusian theory. Unfortunately, Malthusian thought has become entrenched in government policies globally. This is because so many people find apocalyptic thought strangely reassuring. The "fixed pie" theory promoted by Malthus, and later by biologist Paul Erhlich, author of *The Population Bomb*, is the notion that our Earth is a "fixed pie" and, as the world population grows, there will be less and less of the "pie" to go around. Therefore, population must be controlled and reduced so that there is more of the "pie" to go around. This notion, that has influenced government policies globally, also formed the foundation for Eugenics.

Although discussed in theoretical treatises in ancient Greece and Rome, Eugenics got its start in the late 1800s in the United States (and later in Europe). Eugenics is the process of editing the human gene pool by forced sterilization of human beings in order to manage selective breeding to, supposedly, improve the human species.

At its height in Nazi Germany and, later on the African and Asian continents, Eugenics included the extermination of select groups of the population. If select groups of the world population are systematically exterminated, there will be more of the pie left for those considered to be the primary, elite among the human species. This notion that we are running out of nature is bolstered by mainstream media fearmongering.

The truth is this entire world has manifested and is sustained out of God's Love. When this is the case, how can our Earth be anything but endlessly abundant. Despite our best and worst efforts, the Sun and Moon continue to shine, grass, trees, bushes and wild plants continue to grow abundantly and flowers continue to bloom everywhere in the world. Oceans continue to exist. Rivers and streams continue to flow.

The fact is, even in nature, there have always been cycles of endings and beginnings. Everything in form dies, and then the forms are reborn again. Seasons change, disappear and reappear. It is the very nature of our Earth to manifest, sustain and withdraw itself in cycles through time.

The Bet

"Our supplies of natural resources are not finite in any economic sense. Nor does past experience give reason to expect natural resources to become more scarce. Rather, if history is any guide, natural resources will progressively become less costly, hence less scarce, and will constitute a smaller portion of our expenses in future years." [1]

Amid reports in the 1970s of massive starvation in underdeveloped countries around the world, Paul Erhlich's book, *The Population Bomb,* gained worldwide attention and got him on a good number of talk shows. Erlich used his television appearances to make some pretty outrageous claims regarding population growth and the destruction of the world. In one interview, Erlich predicted that England would not exist by the year 2000. In another, Erlich predicted that food riots over food scarcity would become commonplace around the world and he toured and gave lectures on this topic. It was claims such as these that prompted Julian Simon to challenge Erlich to a bet, with the agreement that the bet and its outcome would be publicized.

Erlich formed a group of investors and invested $1,000 on $200 quantities of five metals that were chrome, copper, nickel, tin and tungsten. Then they signed a futures contract that also stipulated that Julian

Simon would sell these same quantities of metal to Erlich's group for the same price in 10 years' time. Price is a reflection of scarcity. So, if population increases made these metals scarcer, Simon would pay, but if they became more abundant with population increases, Erlich would pay. Ten years later, all five metals became cheaper. The prices of three of the metals fell faster than inflation. The price of tin and tungsten fell by more than half. With population growth, all five metals had become more abundant. Erlich sent Simon a check for $567.07 that represented a 36 percent decrease in inflation-adjusted prices. Simon sent Erlich a thank you note with another bet to raise the stakes to $20,000 in a future wager. Erlich refused. [2]

Increased Prosperity Globally

As population has grown on the planet, prosperity has increased globally. In developed nations, incomes have increased and food, health care and education, among other things, have become more affordable. As an example, from 1950 through 2020, the average annual income in the United States rose from $15,183 to $62,941. This is an increase of 315 percent. In the United Kingdom, average annual income has risen from $11,772 to $43,906 in the same period, for an increase of 278 percent. The average global annual income, based on population increases everywhere on the globe for this same period, rose from $4,158 to $16,904. That's an increase of 307 percent (figures quoted are in U.S. dollars). [3]

Some of the world's poorest nations also experienced income growth, side by side with population growth during the same period of 1950 through 2020. In China, these incomes grew from $688 to $14,009. That's an increase of 1,936 percent. India saw an increase from $842 to $6,649, for an increase of 690 percent. In sub-Saharan Africa, the world's poorest region, per capita income rose from $2,214 to $4,025 for an increase of 82 percent (all figures are in U.S.dollars). [4]

The average global life expectancy rose from 52.6 years in 1960 to 72.4 years in 2017, for an increase of 37.6 percent. In the United States, life expectancy rose from 69.8 years to 78.5 years, for an increase of 13 percent. In the United Kingdom, it rose from 71.1 years to 81.2 years, for an increase of 14 percent. The world's poorest nations experienced some of the greatest life expectancy increases for the same period. China went from 43.7 years to 76.4 years, up 75 percent. India went from 41.2 years to 68.8 years for an increase of 67 percent. Sub-Saharan Africa went from 40.4 years to 60.9 years, for an increase of 51 percent. No country in the world has had life expectancy that was lower in 2017 than it was in 1960. [5]

Despite world population growth poverty rates have declined all over the world. The share of people living on less than $1.90 per day has declined from 42 percent in 1981 to less than 10 percent in 2015. In China, it fell from 66 percent in 1990 to 0.5 percent in 2016. For India, it fell from 62 percent in 1977 to 21 percent in 2011. [6]

There has also been an improvement in how we produce goods and services in ways that are less harmful to the environment. Sulphur dioxide (SO_2), is a toxic gas that is produced as a byproduct of copper extraction that requires burning fossil fuels. As an example, SO_2 emissions declined from 152 million metric tons in 1980 to 97 million metric tons in 2010. This is a 36 percent reduction over a period of 30 years and is still declining. [7] SO_2 emissions in the U.S. have been reduced from 31 million metric tons in 1970 to around 2 million metric tons in 2019. This is a reduction of 94 percent. [8]

Andrew McAfee is a Massachusetts Institute of Technology cientist who published some revolutionary findings in his book *The Surprising Story of How We Learned to Prosper Using Fewer Resources – and What Happens Next.* In a free market economy such as the U.S., companies are compelled to decrease the use of natural resources for each dollar of output. One example is aluminum cans. When they were first introduced to market in 1959, they weighed 85 grams. By 2011, they weighed 13 grams. [9] In looking at the U.S. consumption of 72 resources from aluminum to zinc, McAfee discovered that the annual use of 66 resources peaked prior to 2019. Energy use decreased between 2008 and 2017, even though the U.S. economy expanded by 15 percent in the same period. The U.S. economy has reached a point where it is now possible to produce ever-increasing amounts of goods and services using fewer and fewer resources. [10] As other economies become as increasingly advanced as the U.S., they will also reduce their consumption of resources.

Connected to the above, it is important to note that, during the same periods mentioned, the world population has continued to grow while prosperity has only increased.

Personal Resource Abundance and Population Resource Abundance

The great flaw in Malthusian thought and the theories it has produced is that it focuses on measuring scarcity. In this way, it is impossible to get at the truth regarding population growth and material abundance. To understand whether or not nations of the world are enjoying more material abundance, in addition to measuring the effective use of resources in producing more using less, abundance also has to be measured. And, from an economic standpoint, it can be.

Julian Simon created the *Simon Abundance Framework* (SAF). This approach measures and analyzes the relationship between the abundance of resources and population growth over time. SAF measures the benefits of innovation, showing that with population growth we have had increased innovation. SAF bypasses currency fluctuations, the uncertainty of inflation/deflation and purchasing parity adjustments, as these are not stable and consistent measurements of abundance. Instead, SAF consists of two levels of measurement and analysis: personal resource abundance and population resource abundance.

Why measure material abundance rather than scarcity? Human desires are infinite and this is why scarcity will never be eliminated. From the vantage point of ever-increasing desires and cravings there will never be enough of anything to go around. Instead, particularly from an economic standpoint, it is much more useful to measure how many hours a person has to work to afford to buy essential items, along with whether or not that number of hours has increased or decreased over time. This means that from the perspective of abundance, measuring the quantity of resources is not very useful. What is much more useful is an information hierarchy that measures stores of value by quantifying the time it takes to acquire that store of value, along with the cost for acquiring resources with it. This information hierarchy is known as the *Resource Abundance Information Hierarchy*.

SuperAbundance

Gale Pooley is an associate professor of business management at Brigham Young University-Hawaii, coauthor of the *Simon Abundance Index*, and a senior fellow with the Discovery Institute. Marian L. Tupy is a senior fellow at the Cato Institute's Center for Global Liberty and Prosperity, coauthor of *Ten Global Trends Every Smart Person Should Know: And Many Others You Will Find Interesting*, coauthor of the *Simon Abundance Index*, and editor of the website HumanProgress.org. Together, these two have done a remarkable job utilizing the Simon Abundance Index to measure increased material abundance globally that has come hand-in-hand with population growth. The information and references in this section are taken from their book *SuperAbundance. The Story of Population Growth, Innovation, and Human Flourishing On An Infinitely Bountiful Planet.*

Time prices

Why is measuring the quantity of resources practically useless? Gale and Marian make the case that measuring quantity is problematic because, in many cases quantities are not directly observable. For example, we know we have oil and gas on the planet but there is no way of knowing exactly how much of these we have. Then there are varying grades of oil and gas that are not easily measured. Then there is the challenge of knowing where to look in order to measure these and other commodities. Quantity measurement doesn't account for substitutions and replacements and we can't predict future discoveries of new deposits of commodities and how they may increase with improved technology to extract them.

354 DHARMA AND THE PRESERVATION OF LIBERTY

Prices, both nominal and real, provide us with more accurate data with which to practically measure abundance. When you seek to purchase a turkey for Thanksgiving or Christmas dinner, you're usually not concerned with how many turkeys there are in the supermarket, as long as they have one left for you to buy. Your concern is how much the turkey costs. So, if you see hundreds of turkeys in the market cooler, that information is useless to you. Let's say the price of the turkeys is $1,000 each. If you earn a salary equivalent to the average middle class in America, you'll leave the market empty handed. But if you are a Bill Gates whose net worth in 2022 came in at $130 billion dollars, that $1,000 for the turkey is a drop in the bucket for you and you will likely be willing to pay it.

This is a perfect example of that which is a superior measurement to both nominal and real prices – *time prices*. Time is considered to be the scarcest commodity of all. Everyone, whether monetarily wealthy or not, faces the death of the body. Many consider that the more time they spend at their employ, the less time they have for leisure and time spent with family and other loved ones. The Simon Abundance Index measures material abundance in time, rather than money.

Time Price (TP) is defined as the amount of time that you need to work in order to earn enough money to be able to buy something. While prices in money are the same for everyone, TP can differ a lot across people and populations. For example, assuming average expenses are the same, gasoline at $4 per gallon is a lot more expensive for someone earning $10 an hour, than for someone earning $40 an hour.

Time prices (TP) are measured in hours and minutes. The way to calculate TP is to divide the nominal price by the nominal hourly income. For example, if an item costs you $1 and you earn $10 per hour, then that item will cost you 6 minutes of work. [11] If that item increases to $1.10 and your hourly wage increases to $12 per hour, then the item will cost you only 5 minutes and 24 seconds of your time at work. [12] It's important to remember that as long as hourly income is increasing faster than money prices of items you purchase, the TP will decrease. TP always equals the nominal money price divided by your nominal hourly income.

The advantages to using TP when calculating material abundance or scarcity are the following:

- Innovation and productivity gains are always reflected in lower income and higher prices.

- TPs avoid all the complications associated with inflation adjustments that are both subjective and disputed, such as the Consumer Price Index (CPI).

- Because TPs use nominal price and nominal income at every point in time, no inflation adjustments are necessary.

- Analysts can use a variety of hourly income rates (hourly wages with or without nonwage benefits) to calculate TP.

- TPs can be calculated using any currency at any point in time.

- Income and prices are converted to time, which is objective and universal.

Percentage Change In Time Prices

The percentage of change in TP (PCTP) can provide even more valuable data than TP alone can provide. Calculating the percentage of change in TP over time gives us a picture of long-term patterns of availability of goods and services. This helps to understand whether prosperity is increasing or decreasing over time. To calculate the PCTP, first a time period is selected to analyze. Then TPs are calculated for the start-year and the end-year. The time price divisor (TPD) equals the TP at the end of the analyzed period divided by the TP at the beginning of the analyzed period. The calculation is TPD = TP end-year divided by TP start-year.

In 1995, the average nominal price of bananas in the U.S. was $0.45 per pound. Blue-collar workers at that time earned about $16.66 per hour. So, the TP of a pound of bananas in 1995 for blue-collar workers was 0.027 hours or 1 minute 37 seconds of work. [13] In 2018, bananas increased to $0.58 per pound and blue-collar worker salaries increased to $32.06 per hour. The TP of a pound of bananas for such workers in 2018 was 0.018 or 1 minute 5 seconds of paid work. [14] That is a decrease in time equating to an increase in abundance. Applying the TPD would be calculated as 0.018 divided by 0.027 equaling 0.667.

To make this calculation useful for our purposes, we need to apply the percentage change in time price (PCTP). PCTP = TP end-year minus TP start-year divided by TP start-year. To simplify the calculation we'll use PCTP = TP end-year divided by TP start-year minus 1. Then we can calculate PCTP = TPD minus 1. Going back to the banana example, the PCTP would equal 0.667 minus 1 or -0.333. This means that the TP of bananas for blue-collar workers fell by 33.3 percent between 1995 and 2018. [15] This begins to give us an understanding that it cost less paid work time in 2018 to purchase a pound of bananas than in 1995. However, to properly measure whether that equates to an increase or decrease in abundance, we need the personal resource abundance multiplier (pRam).

Personal Resource Abundance Multiplier

The personal resource abundance multiplier (pRAM) tells us how much more of a resource we can acquire for the same amount of paid labor between two points in time. This is an essential step in the formulation of the resource abundance information hierarchy. So, pRAM is the ratio of the time it took to work to earn enough money to purchase something at the start of the analyzed period, divided by the time it took to work to earn enough money to buy something at the end of the analyzed period. pRAM tells us how much more or less of an item we can purchase with the same amount of paid labor. pRAM is calculated in the following way:

pRAM = TP for the start-year divided by TP for the end-year.

Let's go back to our banana example. The TP of a pound of bananas fell from 0.027 hours of work in 1995 to 0.018 hours of work in 2018. So, the pRAM for that period equals 1.5. So, blue collar workers were able to buy 50 percent more bananas in 2018 than they were able to buy in 1995. In this example, as long as pRAM is greater than 1, the abundance of bananas is increasing.

Let's look at the opposite situation. If the TP of a pound of bananas rose from 0.018 hours of paid labor to 0.027 hours of paid labor, then the pRAM would equal 0.667 hours of work. This is less than 1, so the abundance of bananas in this example has decreased to only 3 fifths of the bananas in 2018 that he/she was able to buy for the same amount in 1995. Note that pRAM calculation is geometric and not linear. This is why the above equation is necessary to accurately calculate pRAM, as even a 5% decrease in pRAM can enhance your gains by 100 percent. [16]

Percentage Change In Personal Resource Abundance

With respect to material prosperity, the percentage of change in personal resource abundance (pRA) is a calculation that tells you how much better off you have become between two points in time. Once you have the pRAM, you can then calculate the percentage change in your personal resource abundance over time. Remember that pRAM works like an index. Indexes have a start or base year and a start or base value. With pRAM the start or base value is always 1. So, the percentage change in pRA over time is calculated as pRAM minus 1.

Percentage change in pRA = pRAM minus 1.

Now, back to the bananas. In the banana example, the TP of a pound of bananas in 1995 is 0.027 hours and the TP of a pound of bananas in 2018 is 0.018 hours. The pRAM is equal to 1.5. So, the percentage change in pRA over time is calculated as 1.5 minus 1, which equals 0.50 or 50 percent. This means that bananas became 50 percent more abundant between 1995 and 2018, using blue-collar hourly wages. And, if we look at the opposite circumstance, if the time required to purchase a pound of bananas rose from 0.018 hours to 0.027 hours between 1995 and 2018, then the percentage change over that time period will equal 0.067 minus 1. This would mean that bananas became 33 percent less abundant in that time period, using blue-collar hourly wages. [17]

Compound Annual Growth Rate of Personal Resource Abundance

The compound annual growth rate of personal resource abundance (CAGR-pRA) gives us the rate of improvement between two points in time. With pRAM values calculated, we can then calculate the compound annual growth rate of personal resource abundance. This is an additional step in the resource abundance information hierarchy that tells us how fast pRA is changing. The higher the CAGR-pRA value is, the faster an item increases in affordability. The lower the value, the slower an item increases in affordability. The calculation is as follows:

CAGR-pRA = pRAM to the power of 1, divided by total years of period, minus 1 [18]

To return to the banana example, the pRAM for bananas between 1995 and 2018 came to 1.5. Using the CAGR-pRA calculation, we get 0.0107 or 1.07 percent. This means that the pRA of bananas increased at a rate of 1.07 percent per year. This information will become relevant shortly when I provide you with actual material abundance growth numbers for a variety of items and commodities. [19]

360 DHARMA AND THE PRESERVATION OF LIBERTY

Years to Double
Personal Resource Abundance

Years to double personal resource abundance (YD-pRA) is a calculation that gives the length of time for a resource to become twice as abundant. This is also known as the doubling period. To calculate the doubling period, the NPER ("number of periods") function is used in Excel. NPER is based on the equation (Log(2) minus Log(1) divided by Log(1 + CAGR). This equation approximates 70 divided by CAGR which is known as the rule of the 70s. Going back to the banana example, the CAGR-pRA for bananas between 1995 and 2018 came to 1.07 percent. The NPER function displays that at a CAGR rate at 1.07 percent, bananas will take 65.4 years to double in pRA. If CAGR-pRA were to double to 2.14 percent, the doubling period falls to 32.7 years. If CAGR-pRA falls by half to 0.535 percent, then the doubling period increase to 131 years. [20] Again, the foundation for all of these calculations is time prices.

Calculating the average global nominal GDP per hour worked, along with median incomes and changes in median incomes, is relevant. Because space does not allow for those calculations here, I encourage you to read the book *SuperAbundance* where you will find a detailed analysis of these calculations, relative to this topic.

Personal Resource Abundance
Empirical Evidence and Analysis

"There are many numbers and diagrams in the text. Bear with me, please, the arguments depend on them. If my conclusions were not backed by hard data as proof, some would be laughed away because they violate common sense, and others would be rejected instantly because they starkly contradict the main body of popular writings about population and resources." [21]

Tupy and Pooley do an excellent job of providing a great deal of information in graphs and charts that show increases in personal and population resource abundance over extended periods of time, in just about every resource on the planet. The data is also broken down by country and by blue-collar worker wages, unskilled worker wages, and what they refer to as upskilling worker wages (upskilling workers are employees who develop on-the-job skills that get them an increased wage over time).

Below I will present some of the data, which is quite compelling, that is offered in charts and graphs in *SuperAbundance*. As space is limited here and there is a lot more compelling evidence presented for steady increases in material abundance across all sectors, again I encourage you to read the book.

The Basic 50 Commodities, 1980-2018

This is a view of pRA of 50 individual commodities between 1980 and 2018. The commodities are: aluminum, bananas, barley, beef, chicken, coal, cocoa, coconut oil, coffee, copper, corn, cotton, crude oil, fertilizer, fish meal, gold, groundnuts and groundnut oil, hides, iron ore, lamb, lead, liquefied natural gas (Japan), logs, natural gas (Europe), natural gas (United States), nickel, oranges, palm oil, platinum, plywood, pork, pulpwood, rapeseed, rice, rubber, salmon, sawnwood, shrimp, silver, sorghum, soybeans (including meal and oil), sugar, sunflower oil, tea, tin, tobacco, uranium, wheat, wool, and zinc. [22]

The average global nominal GDP per hour worked rose from $3.24 to $15.88 between 1980 and 2018. We can calculate time prices for this period for the basic 50 commodities by using nominal prices as numerators (the top number of a fraction) and the average nominal GDPs per hour worked as the denominators (the bottom number of a fraction). In this way, the finding is that the average TP of the basic 50 commodities fell by 71.6 percent during this period. The average pRA increased by 252 percent and the average pRA of the basic 50 commodities never fell below its value in 1980. [23]

Using each of the calculations presented earlier in this chapter, here is the basic 50 commodity perspective for the period of 1980 – 2018:

Uranium
Change in resource time price= -87.0%, Personal resource abundance multiplier= 7.69
Change in personal resource abundance= 669%, Compound annual growth rate in personal resource abundance= 5.51%, Years to double personal resource abundance=12.91

Sugar
Change in resource time price= -85.9%, Personal resource abundance multiplier= 7.11
Change in personal resource abundance= 611%, Compound annual growth rate in personal resource abundance= 5.30%, Years to double personal resource abundance=13.43

Coffee
Change in resource time price= -85.4%, Personal resource abundance multiplier= 6.86
Change in personal resource abundance= 586%, Compound annual growth rate in personal resource abundance= 5.20%, Years to double personal resource abundance=13.68

Silver
Change in resource time price= -84.6%, Personal resource abundance multiplier= 6.50

Change in personal resource abundance= 550%, Compound annual growth rate in personal resource abundance= 5.05%, Years to double personal resource abundance=14.07

Pork
Change in resource time price= -84.6%, Personal resource abundance multiplier= 6.50
Change in personal resource abundance= 550%, Compound annual growth rate in personal resource abundance= 5.05%, Years to double personal resource abundance=14.08

Cocoa
Change in resource time price= -82.1%, Personal resource abundance multiplier= 5.57
Change in personal resource abundance= 457%, Compound annual growth rate in personal resource abundance= 4.62%, Years to double personal resource abundance=15.33

Salmon
Change in resource time price= -80.8%, Personal resource abundance multiplier= 5.21
Change in personal resource abundance= 421%, Compound annual growth rate in personal resource abundance= 4.44%, Years to double personal resource abundance=15.96

Cotton
Change in resource time price= -80.1%, Personal resource abundance multiplier= 5.03
Change in personal resource abundance= 403%, Compound annual growth rate in personal resource abundance= 4.34%, Years to double personal resource abundance=16.30

Rice
Change in resource time price= -79.1%, Personal resource abundance multiplier= 4.79
Change in personal resource abundance= 379%, Compound annual growth rate in personal resource abundance= 4.21%, Years to double personal resource abundance=16.81

Palm Oil
Change in resource time price= -77.7%, Personal resource abundance multiplier= 4.49
Change in personal resource abundance= 349%, Compound annual growth rate in personal resource abundance= 4.03%, Years to double personal resource abundance=17.55

Rubber

Change in resource time price= -77.5%, Personal resource abundance multiplier= 4.44
Change in personal resource abundance= 344%, Compound annual growth rate in personal resource abundance= 4.00%, Years to double personal resource abundance=17.67

Wheat
Change in resource time price= -76.00%, Personal resource abundance multiplier= 4.16
Change in personal resource abundance= 316%, Compound annual growth rate in personal resource abundance= 3.82%, Years to double personal resource abundance=18.48

Aluminum
Change in resource time price= -75.8%, Personal resource abundance multiplier= 4.13
Change in personal resource abundance= 313%, Compound annual growth rate in personal resource abundance= 3.80%, Years to double personal resource abundance=18.56

Tin
Change in resource time price= -75.5%, Personal resource abundance multiplier= 4.09
Change in personal resource abundance= 309%, Compound annual growth rate in personal resource abundance= 3.77%, Years to double personal resource abundance=18.71

Shrimp
Change in resource time price= -75.4%, Personal resource abundance multiplier= 4.07
Change in personal resource abundance= 307%, Compound annual growth rate in personal resource abundance= 3.76%, Years to double personal resource abundance=18.78

Hides
Change in resource time price= -74.3%, Personal resource abundance multiplier= 3.89
Change in personal resource abundance= 289%, Compound annual growth rate in personal resource abundance= 3.64%, Years to double personal resource abundance=19.40

Platinum
Change in resource time price= -73.6%, Personal resource abundance multiplier= 3.79
Change in personal resource abundance= 279%, Compound annual growth rate in personal resource abundance= 3.57%, Years to double personal resource abundance=19.77

Sorghum

Change in resource time price= -73.3%, Personal resource abundance multiplier= 3.75
Change in personal resource abundance= 275%, Compound annual growth rate in personal resource abundance= 3.54%, Years to double personal resource abundance=19.92

Corn

Change in resource time price= -73.3%, Personal resource abundance multiplier= 3.74
Change in personal resource abundance= 274%, Compound annual growth rate in personal resource abundance= 3.53%, Years to double personal resource abundance=19.97

Groundnuts etc.

Change in resource time price= -73.1%, Personal resource abundance multiplier= 3.72
Change in personal resource abundance= 272%, Compound annual growth rate in personal resource abundance= 3.52%, Years to double personal resource abundance=20.06

Soybeans etc.

Change in resource time price= -72.0%, Personal resource abundance multiplier= 3.57
Change in personal resource abundance= 257%, Compound annual growth rate in personal resource abundance= 3.41%, Years to double personal resource abundance=20.69

Rapeseed

Change in resource time price= -70.5%, Personal resource abundance multiplier= 3.39
Change in personal resource abundance= 239%, Compound annual growth rate in personal resource abundance= 3.26%, Years to double personal resource abundance=21.59

Coconut Oil

Change in resource time price= -69.9%, Personal resource abundance multiplier= 3.32
Change in personal resource abundance= 232%, Compound annual growth rate in personal resource abundance= 3.21%, Years to double personal resource abundance=21.96

Beef

Change in resource time price= -69.0%, Personal resource abundance multiplier= 3.23

Change in personal resource abundance= 223%, Compound annual growth rate in personal resource abundance= 3.13%, Years to double personal resource abundance=22.49

Logs
Change in resource time price= -68.9%, Personal resource abundance multiplier= 3.21
Change in personal resource abundance= 221%, Compound annual growth rate in personal resource abundance= 3.12%, Years to double personal resource abundance=22.57

Barley
Change in resource time price= -67.2%, Personal resource abundance multiplier= 3.05
Change in personal resource abundance= 205%, Compound annual growth rate in personal resource abundance= 2.98%, Years to double personal resource abundance=23.62

Sunflower Oil
Change in resource time price= -67.0%, Personal resource abundance multiplier= 3.03
Change in personal resource abundance= 203%, Compound annual growth rate in personal resource abundance= 2.96%, Years to double personal resource abundance=23.76

Pulpwood
Change in resource time price= -66.8%, Personal resource abundance multiplier= 3.01
Change in personal resource abundance= 201%, Compound annual growth rate in personal resource abundance= 2.94%, Years to double personal resource abundance=23.90

Bananas
Change in resource time price= -65.8%, Personal resource abundance multiplier= 2.92
Change in personal resource abundance= 192%, Compound annual growth rate in personal resource abundance= 2.86%, Years to double personal resource abundance=24.55

Fertilizer
Change in resource time price= -65.1%, Personal resource abundance multiplier= 2.86
Change in personal resource abundance= 186%, Compound annual growth rate in personal resource abundance= 2.81%, Years to double personal resource abundance=25.04

Tea

Change in resource time price= -65.0%, Personal resource abundance multiplier= 2.86
Change in personal resource abundance= 186%, Compound annual growth rate in personal resource abundance= 2.80%, Years to double personal resource abundance=25.06

Sawnwood

Change in resource time price= -64.8%, Personal resource abundance multiplier= 2.84
Change in personal resource abundance= 184%, Compound annual growth rate in personal resource abundance= 2.79%, Years to double personal resource abundance=25.21

Plywood

Change in resource time price= -63.2%, Personal resource abundance multiplier= 2.72
Change in personal resource abundance= 172%, Compound annual growth rate in personal resource abundance= 2.66%, Years to double personal resource abundance=26.36

Natural Gas, Europe

Change in resource time price= -62.9%, Personal resource abundance multiplier= 2.70
Change in personal resource abundance= 170%, Compound annual growth rate in personal resource abundance= 2.65%, Years to double personal resource abundance=26.55

Crude Oil

Change in resource time price= -62.2%, Personal resource abundance multiplier= 2.65
Change in personal resource abundance= 165%, Compound annual growth rate in personal resource abundance= 2.60%, Years to double personal resource abundance=27.05

Liquified Natural Gas (LNG), Japan

Change in resource time price= -61.9%, Personal resource abundance multiplier= 2.63
Change in personal resource abundance= 163%, Compound annual growth rate in personal resource abundance= 2.57%, Years to double personal resource abundance=27.28

Oranges

Change in resource time price= -59.8%, Personal resource abundance multiplier= 2.49

Change in personal resource abundance= 149%, Compound annual growth rate in personal resource abundance= 2.42%, Years to double personal resource abundance=28.93

Natural Gas, U.S.
Change in resource time price= -59.5%, Personal resource abundance multiplier= 2.47
Change in personal resource abundance= 147%, Compound annual growth rate in personal resource abundance= 2.41%, Years to double personal resource abundance=29.13

Nickel
Change in resource time price= -59.0%, Personal resource abundance multiplier= 2.44
Change in personal resource abundance= 144%, Compound annual growth rate in personal resource abundance= 2.38%, Years to double personal resource abundance=29.53

Lamb
Change in resource time price= -58.5%, Personal resource abundance multiplier= 2.41
Change in personal resource abundance= 141%, Compound annual growth rate in personal resource abundance= 2.34%, Years to double personal resource abundance=29.97

Gold
Change in resource time price= -57.5%, Personal resource abundance multiplier= 2.35
Change in personal resource abundance= 135%, Compound annual growth rate in personal resource abundance= 2.27%, Years to double personal resource abundance=30.81

Tobacco
Change in resource time price= -56.5%, Personal resource abundance multiplier= 2.30
Change in personal resource abundance= 130%, Compound annual growth rate in personal resource abundance= 2.21%, Years to double personal resource abundance=31.67

Lead
Change in resource time price= -49.6%, Personal resource abundance multiplier= 1.98
Change in personal resource abundance= 98%, Compound annual growth rate in personal resource abundance= 1.82%, Years to double personal resource abundance=38.43

Iron Ore

Change in resource time price= -49.4%, Personal resource abundance multiplier= 1.98
Change in personal resource abundance= 98%, Compound annual growth rate in personal resource abundance= 1.81%, Years to double personal resource abundance=38.65

Wool

Change in resource time price= -48.4%, Personal resource abundance multiplier= 1.94
Change in personal resource abundance= 94%, Compound annual growth rate in personal resource abundance= 1.76%, Years to double personal resource abundance=39.77

Coal

Change in resource time price= -45.7%, Personal resource abundance multiplier= 1.84
Change in personal resource abundance= 84%, Compound annual growth rate in personal resource abundance= 1.62%, Years to double personal resource abundance=43.16

Chicken

Change in resource time price= -40.0%, Personal resource abundance multiplier= 1.67
Change in personal resource abundance= 67%, Compound annual growth rate in personal resource abundance= 1.35%, Years to double personal resource abundance=51.64

Copper

Change in resource time price= -39.0%, Personal resource abundance multiplier= 1.64
Change in personal resource abundance= 64%, Compound annual growth rate in personal resource abundance= 1.31%, Years to double personal resource abundance=53.22

Fish Meal

Change in resource time price= -38.4%, Personal resource abundance multiplier= 1.62
Change in personal resource abundance= 62%, Compound annual growth rate in personal resource abundance= 1.28%, Years to double personal resource abundance=54.35

Zinc

Change in resource time price= -21.8%, Personal resource abundance multiplier= 1.28

Change in personal resource abundance= 28%, Compound annual growth rate in personal resource abundance= 0.65%, Years to double personal resource abundance=107.17

AVERAGE FOR ABOVE 50 BASIC COMMODITIES
Change in resource time price= -71.6, Personal resource abundance multiplier= 3.52, Change in personal resource abundance=252%, Compound annual growth rate in personal abundance= 3.37%, Years to double personal resource abundance= 20.94
[24]

As you can see, all of the basic 50 commodities have increased in abundance for the period shown, while population has also increased globally.
Here is the basic 50 commodity perspective for the period of 1980 – 2018, by country and territory:

China
Change in resource time price= -97.5, Personal resource abundance multiplier= 40.30, Change in personal resource abundance=3,930%, Compound annual growth rate in personal abundance= 10.22%, Years to double personal resource abundance= 7.1

South Korea
Change in resource time price= -92.1, Personal resource abundance multiplier= 12.67, Change in personal resource abundance=1,167%, Compound annual growth rate in personal abundance= 6.91%, Years to double personal resource abundance= 10.4

Sri Lanka
Change in resource time price= -88.4, Personal resource abundance multiplier= 8.61, Change in personal resource abundance=761%, Compound annual growth rate in personal abundance= 5.83%, Years to double personal resource abundance= 12.2

Ireland
Change in resource time price= -88.1, Personal resource abundance multiplier= 8.42, Change in personal resource abundance=742%, Compound annual growth rate in personal abundance= 5.77%, Years to double personal resource abundance= 12.4

Thailand
Change in resource time price= -87.5, Personal resource abundance multiplier= 8.02, Change in personal resource abundance=702%,

Compound annual growth rate in personal abundance= 5.63%, Years to double personal resource abundance= 12.7

Singapore
Change in resource time price= -84.2, Personal resource abundance multiplier= 6.34, Change in personal resource abundance=534%, Compound annual growth rate in personal abundance= 4.98%, Years to double personal resource abundance= 14.3

Hong Kong
Change in resource time price= -83.2, Personal resource abundance multiplier= 5.95, Change in personal resource abundance=495%, Compound annual growth rate in personal abundance= 4.81%, Years to double personal resource abundance= 14.8

India
Change in resource time price= -82.0, Personal resource abundance multiplier= 5.55, Change in personal resource abundance=455%, Compound annual growth rate in personal abundance= 4.61%, Years to double personal resource abundance= 15.4

Portugal
Change in resource time price= -78.1, Personal resource abundance multiplier= 4.58, Change in personal resource abundance=358%, Compound annual growth rate in personal abundance= 4.08%, Years to double personal resource abundance= 17.3

Bangladesh
Change in resource time price= -77.3, Personal resource abundance multiplier= 4.41, Change in personal resource abundance=341%, Compound annual growth rate in personal abundance= 3.98%, Years to double personal resource abundance= 17.8

Indonesia
Change in resource time price= -77.0, Personal resource abundance multiplier= 4.35, Change in personal resource abundance=335%, Compound annual growth rate in personal abundance= 3.94%, Years to double personal resource abundance= 17.9

Turkey
Change in resource time price= -75.7, Personal resource abundance multiplier= 4.12, Change in personal resource abundance=312%, Compound annual growth rate in personal abundance= 3.80%, Years to double personal resource abundance= 18.6

New Zealand

Change in resource time price= -75.1, Personal resource abundance multiplier= 4.01, Change in personal resource abundance=301%, Compound annual growth rate in personal abundance= 3.72%, Years to double personal resource abundance= 19.0

Australia

Change in resource time price= -73.8, Personal resource abundance multiplier= 3.82, Change in personal resource abundance=282%, Compound annual growth rate in personal abundance= 3.59%, Years to double personal resource abundance= 19.7

Finland

Change in resource time price= -73.7, Personal resource abundance multiplier= 3.80, Change in personal resource abundance=280%, Compound annual growth rate in personal abundance= 3.58%, Years to double personal resource abundance= 19.7

Norway

Change in resource time price= -73.2, Personal resource abundance multiplier= 3.73, Change in personal resource abundance=273%, Compound annual growth rate in personal abundance= 3.53%, Years to double personal resource abundance= 20.0

Pakistan

Change in resource time price= -72.9, Personal resource abundance multiplier= 3.69, Change in personal resource abundance=269%, Compound annual growth rate in personal abundance= 3.50%, Years to double personal resource abundance= 20.2

Iceland

Change in resource time price= -72.7, Personal resource abundance multiplier= 3.67, Change in personal resource abundance=267%, Compound annual growth rate in personal abundance= 3.48%, Years to double personal resource abundance= 20.3

Austria

Change in resource time price= -72.3, Personal resource abundance multiplier= 3.60, Change in personal resource abundance=260%, Compound annual growth rate in personal abundance= 3.43%, Years to double personal resource abundance= 20.5

Malaysia

Change in resource time price= -70.9, Personal resource abundance multiplier= 3.43, Change in personal resource abundance=243%, Compound annual growth rate in personal abundance= 3.30%, Years to double personal resource abundance= 21.4

United States

Change in resource time price= -70.6, Personal resource abundance multiplier= 3.40, Change in personal resource abundance=240%, Compound annual growth rate in personal abundance= 3.28%, Years to double personal resource abundance= 21.5

Denmark

Change in resource time price= -70.5, Personal resource abundance multiplier= 3.39, Change in personal resource abundance=239%, Compound annual growth rate in personal abundance= 3.27%, Years to double personal resource abundance= 21.6

Germany

Change in resource time price= -70.5, Personal resource abundance multiplier= 3.39, Change in personal resource abundance=239%, Compound annual growth rate in personal abundance= 3.27%, Years to double personal resource abundance= 21.6

Japan

Change in resource time price= -70.2, Personal resource abundance multiplier= 3.35, Change in personal resource abundance=235%, Compound annual growth rate in personal abundance= 3.23%, Years to double personal resource abundance= 21.8

Chile

Change in resource time price= -69.5, Personal resource abundance multiplier= 3.28, Change in personal resource abundance=228%, Compound annual growth rate in personal abundance= 3.18%, Years to double personal resource abundance= 22.2

Luxembourg

Change in resource time price= -68.7, Personal resource abundance multiplier= 3.20, Change in personal resource abundance=220%, Compound annual growth rate in personal abundance= 3.11%, Years to double personal resource abundance= 22.7

Spain

Change in resource time price= -68.7, Personal resource abundance multiplier= 3.20, Change in personal resource abundance=220%, Compound annual growth rate in personal abundance= 3.10%, Years to double personal resource abundance= 22.7

Switzerland

Change in resource time price= -68.4, Personal resource abundance multiplier= 3.16, Change in personal resource abundance=216%, Compound annual growth rate in personal abundance= 3.08%, Years to double personal resource abundance= 22.9

Peru

Change in resource time price= -68.3, Personal resource abundance multiplier= 3.16, Change in personal resource abundance=216%, Compound annual growth rate in personal abundance= 3.07%, Years to double personal resource abundance= 22.9

Brazil

Change in resource time price= -68.0, Personal resource abundance multiplier= 3.13, Change in personal resource abundance=213%, Compound annual growth rate in personal abundance= 3.05%, Years to double personal resource abundance= 23.1

United Kingdom

Change in resource time price= -66.5, Personal resource abundance multiplier= 2.98, Change in personal resource abundance=198%, Compound annual growth rate in personal abundance= 2.92%, Years to double personal resource abundance= 24.1

Philippines

Change in resource time price= -65.8, Personal resource abundance multiplier= 2.92, Change in personal resource abundance=192%, Compound annual growth rate in personal abundance= 2.86%, Years to double personal resource abundance= 24.6

Argentina

Change in resource time price= -65.7, Personal resource abundance multiplier= 2.92, Change in personal resource abundance=192%, Compound annual growth rate in personal abundance= 2.86%, Years to double personal resource abundance= 24.6

Italy

Change in resource time price= -64.8, Personal resource abundance multiplier= 2.84, Change in personal resource abundance=184%, Compound annual growth rate in personal abundance= 2.79%, Years to double personal resource abundance= 25.2

Canada

Change in resource time price= -64.6, Personal resource abundance multiplier= 2.83, Change in personal resource abundance=183%, Compound annual growth rate in personal abundance= 2.77%, Years to double personal resource abundance= 25.3

Colombia

Change in resource time price= -63.6, Personal resource abundance multiplier= 2.75, Change in personal resource abundance=175%, Compound annual growth rate in personal abundance= 2.70%, Years to double personal resource abundance= 26.0

France

Change in resource time price= -62.7, Personal resource abundance multiplier= 2.68, Change in personal resource abundance=168%, Compound annual growth rate in personal abundance= 2.63%, Years to double personal resource abundance= 26.7

Belgium

Change in resource time price= -61.8, Personal resource abundance multiplier= 2.62, Change in personal resource abundance=162%, Compound annual growth rate in personal abundance= 2.56%, Years to double personal resource abundance= 27.4

Greece

Change in resource time price= -59.3, Personal resource abundance multiplier= 2.46, Change in personal resource abundance=146%, Compound annual growth rate in personal abundance= 2.39%, Years to double personal resource abundance= 29.3

Netherlands

Change in resource time price= -58.5, Personal resource abundance multiplier= 2.41, Change in personal resource abundance=141%, Compound annual growth rate in personal abundance= 2.34%, Years to double personal resource abundance= 29.9

Sweden

Change in resource time price= -55.3, Personal resource abundance multiplier= 2.23, Change in personal resource abundance=123%, Compound annual growth rate in personal abundance= 2.14%, Years to double personal resource abundance= 32.8

Mexico

Change in resource time price= -40.8, Personal resource abundance multiplier= 1.69, Change in personal resource abundance=69%, Compound annual growth rate in personal abundance= 1.39%, Years to double personal resource abundance= 50.3

AVERAGE FOR ABOVE COUNTRIES/TERRITORIES

Change in resource time price= -71.6, Personal resource abundance multiplier= 3.52, Change in personal resource abundance=252%, Compound annual growth rate in personal abundance= 3.37%, Years to double personal resource abundance= 20.9

[25]

Across the globe, countries and territories have experienced increased prosperity for the time period indicated. Again, the purpose of providing this data is to show that there is a direct correlation between population growth and increases in prosperity and the material abundance of resources.

Chapter 10
Upholding Dharma and
Protecting Human Dignity
Is The Only Way Forward

Imagine a life where, under the disguise of protecting your life, government engages in denigrating your existence. Imagine a life where you, a human being, are considered to be nothing more than a dollar sign, enshrined in an algorithm that ensures that you are a commodity for the greedy, wealthy elite to trade.

Imagine a life where what you think, say and are allowed to feel is dictated by government, in partnership with Big Business. Imagine a life where unelected bureaucrats and the wealthy elite get to decide whether you live or die, depending on your ethnicity and culture. Now, imagine your body being the property of your government, managed by the wealthy elite who have taken socio-economic control of your life - and dissent is not allowed.

Now examine your existence under Covid mandates, the Pandemic Era and the Great Reset that is already in motion. I think you will agree that, with respect to the above, we are already there. What are we prepared to do about it? *Because we can't comply our way out of tyranny.*

No One Asked Us

Throughout this book I have been sharing

information and data regarding the plan governments of the world have for passing legislation and instituting protocols for increased control over our minds, bodies and speech. They say these are necessary for the welfare of the people. However, all of these plans have one thing in common. Before even considering them, we the people were never asked what we want or how we feel about the plans that they have made no attempt to hide. *No one asked us.* And this is indicative of the fact that they don't care what we think or what we want.

Sacred Law

We live on a rock that hangs in a void of space without anything material with which to hold it there. This rock spins on an axis back and forth, in an orbit around a fireball. This phenomenon has taken place for longer than anyone knows. And no government, no standing army, no sovereign wealth trust, no nation, no drug cartel – nothing and no one can alter or manipulate the fact that we live on a rock that hangs in a void of space without anything material with which to hold it there - spinning on an axis back and forth, in an orbit around a fireball. This does infer, in a most compelling way, that there is a sacred law that governs here. The orderliness of this phenomenon infers it.

In the words of Mahatma Gandhi, "Where there is law, there is a lawgiver." So, there is a sacred law here and a lawgiver, the understanding and experience of which we must fashion our governance on. Whether you refer to that lawgiver as God, Jesus Christ, Mohammed, the Self, the Lord, the Absolute – the labels don't really matter. That there is such a phenomenon that infers a lawgiver is scientifically sound, by way of the consequence of direct experience.

Science without recognition of God as the energy substratum of everything and everyone is no science at all. Therefore, science, whether spiritual or secular, must start with an examination and acknowledgement of the fact that there is a force, an energy substratum of everything that rules here by God's will, and on which societies are superimposed. Greed begins to fester when this power, a spiritual power that is all-pervasive, is not embraced.

Greed

The human form is sacred. For it is only through the intelligence of the human being that the Truth with respect to this phenomenon can be embraced and upheld. And yet, in an ever-increasing fashion, human beings have become the most sought after commodity, to be controlled, manipulated and traded. Human dignity is being extinguished in the maniacal egoism of greed. Socio-economic dominance is now the flavor of our present times, and attaining this dominance has gotten easier as nations prosper.

Manifesting out of socialism, a hybrid of communism and fascism has become the mechanism for this travesty. For example, a Republic operating democratically that does not have the active participation of its citizens in shaping policy and law is no different than a communist or fascist regime. And we have to remember that governments are made up of people and "systems" are created, run and managed by people. So, who are the people responsible for the greed that is eroding free societies? This question must be answered because the human species is at risk.

Our Liberty is being forced into extinction. Humanity is at a crossroads like never before. With respect to the environment, public health policy, food, water and energy, we are putting the human species at ever-increasing risk. The Covid crisis that has ushered in the Coronavirus Era brings with it the corruption of our most trusted institutions and government itself. Never before in recent history have we seen such a rapid decline in human and civil rights around the globe, with entire governments and nations acting in lockstep to dictate what we put on and in our bodies. My Guru once said that the source of the destruction of humanity will not require bombs, but will proceed from greed.

If not arrested, greed corrupts, both individually and collectively. It strikes at the heart of humankind by destroying human dignity and overriding conscience – our natural connection to ethics and morality, to God. This can only degrade the quality of life by dehumanizing entire populations.

To be clear, greed is a spiritual disease. Therefore, it is important to understand how greed corrupts so that we can embrace and nurture principles for wholistic living, in recognition of God, the Self, the true possessor of this place we call Earth.
Honoring God is a necessity for upholding Human Dignity, protecting Humanity and cherishing all of Life. When we don't embrace Honor in this way, maniacal egoism becomes the order of the day, reigning down havoc, hysteria and tyranny everywhere.

Maniacal Egoism

It appears that the world has, indeed, gone mad! And the overwhelming push for socio-economic control of the masses is greater now than it ever has been in recent history. This push for socio-economic control of the masses by a small group of wealthy elite and government bureaucrats has now taken the form of the complete commoditization of all human beings, everywhere. It is oppression of an entirely different nature, the likes of which we have never seen before in recent history.

This is no longer just a matter of profits before people. They now want to own our minds and bodies. The declaration of a world-wide pandemic, based on a virus that, by the numbers, is no more dangerous or widespread than the annual flu virus has set the stage for this commoditization of human beings everywhere, for socio-economic dominance of the world. In order to defeat this madness, it is essential to study the mindset of these oppressors.

Although there are many examples of this mindset in today's post-Covid crisis, I want to share with you two examples that are indicative of this clear intention toward mounting oppression. The following are quotes of Yuval Noah Harari taken from video presentations he has posted online [1,2,3]. Harari is the chief advisor to Klaus Schwab and is credited with designing the World Economic Forum (WEF) and the plan for the Great Reset [4].

"There is no such thing as free will. Science is familiar with just two kinds of processes in nature. You have deterministic processes and you have random processes, and of course you have combinations of randomness and determinism which result in a probabilistic outcome, but none of that is freedom. Freedom has absolutely no meaning from a physical or biological perspective. It's just another myth, another empty term that humans have invented. Humans have invented God, and humans have invented heaven and hell, and humans have invented free will. But there is no more truth to free will than there is to heaven and hell. And as for feelings, they are definitely real; they are not a fiction of our imagination. But feelings are really just biochemical algorithms, and there is nothing metaphysical or supernatural about them. There is no obvious reason to consider them as the highest authority in the world. And most importantly, what scientists and engineers are telling us more and more, is that if we only have enough data, and enough computing power, we can create external algorithms that understand humans and their feelings much better than humans can understand themselves. And once you have an algorithm that understands you, and understands your feelings better than you understand yourself, this is the point when authority really shifts away from humans to algorithms."

"Covid is critical because this is what convinces people to accept, to legitimize, total biometric surveillance. If we want to stop this epidemic, we need not just to monitor people, we need to monitor what's happening under their skin. .....What we have seen so far is corporations and governments collecting data about where we go, who we meet, what movies we watch. The next phase is the surveillance going under our skin."

"We now see mass surveillance systems established even in democratic countries, which previously rejected them. And we also see a change in the nature of surveillance. Previously, surveillance was mainly above the skin; now it's going under the skin. Governments want to know not just where we go or who we meet; above all, they want to know what is happening under our skin: what's our body temperature? What's our blood pressure? What is our medical condition? ....Now humans are developing even bigger powers than ever before. We are really acquiring Divine powers of creation and destruction. We are really upgrading humans into gods; we are acquiring, for instance, the power to re-engineer life."

"Humans are now hackable animals. You know, the whole idea that humans have this soul or spirit, and they have free will, and nobody knows what's happening inside me, so, whatever I choose, whether in the election or whether in the supermarket, this is my free will. That's over."

"In the industrial revolution of the 19th century, what humanity basically learned to produce was all kinds of stuff, like textiles and shoes, and weapons and vehicles. This was enough for very few countries that underwent the revolution fast enough to subjugate everybody else. What we are talking about now is like a second industrial revolution, but the product this time will not be textiles or machines, or vehicles, or even weapons; the product this time will be humans themselves. We are basically learning to produce bodies and minds. Bodies and minds are going to be, I think, the two main products of the next wave of all these changes."

"If there is a gap between those that know to produce bodies and minds, and those that do not, then this is far greater than anything we saw before in history. This time, if you are not part of the revolution fast enough, then you probably become extinct. Once you know how to produce bodies and brains and minds— cheap labor in Africa or South Asia or wherever, it simply counts for nothing."

"Again, I think the biggest question in maybe economics and politics of the coming decade, will be what to do with all these useless people. I don't think we have an economic model for that. My best guess, which is just a guess, is that food will not be a problem. With that kind of technology, you will be able to produce food to feed everybody. The problem is more boredom, and what to do with them and how will they find some sense of meaning in life when they are basically meaningless, worthless? My best guess at present is a combination of drugs and computer games."

These quotes are so repulsive that you may make the mistake of discounting Harari as a raving lunatic, completely harmless. Not so fast! Now, consider the following headline:
Orwell's "Ministry of Truth" Materializes as Biden's DHS Announces "Disinformation Governance Board." Since the ineffective, cruel and oppressive response by world governments to the SARS-COV2 Pandemic called Covid-19, there have been comparisons to George Orwell's 1984. Some claim that we are far from the dystopian world that Orwell warns us about.

However, the latest moves by the Biden administration seem as if they've been taken directly from the novel. For example, just after being elected President of the U.S., Biden ordered the Department of Homeland Security (DHS) to create a board that will focus on countering misinformation and disinformation. It was given the name the "Disinformation Governance Board (DGB)." There was a flood of public outrage when the DGB was announced. So, the Biden administration has put the DGB on hold while Biden searches for someone to replace Nina Jankowicz.

Some say that the DGB is a non-starter. The truth is the DGB is simply being reorganized, away from the prying eyes of the public. We know this now due to the fact that, at the same time the DGB was being dismantled, Biden engaged other agencies within the U.S. Federal government to execute censorship by proxy on Facebook, X, Instagram and Google. The Supreme Court is now hearing a case on this that has been brought against the Biden administration (see Chapter 7).

Full Government Control Over the Citizenry

In the novel 1984 (published in 1949), Orwell describes a dystopian future in which the government has almost full control over its citizens. The government is represented primarily by 4 ministries, one of them being the Ministry of Truth (Minitrue). This is described in the novel as the government's propaganda wing. One of the primary roles of MiniTrue is to falsify historical records to present a new version of history that better serves the government's needs.

The Ministry of Truth manages news media, entertainment, the fine arts, and educational books. Its purpose is to rewrite history and change the facts to fit Party doctrine for propaganda effect. For example, if Big Brother (the personification of Orwell's fictional totalitarian regime) makes a prediction that turns out to be wrong, the employees of the Ministry of Truth correct the record to make it accurate. Changing history, words and facts in books, articles and other media about current and past events is part of the strategy to ensure that government is always seen in a favorable light and can do no harm. This is propaganda at its worst.

China has become the model for government control of the masses that governments of other countries are now using. The Chinese model is being hailed by the WEF and the UN, and is being used by the European Union. The Biden administration is also using this model in the adoption of its policies. In China, the CCP decided that government should become God. To accomplish this, the CCP has destroyed the nuclear family in China, along with religion and spirituality. The CCP has accomplished this by making people's minds and bodies the property of the Chinese government. Health freedom and bodily autonomy are non-existent in China and government censorship of free speech is the law. The replication of this model in other countries, including the U.S., has begun with the deterioration of health freedom and bodily autonomy, along with growing censorship.

What It Means To Be Human

The World Economic Forum (WEF), led by Klaus Schwab, recently held their annual conference in China. During the conference, Schwab praised the CCP and the Chinese government for their form of governance and stated that it is a pillar for the advancement of the WEF's 4th Industrial Revolution (4IR) plan. That plan includes merging human beings with AI as part of a broad, planned transhumanist effort to change what it means to be human.

This plan coincides with what is known as the Internet of Bodies (IoB), a Big Tech push to have all human bodies connected to the Internet by way of devices implanted in our bodies, beginning with our brains. You can read more about IoB here: https://www.weforum.org/agenda/2020/06/internet-of-bodies-covid19-recovery-governance-health-data/ and here: https://www.rand.org/multimedia/video/2020/10/29/what-is-the-internet-of-bodies.html. With regard to this link, take note that the RAND corporation used to be one of the largest military contractors on the planet, in partnership with Douglas Aircraft and the U.S. Air Force. They are now a global think tank and, if you don't know, RAND developed what we now know as the Internet.

They are a major party to securing one world government via, among other things, Big Tech and are one of the primary forces behind AI development.

One of the first executive orders that President Biden executed is the EO on *Advancing Biotechnology and Biomanufacturing Innovation for a Sustainable, Safe, and Secure American Bioeconomy.* [5] Among other things, the order states:

"For biotechnology and biomanufacturing to help us achieve our societal goals, the United States needs to invest in foundational scientific capabilities. We need to develop genetic engineering technologies and techniques to be able to write circuitry for cells and predictably program biology in the same way in which we write software and program computers; unlock the power of biological data, including through computing tools and artificial intelligence."

Here, the intention is clear – to write circuitry for cells that will allow for our biology to be fully controlled through AI. In signing this order, Biden has brought the U.S. Federal government into alignment with WEF objectives for changing what it means to be human. There is a short video clip on this produced by The High Wire that you can view here: https://thehighwire.com/ark-videos/biden-executive-order-signals-alignment-with-wef/.
The transhumanism push aims to merge humanity with artificial intelligence.

Dr. Carrie Madej is an Osteopathic and Internal Medicine physician. Originally from Dearborn, Michigan, she received her medical degree from Kansas City University of Medical Biosciences in 2001. She currently dedicates her time educating others on vaccines, nanotechnology, and human rights via multiple platforms and speaking engagements. Dr.

Madej has also spent many years researching and speaking on Transhumanism and the sweeping developments in connecting it to AI. As the public's understanding of Transhumanism and AI is very limited, there are several video presentations of hers that I encourage you to watch. You can begin viewing these here:

Carrie Madej - Human 2.0
https://vimeo.com/773612617/9e213c713c

Dr. Carrie Madej – Nanobots, Transhumanism, Never-Ending Vaccines, HIV, Shedding, & Detox
https://zeeemedia.com/interview/dr-carrie-madej-nanobots-transhumanism-never-ending-vaccines-hiv-shedding-detox/

Transhumanism and AI with Carrie Madej
https://www.youtube.com/watch?v=57b52l_pJfA

BATTLE FOR HUMANITY – How the new vaccines prepare humanity for transhumanism.
https://bhaktaschool.org/battle-for-humanity/

After viewing these, lest you think Dr. Madej is a quack who has manufactured facts out of thin air, I suggest you view the information using the following links so that you understand that what she speaks of is already in play, beginning with the U.S. military and China's military.

https://www.nbcnews.com/politics/national-security/china-has-done-human-testing-create-biologically-enhanced-super-soldiers-n1249914

https://www.globalpolicyjournal.com/blog/18/05/2015/transhumanism-and-war

https://sociable.co/military-technology/pentagon-gene-editing-internet-of-bodies-ai-enhance-human-performance/

Then, when you get done with these, *The Manchurian Candidate* is a movie starring Denzel Washington, Liv Schreiber and Meryl Streep that was released in 2004. The plot eerily reflects the current development of Transhumanism.

Respect, Love and Human Dignity

Human beings are sacred and a human birth is sacred. This is so because it is only in a human form that we can fully realize our God-nature while becoming established in Love and Respect for Humanity and Human Dignity. My Shri Gurudev spoke constantly about Love and Respect and would open and close all his talks by saying "With great Respect and Love, I welcome you with all my heart."

Respect is the highest invocation to God! It is steeped in Human Dignity and Equality Consciousness. Therefore, without the direct knowledge and experience of these spiritual principles, it is not possible to respect yourself and command respect from others. *You are so much greater than you think you are!* You can truly respect yourself and others in a way that easily commands Love and Respect for human dignity.

What is human dignity? Human dignity is first the recognition that you are not the body, the mind or the senses. This recognition must culminate in the direct and ongoing experience of your true nature. Otherwise, human dignity gets lost in a sea of attachment, attraction and aversion. Limiting desire and craving is the glue that tears down human dignity over and over again, in the false notion of individuality, imprisoned in the ego idea.

Equality Consciousness

What Is Equality? When you think of equality, several things may come to mind. Freedom of speech, freedom of expression, free thinking and the freedom to pursue personal gain. Liberty may also come to mind – being at liberty to do what you want, the equal opportunity to live as others do, respect for your liberty and privacy. These are great principles, but approached in the wrong way, each brings entanglement and suffering.

Humility is the first step in the experience of Equality Consciousness, out of which comes a natural and spontaneous desire to protect human dignity. Humility is a state of Grace, born of Equality Consciousness and steeped in awe. To be humble, the complete recognition of God's Grace in daily mundane existence and spiritual life is an absolute necessity. Humility is born of Equality Consciousness. This is the constant remembrance that you are neither greater or lesser than anything or anyone else. You are equal in God. You respect yourself and you respect others as the Self, as God. Indeed, God dwells in everything and everyone, everywhere. The manifestation of the world of forms is proof of God's existence and power of Grace.

With this Equality Consciousness you are able to honor and respect all beings, all creatures as your very own Self. Then you are able to experience that everything and everyone in God's creation has something to offer you. Living in this awareness is Humility and out of this Humility, Reverence and Respect comes Love.

Love

Love is the highest of all principles and is the foundation for Nityananda Shaktipat Yoga. Shri Bhagawan Nityananda of Ganeshpuri, the master of our lineage in these modern times, states, "The Heart is the hub of all sacred places. Go there and roam." And one of the greatest sages of our lineage, Shri Narada, defines Love in the following way: "When Love comes, God reveals himself. By attaining it, a person becomes perfect, immortal and satisfied forever. This is how you know that it is Love." Jalal al-Din Rumi, the great Persian Sufi mystic whose writings have been embraced in nearly every spiritual path and religion on the planet, tells us, "Your task is not to seek for love, but merely to seek and find all the barriers within yourself that you have built against it."

These barriers dissolve when we embrace Equality Consciousness and recognize the importance of respecting and honoring each other by seeing God in each other. Then we can act accordingly in our daily mundane existence to protect and nurture Human Dignity and the sacredness of all of life here. This is Dharma, our duty to each other.

Dharma is the only way forward in addressing and overcoming the challenges detailed in this book.

REFERENCES

Introduction References

1. https://www.patrioticviralnews.com/articles/meta-hires-cia-agent-to-head-up-their-election-censorship-division/
2. https://www.foxnews.com/politics/biden-likely-violated-first-amendment-covid-19-pandemic-federal-judge-says
3. TNI, https://www.bbc.com/beyondfakenews/trusted-news-initiative/
4. Breaking: Landmark Lawsuit Slaps Legacy Media With Antitrust, First Amendment Claims for Censoring COVID-Related Content https://www.villagenews.com/story/2023/01/05/news/breaking-landmark-lawsuit-slaps-legacy-media-with-antitrust-first-amendment-claims-for-censoring-covid-related-content/71968.html
5. Meta Quest, https://www.meta.com/
6. Implanted Microchip, Klaus Schwab, World Economic Forum and The Great Reset https://www.youtube.com/watch?v=UmQNA0HL1pw
7. Neuralink: Elon Musk's brain chip firm wins US approval for human study, https://www.bbc.com/news/health-65717487
8. Elon Musk's brain chip firm Neuralink lines up clinical trials in humans, https://www.theguardian.com/technology/2022/jan/20/elon-musk-brain-chip-firm-neuralink-lines-up-clinical-trials-in-humans
9. FDA Approves First Implantable Identification Chip for Medical Use, https://californiahealthline.org/morning-breakout/fda-approves-first-implantable-identification-chip-for-medical-use/

10. https://rumble.com/vxyfo5-yuval-noah-harari-the-covid-crisis-was-the-moment-when-surveillance-started.html

11. Yuval Noah Harari, "There Is No Such Thing As Free Will" & "Humans Have Invented God," https://frankspeech.com/video/yuval-noah-harari-there-no-such-thing-free-will-humans-have-invented-god

Chapter 1

1. Truth and Reconciliation Commission, South Africa, https://www.britannica.com/topic/Truth-and-Reconciliation-Commission-South-Africa

2. Twenty years ago, the U.S. warned of Iraq's alleged 'weapons of mass destruction,' https://www.npr.org/2023/02/03/1151160567/colin-powell-iraq-un-weapons-mass-destruction

3. Edward Snowden: the whistleblower behind the NSA surveillance revelations, https://www.theguardian.com/world/2013/jun/09/edward-snowden-nsa-whistleblower-surveillance

4. America's Pandemic War Games Don't End Well, https://foreignpolicy.com/2020/04/01/coronavirus-pandemic-war-games-simulation-dark-winter/

5. SARS Pandemic: How the Virus Spread Around the World in 2003, https://www.history.com/news/sars-outbreak-china-lessons

6. Pandemic 1, https://plandemicseries.com/plandemic-1/

7. New research shows CDC exaggerated the evidence for masks to fight COVID, https://chicago.suntimes.com/columnists/2023/2/8/23591132/cdc-exaggerated-evidence-supporting-mask-mandates-column-jacob-sullum

8. Mask Facts, https://aapsonline.org/mask-facts/

9. More than 170 Comparative Studies and Articles on Mask Ineffectiveness and Harms, By Paul Elias Alexander, December 20, 2021, https://brownstone.org/articles/studies-and-articles-on-mask-ineffectiveness-and-harms/
10. https://drive.google.com/file/d/1HCT4D96uJ6I9HlpOfoGTMm2pOmkQeXSn/view, pgs 8-9.

Chapter 2

1. Kennedy Jr., Robert F., The Real Anthony Fauci, Skyhorse Publishing, NY, NY, pg. 1
2. Kennedy Jr., Robert F., The Real Anthony Fauci, Skyhorse Publishing, NY, NY, pgs. 1-2
3. Kennedy Jr., Robert F., The Real Anthony Fauci, Skyhorse Publishing, NY, NY, pg. 2
4. 3. Kennedy Jr., Robert F., The Real Anthony Fauci, Skyhorse Publishing, NY, NY, pg. 4
5. https://www.msn.com/en-us/health/medical/scientific-and-public-health-failure-fauci-admits-covid-shots-didn-t-have-a-chance-of-controlling-the-pandemic/ar-AA17dv2d
6. https://www.uspresidentialelectionnews.com/2023/02/fauci-now-admits-why-covid-vaccine-was-never-able-to-slow-the-spread/
7. https://pandemictimeline.com/2015/03/peter-daszak-addresses-workshop/
8. Huff, Dr. Andrew G., The Truth About Wuhan, Skyhorse Publishing, NY, NY, pgs. 194-195
9. Huff, Dr. Andrew G., The Truth About Wuhan, Skyhorse Publishing, NY, NY, pgs. 93-94
10. Huff, Dr. Andrew G., The Truth About Wuhan, Skyhorse Publishing, NY, NY, pgs. 172-177
11. https://www.iqt.org/

12. https://www.scientificamerican.com/article/3-human-chimeras-that-already-exist/?print=true

13. Fleming, Dr. Richard M., Is Covid-19 A Bioweapon?, Skyhorse Publishing, NY, NY, pg. 2

14. Baric, Ralph S., Directional Assembly of Large Viral Genomes and Chromosomes. US Patent 6,593,111, issued July 15, 200315.

15. Fleming, Dr. Richard M., Is Covid-19 A Bioweapon?, Skyhorse Publishing, NY, NY, pg. 3

16. Fleming, Dr. Richard M., Is Covid-19 A Bioweapon?, Skyhorse Publishing, NY, NY, pg. 3-4

17. https://uscode.house.gov/view.xhtml?req=(title:21%20section:360bbb%20edition:prelim

18. https://uscode.house.gov/view.xhtml?req=(title:21%20section:360bbb-3a%20edition:prelim

19. https://www.theepochtimes.com/us/pediatrician-fired-after-raising-alarm-on-covid-19-vaccines-during-us-senate-event-5431515

20. Leake, John and McCullough, Dr. Peter A., The Courage to Face COVID-19. Pgs. 20-21

21. Leake, John and McCullough, Dr. Peter A., The Courage to Face COVID-19. Pg. 26

22. Leake, John and McCullough, Dr. Peter A., The Courage to Face COVID-19. Pg. 27

23. https://www.ncbi.nlm.nih.gov/pmc/articles/PMC7102549/

24. https://www.ncbi.nlm.nih.gov/pmc/articles/PMC7102549/

25. Bruesewitz v. Wyeth LLC, 562 U.S. 223 (2011) https://supreme.justia.com/cases/federal/us/562/223/)

26. https://cdn.who.int/media/docs/default-source/classification/icd/covid-19/guidelines-cause-of-death-covid-19-20200420-en.pdf

27. CDC director admits hospitals, medical folks have 'perverse incentive' to falsely count Covid deaths (video) https://www.bizpacreview.com/2020/08/02/cdc-director-admits-hospitals-medical-folks-have-perverse-incentive-to-falsely-count-covid-deaths-954633/
28. Fact check: Hospitals get paid more if patients listed as COVID-19, on ventilators https://www.usatoday.com/story/news/factcheck/2020/04/24/fact-check-medicare-hospitals-paid-more-covid-19-patients-coronavirus/3000638001/

Chapter 3

1. Kennedy Jr., Robert F. and Hooker, Brian, Vax-Unvax – Let the Science Speak, Skyhorse Publishing, NY, NY, Pg. xviii
2. Kennedy Jr., Robert F. and Hooker, Brian, Vax-Unvax – Let the Science Speak, Skyhorse Publishing, NY, NY, Pg. 1
3. Kennedy Jr., Robert F. and Hooker, Brian, Vax-Unvax – Let the Science Speak, Skyhorse Publishing, NY, NY, Pg. 3
4. Kennedy Jr., Robert F. and Hooker, Brian, Vax-Unvax – Let the Science Speak, Skyhorse Publishing, NY, NY, Pg. 3
5. Kennedy Jr., Robert F. and Hooker, Brian, Vax-Unvax – Let the Science Speak, Skyhorse Publishing, NY, NY, Pgs. 3-4
6. Kennedy Jr., Robert F. and Hooker, Brian, Vax-Unvax – Let the Science Speak, Skyhorse Publishing, NY, NY, Pg. 4
7. Kennedy Jr., Robert F. and Hooker, Brian, Vax-Unvax – Let the Science Speak, Skyhorse Publishing, NY, NY, Pg. 4
8. Kennedy Jr., Robert F. and Hooker, Brian, Vax-Unvax – Let the Science Speak, Skyhorse Publishing, NY, NY, Pgs. 4-5

9. Kennedy Jr., Robert F. and Hooker, Brian, Vax-Unvax – Let the Science Speak, Skyhorse Publishing, NY, NY, Pg. 6

10. Kennedy Jr., Robert F. and Hooker, Brian, Vax-Unvax – Let the Science Speak, Skyhorse Publishing, NY, NY, Pgs. 6-7

11. Kennedy Jr., Robert F. and Hooker, Brian, Vax-Unvax – Let the Science Speak, Skyhorse Publishing, NY, NY, Pg. 14

12. Kennedy Jr., Robert F. and Hooker, Brian, Vax-Unvax – Let the Science Speak, Skyhorse Publishing, NY, NY, Pg. 15

13. Kennedy Jr., Robert F. and Hooker, Brian, Vax-Unvax – Let the Science Speak, Skyhorse Publishing, NY, NY, Pg. 16

14. Kennedy Jr., Robert F. and Hooker, Brian, Vax-Unvax – Let the Science Speak, Skyhorse Publishing, NY, NY, Pg. 19

15. Kennedy Jr., Robert F. and Hooker, Brian, Vax-Unvax – Let the Science Speak, Skyhorse Publishing, NY, NY, Pg. 21

16. Kennedy Jr., Robert F. and Hooker, Brian, Vax-Unvax – Let the Science Speak, Skyhorse Publishing, NY, NY, Pg. 23

17. Kennedy Jr., Robert F. and Hooker, Brian, Vax-Unvax – Let the Science Speak, Skyhorse Publishing, NY, NY, Pg. 24

18. Kennedy Jr., Robert F. and Hooker, Brian, Vax-Unvax – Let the Science Speak, Skyhorse Publishing, NY, NY, Pg. 26

Chapter 4

1. Center for Human Rights and Global Justice, New York University School of Law, Paving a Digital Road to Hell?, Pgs. 2-4

2. Schwab, Klaus and Malleret, Thierry, COVID-19: The

Great RESET, World Economic Forum, Geneva, Switzerland, Pgs. 89-93

3. World Council for Health, Effects of Unregulated Digitalization on Health and Democracy, pg. 18

4. Internet of Things; https://mitpress.mit.edu/books/internet-things

5. California tests, Iowa launches digital IDs, while Michigan considers legislation https://www.biometricupdate.com/202308/california-tests-iowa-launches-digital-ids-while-michigan-considers-legislation

6. https://www.biometricupdate.com/companies/iproov-limited

7. Amazon One https://one.amazon.com/

8. WO2020060606 - CRYPTOCURRENCY SYSTEM USING BODY ACTIVITY DATA https://patentscope.wipo.int/search/en/detail.jsf?docId=WO2020060606

9. Corbishley, Nick, Scanned, Chelsea Green Publishing, White River Junction, VT, Pgs. 92-94

10. Wolf, Naomi, The End of America, Chelsea Green Publishing, White River Junction, VT, Pg. 81

11. https://www.history.com/this-day-in-history/office-of-homeland-security-founded

12. https://www.history.com/topics/21st-century/patriot-act

13. https://www.wikiwand.com/en/Operation_TIPS

14. James Risen and Eric Lichtblau, "Bank Data Sifted in Secret by U.S. to Block Terror" New York Times, June 23, 2006, A1

15. President Biden tests positive for COVID, a year after he said vaccines prevent infections https://www.poynter.org/reporting-editing/2022/president-joe-biden-coronavirus-vaccinated/

16. Jill Biden tests positive for Covid-19

https://www.politico.com/news/2023/09/04/jill-biden-tests-positive-covid-19-00113923

17. Conflicting Evidence of mRNA Technology Raises Serious Concerns About Rush for Use in New Vaccine Development
https://www.theepochtimes.com/health/conflicting-evidence-of-mrna-technology-raises-serious-concerns-about-rush-for-use-in-new-vaccine-development-5480328

18. The EMA covid-19 data leak, and what it tells us about mRNA instability
https://www.bmj.com/content/372/bmj.n627

19. Study: 74% of Post-Jab Deaths Caused by the Shot
https://articles.mercola.com/sites/articles/archive/2023/07/18/post-covid-vaccination-deaths.aspx

20. Doctors Censored by The Lancet in Paper that Found 74% mRNA Vaccine-Related Cause of Death
https://rumble.com/v2ykrv8-doctors-censored-by-lancet-in-paper-that-found-74-mrna-vaccine-related-caus.html

21. Serious adverse events from Pfizer's mRNA vaccine are not "rare" (MARYANNE DEMASI, PHD JUN 27
https://rwmalonemd.substack.com/

22. 'Serious Doubt' About COVID-19 Vaccine Safety After Forced Release of 15,000 Pages of Clinical Trial Data: https://www.theepochtimes.com/article/serious-doubt-raised-about-covid-19-vaccine-safety-after-forced-release-of-15000-pages-of-clinical-trial-data-5414614

23. Budi Sadiki, Indonesian Health Minister
https://www.dropbox.com/s/xbfrdcubmsx6ve7/Updated%20Budi%20Sadikin%20Video.mp4?dl=0

24. WHO to seek global certificate system, inspired by EU's COVID pass
https://medicalxpress.com/news/2023-06-global-certificate-eu-covid.html

25. Corbishley, Nick, Scanned, Chelsea Green

Publishing, White River Junction, VT, Pgs. 91-92

26. The WHO's Proposed Amendments Will Increase Man-Made Pandemics https://brownstone.org/articles/who-amendments-increase-man-made-pandemics/

Chapter 5

1. The Creature From Jekyll Island, Griffin, G. Edward, American Media Publishing, September 2010; pg. 139
2. The Creature From Jekyll Island, Griffin, G. Edward, American Media Publishing, September 2010; pg. 140
3. The Creature From Jekyll Island, Griffin, G. Edward, American Media Publishing, September 2010; pgs. 143-144
4. The Creature From Jekyll Island, Griffin, G. Edward, American Media Publishing, September 2010; pgs. 155-156
5. The Tyranny of the Federal Reserve, Brian O'Brien, August 2015, Brian O'Brien; pgs. 99-104
6. The Death of Money, James Rickards, Portfolio/Penguin, 2017, pgs. 168-169
7. The Tyranny of the Federal Reserve, Brian O'Brien, August 2015, Brian O'Brien; pgs. 56-57 & 72-78
8. The Creature From Jekyll Island, Griffin, G. Edward, American Media Publishing, September 2010; pgs. 165-168
9. Ibid.
10. The Creature From Jekyll Island, Griffin, G. Edward, American Media Publishing, September 2010; pgs. 3-11
11. The Creature From Jekyll Island, Griffin, G. Edward, American Media Publishing, September 2010; pgs. 85-87
12. The Death of Money, James Rickards, Portfolio/Penguin, 2017, pgs. 168-169
13. The Death of Money, James Rickards, Portfolio/Penguin, 2017, pgs. 1-2

14. The Creature From Jekyll Island, Griffin, G. Edward, American Media Publishing, September 2010; pgs. 85-87

15. The Creature From Jekyll Island, Griffin, G. Edward, American Media Publishing, September 2010; pg. 88

16. The Death of Money, James Rickards, Portfolio/Penguin, 2017, pgs. 198-214

17. The Creature From Jekyll Island, Griffin, G. Edward, American Media Publishing, September 2010; pg. 74

18. Zimbabwe and the IMF, Rangarirai Machemedze is the Programmes Coordinator for the Southern and Eastern African Trade, Information and Negotiations institute (SEATINI); https://sarpn.org/documents/d0000758/P852-Zimbabwe_IMF.pdf

19. The Creature From Jekyll Island, Griffin, G. Edward, American Media Publishing, September 2010; pgs. 98-99

20. The Creature From Jekyll Island, Griffin, G. Edward, American Media Publishing, September 2010; pg. 107

21. The Creature From Jekyll Island, Griffin, G. Edward, American Media Publishing, September 2010; pg. 119-120

22. The House of Morgan; An American Banking Dynasty and the Rise of Modern Finance, Chernow, Ron, Atlantic Monthly Press, 1990

23. The Creature From Jekyll Island, Griffin, G. Edward, American Media Publishing, September 2010; pg. 185-200

24. Fabian Society; https://fabians.org.uk/

25. The Smallest Voice; https://thesmallestvoice.com/fabian-socialists-taking-over-america/

26. The Secret History of the War On Caner, Davis, Devra, Basic Books, 2007; pgs. 47-53

27. American Eugenics Society; https://embryo.asu.edu/pages/american-eugenics-society-1926-1972

28. Margaret Sanger and the eugenics movement;
https://www.denverpost.com/2010/06/02/margaret-sanger-and-the-eugenics-movement/
29. American Eugenics Society (AES);
https://eugenicsarchive.ca/discover/connections/5233e53d5c2ec500000000e2
30. Scanned, Corbishley, Nick; Chelsea Green Publishing, February 2022; pgs. 119-125.
31. Scanned, Corbishley, Nick; Chelsea Green Publishing, February 2022; pgs. 113-119.
32. Digital fiat currency;
https://patents.google.com/patent/US20200151682A1/en
33. Bill Gates Champions His Own 'Digital Money' - But What Is It?;
https://cryptonews.com/news/bill-gates-champions-his-own-digital-money-but-what-is-it-9316.htm
34. Visa Files Patent for Digital Fiat Currency;
https://dailycoin.com/digital-fiat-currency/
35. The Tyranny of the Federal Reserve, Brian O'Brien, August 2015, Brian O'Brien; pgs. 61-62
36. The Tyranny of the Federal Reserve, Brian O'Brien, August 2015, Brian O'Brien; pgs. 62-63
37. The Creature From Jekyll Island, Griffin, G. Edward, American Media Publishing, September 2010; pg. 185-200

Chapter 6

1. Global Warming? North America Snow Coverage Hits "Decadal Highs"
https://www.zerohedge.com/weather/global-warming-north-america-snow-coverage-hits-decadal-highs
2. https://www.macrotrends.net/countries/USA/united-states/gdp-per-capita
3. https://www.macrotrends.net/countries/USA/united-states/gdp-per-capita

4. https://unctad.org/press-material/least-developed-countries-report-2021-least-developed-countries-post-covid-world

5. https://www.researchgate.net/figure/Savings-and-Investment-All-Countries_fig1_343358976

6. https://www.statista.com/statistics/279777/global-unemployment-rate/

7. https://www.fao.org/3/CC2211EN/online/CC2211EN.html#chapter-2

8. https://www.macrotrends.net/countries/WLD/world/gnp-gross-national-product

9. https://www.worldometers.info/world-population/world-population-by-year/

10. https://www.macrotrends.net/countries/WLD/world/fertility-rate

11. https://www.statista.com/chart/30671/number-of-millionaires-and-share-of-the-population/

12. https://www.macrotrends.net/1319/dow-jones-100-year-historical-chart

13. https://www.ipcc.ch/assessment-report/ar6/

14. Bill Gates SLAMMED By Joe Rogan, Russel Brand For Driving Vaccine Conversations, Motivated By Profit https://www.youtube.com/watch?v=wxq78OUtB5I

15. Crok, Marcel and May, Andy, The Frozen Climate views of the IPCC, Clintel Foundation, Amsterdam, Netherlands, Pgs. 38-39

16. https://earth.org/environmental-impact-of-battery-production/

17. https://www.instituteforenergyresearch.org/renewable/the-environmental-impact-of-lithium-batteries/

18. https://www.theguardian.com/us-news/2023/jan/24/us-electric-vehicles-lithium-consequences-research

19. https://earth.org/environmental-impact-of-battery-production/

20. https://www.instituteforenergyresearch.org/renewable/the-environmental-impact-of-lithium-batteries/

21. https://www.theguardian.com/us-news/2023/jan/24/us-electric-vehicles-lithium-consequences-research

22. https://earth.org/environmental-impact-of-battery-production/

23. https://www.instituteforenergyresearch.org/renewable/the-environmental-impact-of-lithium-batteries/

24. https://www.theguardian.com/us-news/2023/jan/24/us-electric-vehicles-lithium-consequences-research

25. https://earth.org/environmental-impact-of-battery-production/

26. https://www.instituteforenergyresearch.org/renewable/the-environmental-impact-of-lithium-batteries/

27. https://www.theguardian.com/us-news/2023/jan/24/us-electric-vehicles-lithium-consequences-research

28. https://earth.org/environmental-impact-of-battery-production/

29. https://www.instituteforenergyresearch.org/renewable/the-environmental-impact-of-lithium-batteries/

30. https://chesleybrown.com/the-hazards-of-ev-charging-stations/

31. https://earth.org/environmental-impact-of-battery-production/

32. https://www.instituteforenergyresearch.org/renewable/the-environmental-impact-of-lithium-batteries/

33. https://www.theguardian.com/us-news/2023/jan/24/us-electric-vehicles-lithium-consequences-research

34. https://earth.org/environmental-impact-of-battery-production/

35. https://www.instituteforenergyresearch.org/renewable/the-environmental-impact-of-lithium-batteries/

36. https://www.theguardian.com/us-news/2023/jan/24/us-electric-vehicles-lithium-consequences-research

37. https://www.theepochtimes.com/us/the-high-cost-of-electric-vehicles-mining-for-minerals-puts-us-water-supplies-in-danger-5491463

38. https://www.kbb.com/car-advice/how-much-electric-car-cost/

39. https://www.carfax.com/blog/car-depreciation

40. https://www.forbes.com/sites/forbesbusinesscouncil/2023/03/10/can-the-us-electric-grid-handle-the-load-from-ev-charging/?sh=516cdb504d2a

41. https://spectrum.ieee.org/the-ev-transition-explained-2658463709

42. https://www.usatoday.com/story/money/cars/2022/04/30/electric-vehicle-charging-station-demand/7449847001/?gnt-cfr=1

43. https://www.msn.com/en-us/autos/news/here-s-why-ev-charging-stations-are-failing-and-what-automakers-plan-to-do-about-it/ar-AA1hsVfY

44. https://www.newsweek.com/california-facing-power-crisis-frets-over-electric-car-charging-routines-1602755

45. https://abcnews.go.com/Business/broken-machines-long-waits-reality-charging-electric-vehicle/story?id=97389275

46. https://chesleybrown.com/the-hazards-of-ev-charging-stations/

47. https://www.tomsguide.com/news/how-long-does-it-take-to-charge-an-electric-car-what-you-need-to-know

48. https://www.howtogeek.com/125602/what-happens-when-an-electric-vehicle-battery-dies/

49. https://www.pcmag.com/news/ev-batteries-101-degradation-lifespan-warranties-and-more

50. https://www.theepochtimes.com/opinion/mega-jolt-the-costs-and-logistics-of-plugging-in-evs-are-about-to-become-supercharged-5521869#/find/nearest?country=US

51. https://www.theepochtimes.com/article/true-cost-of-ev-fueling-equivalent-to-17-33-per-gallon-of-gas-report-5518233

52. https://www.theepochtimes.com/us/biden-admin-climate-regulations-add-9100-to-typical-american-household-consumer-watchdog-5518223

53. https://www.theepochtimes.com/us/chinese-green-tech-companies-pose-national-security-risks-to-us-report-says-5516290

54. https://www.wired.com/story/solar-panels-are-starting-to-die-leaving-behind-toxic-trash/

55. https://www.instituteforenergyresearch.org/renewable/solar/solar-waste-a-looming-problem/

56. https://fee.org/articles/solar-panels-produce-tons-of-toxic-waste-literally/

57. https://www.treehugger.com/how-much-co-does-one-solar-panel-create-4868753

58. https://scitechdaily.com/wind-farms-cause-more-environmental-impact-than-previously-thought/

59. https://www.forbes.com/sites/christopherhelman/2021/04/28/how-green-is-wind-power-really-a-new-report-tallies-up-the-carbon-cost-of-renewables/?sh=41556cd573cd

60. https://spectrum.ieee.org/to-get-wind-power-you-need-oil

61. Trees Are Climate Change, Carbon Storage Heroes
https://www.fs.usda.gov/features/trees-are-climate-change-carbon-storage-heroes
62. How many new trees would we need to offset our carbon emissions?
https://climate.mit.edu/ask-mit/how-many-new-trees-would-we-need-offset-our-carbon-emissions
63. The best trees to reduce air pollution
https://www.bbc.com/future/article/20200504-which-trees-reduce-air-pollution-best
64. Trees Help Protect the Planet From Climate Change. But The World Isn't Doing Enough to Protect Forests
https://time.com/6213444/how-do-trees-affect-climate-change/
65. How to erase 100 years of carbon emissions? Plant trees—lots of them.
https://www.nationalgeographic.com/environment/article/how-to-erase-100-years-carbon-emissions-plant-trees
66. Examining the Viability of Planting Trees to Help Mitigate Climate Change
https://climate.nasa.gov/news/2927/examining-the-viability-of-planting-trees-to-help-mitigate-climate-change/
67. A conversation about how trees soak up carbon with Ronnie Drever, senior conservation scientist for Nature United. https://www.nature.org/en-us/magazine/magazine-articles/forest-carbon-101/

Chapter 7

1. https://www.washingtonexaminer.com/news/adam-schiff-urges-tech-companies-to-combat-spread-of-misinformation-during-pandemic
2. Adam Schiff pushes YouTube and Twitter on coronavirus misinformation –

https://www.theverge.com/2020/4/30/21243026/facebook-twitter-youtube-coronavirus-covid-19-misinformation-adam-schiff

3. Schiff Sends Letter to Google and Facebook Regarding Anti-Vaccine Misinformation https://schiff.house.gov/news/press-releases/schiff-sends-letter-to-google-facebook-regarding-anti-vaccine-misinformation

4. An Anti-Vaccine Book Tops Amazon's COVID Search Results. Lawmakers Call Foul https://www.npr.org/2021/09/09/1035559330/democrats-slam-amazon-for-promoting-false-covid-cures-and-anti-vaccine-claims

5. https://www.dailywire.com/news/biden-says-these-12-people-are-responsible-for-most-covid-misinformation-never-says-who-they-are

6. CCDH CEO Imran Ahmed Violates Chatham House Rule, Refuses to Cooperate In Response to Congressional Inquiry - https://greenmedinfo.com/blog/ccdh-ceo-imran-ahmed-violates-chatham-house-rule-response-congressional-inquiry2

7. Democrats want to monitor your TEXTS and use 'aggressive' fact-checkers to dispel vaccine misinformation, report claims https://www.dailymail.co.uk/news/article-9784099/Biden-ramps-war-anti-vaxxers-aggressive-fact-checkers.html

8. Biden's FBI has classified MAGA as terrorists - https://hotair.com/david-strom/2023/10/05/bidens-fbi-has-classified-maga-as-terrorists-n582414

9. Donald Trump Followers Targeted by FBI as 2024 Election Nears - https://www.newsweek.com/2023/10/13/exclusive-fbi-targets-trump-followers-2024-election-nears-1831836.html

10. 'Kick People Off': Rep. Jordan Releases New Info on Biden-Facebook COVID-19 Censorship - https://www.theepochtimes.com/us/kick-people-off-rep-jordan-releases-new-info-on-biden-facebook-covid-19-censorship-5443006

11. Biden likely violated First Amendment during COVID-19 pandemic, federal judge says - Google, Meta and Twitter were all named in the lawsuits - https://www.foxnews.com/politics/biden-likely-violated-first-amendment-covid-19-pandemic-federal-judge-says

12. Court Order Halts Government-Instigated Censorship by Big Tech - https://www.theepochtimes.com/in-depth-court-order-halts-government-instigated-censorship-by-big-tech_5376073.html

13. 'Nerve Center' of Government Censorship Blocked by Court Order - https://www.theepochtimes.com/epochtv/nerve-center-of-government-censorship-blocked-by-court-order-5504103

14. Meta Hires CIA Agent to Head Up Their Election Censorship Division - https://www.patrioticviralnews.com/articles/meta-hires-cia-agent-to-head-up-their-election-censorship-division/

15. Retail health company has Chase accounts suddenly terminated, owner critical of COVID vaccines, FDA, https://flvoicenews.com/retail-health-company-has-chase-accounts-suddenly-terminated-owner-critical-of-covid-vaccines-fda/

16. UK banks are closing more than 1,000 accounts every day https://www.theguardian.com/business/2023/jul/30/uk-banks-closing-more-than-1000-accounts-every-day

17. The EU's Mass Censorship Regime Is Almost Fully Operational. Will It Go Global?

https://www.zerohedge.com/political/eus-mass-censorship-regime-almost-fully-operational-will-it-go-global
18. The Social Dilemma; https://watchdocumentaries.com/the-social-dilemma/

Chapter 8

1. Watching Biden Try To Recite the Declaration Is Worse Than Barney Fife Trying To Recite the Preamble; https://www.westernjournal.com/watching-biden-try-recite-declaration-worse-barney-fife-trying-recite-preamble
2. Biden exposes the truth about progressives and the Constitution; https://nypost.com/2022/02/02/biden-exposes-the-truth-about-progressives-and-the-constitution/
3. Biden: Your Constitutional Rights Are 'Not Absolute'; https://sfcmac.com/biden-your-constitutional-rights-are-not-absolute/
4. https://www.whitehouse.gov/briefing-room/presidential-actions/2021/04/15/executive-order-on-blocking-property-with-respect-to-specified-harmful-foreign-activities-of-the-government-of-the-russian-federation/
5. Biden's Tyrannical Attack on Private Property Rights; https://townhall.com/columnists/katiepavlich/2021/08/06/bidens-tyrannical-attack-on-private-property-rights-n2593731
6. Monkeypox Simulation In 2021 Predicted Current Outbreak; https://nypost.com/2022/05/28/monkeypox-simulation-in-2021-predicted-current-outbreak/
7. Monkeypox Scenarios, Germ Games and Vaccines; https://lightonlight.education/monkeypox-scenarios-germ-games-and-vaccines/
8. What If I Were to Tell You They Ran the Monkeypox War Game In March 2021?;

https://nonvenipacem.com/2022/05/22/what-if-i-were-to-tell-you-they-ran-the-monkeypox-war-game-in-march-2021/

9. Strengthening Global Systems to Prevent and Respond to High-Consequence Biological Threats; https://www.nti.org/wp-content/uploads/2021/11/NTI_Paper_BIO-TTX_Final.pdf

10. Biden likely violated First Amendment during COVID-19 pandemic, federal judge says - Google, Meta and Twitter were all named in the lawsuits - https://www.foxnews.com/politics/biden-likely-violated-first-amendment-covid-19-pandemic-federal-judge-says

11. Inside the Facebook Files: Emails Reveal the CDC's Role in Silencing COVID-19 Dissent https://reason.com/2023/01/19/facebook-files-emails-cdc-covid-vaccines-censorship/

12. How the CDC Coordinated With Big Tech To Censor Americans https://freebeacon.com/biden-administration/how-the-cdc-coordinated-with-big-tech-to-censor-americans/

13. 5th Circuit finds Biden White House, CDC likely violated First Amendment https://www.washingtonpost.com/technology/2023/09/08/5th-circuit-ruling-covid-content-moderation/

14. 'A republic, if you can keep it'; https://www.washingtonpost.com/history/2019/12/18/republic-if-you-can-keep-it-did-ben-franklin-really-say-impeachment-days-favorite-quote/

15. https://www.cnn.com/2020/08/19/health/gmo-mosquitoes-approved-florida-scn-wellness/index.html

16. History of MK Uktra; https://www.history.com/topics/us-government/history-of-mk-ultra

17. Freeway. Crack In the System – Freeway Rick Ross; https://www.primevideo.com/detail/Freeway-Crack-in-the-System/0OSC61W6R20CZ1VFAW2LVVBC2R

18. THE CIA-CONTRA-CRACK COCAINE CONTROVERSY: A REVIEW OF THE JUSTICE DEPARTMENT'S INVESTIGATIONS AND PROSECUTIONS; https://oig.justice.gov/sites/default/files/archive/special /9712/ch01p1.htm

19. Tech Apps Are Spying On Kids; https://childrenshealthdefense.org/defender/tech-apps-spying-kids/

Chapter 9

1. Simon, Julian L., The Ulitmate Resource 2, Princeton University Press, 1996, pg. 6

2. Tupy, Marian L. and Pooley, Gale L., SuperAbundance, Cato Institute, Washington DC

3. Total Economy Database, The Conference Board (online data set: TED 1), https://www.conference-board.org/data/economydatabase/total-economy-database-productivity

4. Total Economy Database, The Conference Board (online data set: TED 1), https://www.conference-board.org/data/economydatabase/total-economy-database-productivity

5. Life Expectancy at Birth, Total (Years), World Bank (online data set

6. Poverty Headcount Ratio at a $1.90 a Day (2011 PPP) (% of Population), World Bank (online data set), https://databank.worldbank.org/metadataglossary/jobs/series/SI.POV.DDAY

7. Jan Luiten van Zanden, How Was Life? Global Well-being Since 1820 (Paris: OECD Publishing, 2014) (Global SO2 Emissions, Our World In Data) (Z. Klimont, S. J. Smith, and J. Cofala, The Last Decade of Global Anthropogenic Sulfur Dioxide: 2000-2011 Emissions, Enviornmental Research letters 8, no. 1 (January 9, 2013), https://doi.org/10.1088/1748-9326/8/1/014003

8. Volume of Sulfur Dioxide Emissions in the U.S. from 1970 to 2019, Statista (online data set), April 2020, https://www.statista.com/statistics/501303/volume-of-sulfur-dioxide-emissions-us/

9. Andrew McAfee, The Surprising Story of How We Learned to Prosper Using Fewer Resources – and What Happens Next, New York: Charles Scribner & Sons, pg. 101

10. The Paradoxical Malthusian. A Promethean Perspective on Vaclav Smil's Growth: From Microorganisms to Megacities (MIT Press 2019) and Energy and Civilization: A History, (MIT Press, 2017) – Energies 13, no. 20: 5306, https://doi.org/10.3390/en13205306

11. Tupy, Marian L. and Pooley, Gale L., SuperAbundance, Cato Institute, Washington DC. Pg. 113

12. Tupy, Marian L. and Pooley, Gale L., SuperAbundance, Cato Institute, Washington DC. Pg. 113

13. Tupy, Marian L. and Pooley, Gale L., SuperAbundance, Cato Institute, Washington DC. Pg. 114

14. Tupy, Marian L. and Pooley, Gale L., SuperAbundance, Cato Institute, Washington DC. Pg. 114

15. Tupy, Marian L. and Pooley, Gale L., SuperAbundance, Cato Institute, Washington DC. Pg. 114

16. Tupy, Marian L. and Pooley, Gale L., SuperAbundance, Cato Institute, Washington DC. Pgs. 116-117, Table 4.1 and Figure 4.1

17. Tupy, Marian L. and Pooley, Gale L., SuperAbundance, Cato Institute, Washington DC. Pgs. 117-118

18. Tupy, Marian L. and Pooley, Gale L., SuperAbundance, Cato Institute, Washington DC. Pg. 118

19. Tupy, Marian L. and Pooley, Gale L., SuperAbundance, Cato Institute, Washington DC. Pgs. 118-119

20. Tupy, Marian L. and Pooley, Gale L., SuperAbundance, Cato Institute, Washington DC. Pg. 119

21. Simon, Julian L., The Ultimate Resource 2, Princeton University Press, 1996, Pg. 9

22. Tupy, Marian L. and Pooley, Gale L., SuperAbundance, Cato Institute, Washington DC. Pgs. 136-137

23. Tupy, Marian L. and Pooley, Gale L., SuperAbundance, Cato Institute, Washington DC. Pg. 137

24. Tupy, Marian L. and Pooley, Gale L., SuperAbundance, Cato Institute, Washington DC. Pg. 138

25. Tupy, Marian L. and Pooley, Gale L., SuperAbundance, Cato Institute, Washington DC. Pg. 141

Chapter 10

1. Harari, Yuval Noah; https://www.ynharari.com/

2. https://www.youtube.com/watch?v=8vsg_kR9e7Y

3. https://www.youtube.com/hashtag/yuvalnoahharari

4. Schwab, Klaus; Malleret, Thierry: Covid-19: The Great Reset, 2020 World Economic Forum

5. https://www.whitehouse.gov/briefing-room/presidential-actions/2022/09/12/executive-order-on-advancing-biotechnology-and-biomanufacturing-innovation-for-a-sustainable-safe-and-secure-american-bioeconomy/

INDEX

Hydroxychloroquine (HCQ). x, 28, 68-71, 147-148, 156, 162, 237, 247.

Industrial/Factory Farming. 210, 222, 224, 226, 230.
Instagram. 127, 240, 242, 290, 302, 342.
Integrity. 2, 58, 244-245.
International Covenant on Civil and Political Rights Treaty (ICCPR). 43.
In-Q-tel (IQT). 40.
Ivermectin (IVM). x, 28, 68, 72, 148, 157, 162, 236, 238-239, 246.

Jnaneshwar Maharaj. v-vi.

Kali Yuga. vi, vii.
Klaus Schwab. xi, xiii, 120, 126, 201, 289-290, 339, 343.

Liberty. vii, xiv, xv, 1, 4, 5-6, 8-11, 13, 15-18, 74, 76, 85, 118, 120, 129, 130, 169, 170-172, 221, 231, 234, 249, 252-255, 257-259, 260, 263-264, 267, 275-278, 280, 282-283, 285-288, 292-293, 298-300, 314, 337, 346-347.
Liberty Action Council. 260, 263, 267, 275, 277-278, 280, 282-283, 285-288, 292-293, 299.
Lockdowns. xiii, 11-12, 14, 19-20, 22, 28, 64, 73, 83, 84, 86-87, 202, 204.
Love. vi, xii, 2, 4, 171, 194, 262-263, 309, 346-348.

Mahabharata. 1-2.
Maniacal Egoism. xiv, 19, 124, 337, 338.
Mask Mandates. 6, 10, 19, 23, 83-84, 86-87, 169.
Muktananda Paramahamsa. xv, 2.
Meta. ix, xi, xii, 127, 242.
Meta Quest. xi.
Ministry of Truth (Minitrue). 249, 341, 342.

National Security Agency (NSA). 5, 131, 168, 249, 305.

U.S. Defense Advanced Research Projects Agency (DARPA). 31.
U.S. Department of Agriculture (USDA). 82-83, 87, 223.
U.S. Department of Defense (DOD). 22, 29, 40, 48-51, 56, 63, 168, 249.
U.S. Department of Health and Human Services (DHHS) (HHS). 24, 44, 49-50, 61-63, 83, 99, 103, 140, 295-296.
U.S. Department of Homeland Security (DHS). x, 341.
U.S. Food and Drug Administration (FDA). viii, 33, 35, 46, 48-50, 56, 67-69, 71-72, 76, 80, 82-83, 86-87, 102, 116, 141, 156, 162, 223, 296.
U.S. Federal Reserve Bank. 87, 121, 172, 175-179, 181-184, 188-191, 294.
United Nations (UN). vii, viii, 9, 120-121, 128, 180, 197, 231.
United Nations Development Program (UNDP). 121, 231.
United States Agency for International Development (USAID). 39, 40, 80, 121.

Vanguard. viii.
Vaccine Mandates. 19-20, 34, 76, 81, 86-87, 145, 169.
Vaccine Passports. ix, 74, 81-82, 86, 118-119, 121, 133, 139, 142-143, 152, 168-169, 185, 187, 266.

World Council For Health. 126.
World Economic Forum (WEF). vii, viii, xi, xiii, 20, 64, 120-121, 124-127, 130, 133-134, 200-201, 289, 308, 339, 342-344.
World Health Organization (WHO). vii, viii, 70, 78-79, 97, 121, 155, 157, 162, 164-167.
Wuhan. 24, 30, 32, 35-38, 40-41, 44, 56-58, 60-61, 63, 69, 70, 164.
Wuhan Institute of Virology (WIV). 32, 36-37, 40-41, 44, 56, 58, 60-62, 164.

Yuval Noah Harari. xi, xiii, 289, 339.

About Kedarji

Kedarji is the Founder of The Bhakta School of Transformation, an Ohio-based not-for-profit public charity devoted to lasting Inner Peace and permanent spiritual transformation. The curriculum offering here is based on Kedaji's 4 Pillars of Joy In Daily Living.

He had an early career in the Performing Arts as an actor and singer in Broadway musicals, plays, movies and television. He went on to study violin and conducting at the Juilliard School of Music and graduated with degrees in performance and composition from the Manhattan School of Music. Later, he studied Eastern and Oriental Medicine, graduated with degrees in both from the Kushi Institute, and had a practice in New York City for many years.

Leading With Love

Kedarji helps people embrace the Grace in life's joys and challenges in a way that causes lasting happiness and peace. In a world seemingly mad with greed and corruption, Kedarji has a long track record of helping people affirm and expand the best parts of their lives.

He is a Siddha in the lineage of the great sage and saint, Bhagawan Nityananda of Ganeshpuri. He imparts the same instruction and leadership he was taught— the same methods used by a line of spiritually proven and powerful masters who have uplifted people's lives for thousands of years.

A Siddha is one who has made the commitment to live as an ascetic, renouncing the pursuit of worldly pleasures and fantasies to serve the greater good and to work to uplift humanity. In this regard, Kedarji is known as a true spiritual leader, and a Shaktipat Guru (see below) who leads by example in becoming both wise and well with a powerful, heart-centered approach.

Practical Leadership In A Shaktipat Guru

Kedarji has a reputation for leading without insisting that people follow. This allows students and seekers to come to our approach in their own way. Kedarji is in a lineage of Sadgurus on whose shoulders he stands and takes refuge in. This is the great Shiva lineage that Bhagawan Nityananda of Ganeshpuri also made, of which Kedarji is a part.

Wise, Happy and Well

Many of Kedarji's students say that, through his leadership, he has transformed their lives in profound ways not experienced in other modalities or on other paths.

His students blossom and uncover hidden strengths through a well-integrated and time-tested approach. Through his leadership, it's possible for anyone and everyone to experience life's magic in a way that they come to know their true nature and attain a state of lasting happiness, peace and joy.

With his 4 Pillars of Joy In Daily Living as the foundation (the Spiritual Power, Improved Mental State, Emotional Resilience and Vibrant Health), he combines the power of Grace of his spiritual lineage with the time-honored, Siddha Science of the Yoga of the Siddhas. This powerful combination includes his skill as a Shaktipat Meditation master and his many years of practice as a practitioner of Eastern and Oriental medicine.

Authentic Shaktipat Guru – Shaktipat Meditation Master

Kedarji is a Shaktipat Guru. He has been vested with the power and authority to fully awaken and nurture the dormant spiritual awareness known as Kundalini. Specifically, this awakening occurs by way of the transmission of the Grace-bestowing power inherent in the Blessing of Shaktipat. In particular, you will find that Kedarji is a recognized and very skilled spiritual leader and Shaktipat Meditation Master. Additionally, he has the ability to lead you on the journey to the realization of your true nature. Indeed, this is a journey in which you retrace your steps back to God.

Author/Producer

Kedarji is the author of several other books and courses, including:
- Vibration of Divine Consciousness. A Spiritual Autobiography.
- The Verses On Witness Consciousness.
- The Abode of Grace – Bhagawan Nityananda of Ganeshpuri.
- Contemplations On the Amritanubhava of Shri Jnaneshwar Maharaj.
- How To Be Fearless, Happy and Resilient In The Age of Noise and Distractions. (a video home-study course and weekend retreat).
- The Sutras On The 5-Fold Act of Divine Consciousness.
- Live Strong and Be Happy. Learn The Daily Rituals of The Most Spiritually-Powerful, Happiest and Healthiest People On The Planet.

Spiritual Journey

Kedarji began his quest to understand and fully imbibe Yoga Science at an early age. Feeling incomplete, he began an intense spiritual journey that took him to India and Asia. Soon after, he experienced an initiation, an awakening into the power of true Meditation, Chanting and Contemplation that formed the foundation for putting all the pieces together.

Due to this event and ongoing application of the methods taught connected to it, Kedarji was able to fully apply the science behind well-being that is based on the Spiritual Power. He calls it the energy substratum of everything. His direct, unfolding experience of this power is the basis for the integration of his 4 Pillars of Joy In Daily Living embodied in his unique approach; an approach that combines Siddha Science and the science of a holistic lifestyle of health and well-being with the transmission of Grace that he extends as a God-realized, Shaktipat Guru.

Come Join Us

You can find out who Kedarji is by spending some time in the company of this Shaktipat Guru. Moreover, this is also the best way for you to experience how the power of Grace and Siddha Science skills mastery that he transmits can impact your life for the better.

Come join us to be with Kedarji and our spiritual & well-being community. Doing so, you will experience the profound leadership that awaits you here. You will find Kedarji to be an outgoing, warm and accessible leader with a great sense of humor. Equally welcoming and skilled is our staff of teachers. We hope to welcome you soon to our programs.